STILL PROCLAIMING YOUR WONDERS

also by Walter J. Burghardt, S.J.
published by Paulist Press

TELL THE NEXT GENERATION
SIR, WE WOULD LIKE TO SEE JESUS
SEASONS THAT LAUGH OR WEEP

STILL PROCLAIMING YOUR WONDERS

Homilies for the Eighties

WALTER J. BURGHARDT, S.J.
Theologian in Residence
Georgetown University

Marilyn
In gratitude
for
your friendship
Walter J. Burghardt,

PAULIST PRESS
New York/Ramsey

Library of Congress
Catalog Card Number: 84-80353

ISBN: 0-8091-2632-X

Published by Paulist Press
545 Island Road, Ramsey, N.J. 07446

Printed and bound in the
United States of America

TABLE OF CONTENTS

FEASTS

MEDLEY

"O God, from my youth you have taught me,
and I am still proclaiming your wonders."

(Ps 71:17)

*for
Georgetown's young,
yesterday and today,
who have revealed to me
the wealth of God's wonders
and have given youth
to my joy*

PREFACE

In 1960 my first book of sermons appeared. It had for title *All Lost in Wonder*, a phrase borrowed from the Jesuit poet Gerard Manley Hopkins' striking version of St. Thomas Aquinas' hymn to the Blessed Sacrament *Adoro te*. Almost a quarter century later a fifth book of sermons is ready, and my search for a title has ended with the same wondrous word, this time in a phrase taken from the Psalms that have inspired much of my own living and preaching. The intervening years, with their tears and laughter, have lent depth and meaning to what was in 1960 primarily a catchword, calculated to seize the eye. Today wonder is my ceaseless reaction to the endless series of God's wonderful works in the story of salvation, the story of a God who, as the Book of Job tells us, "does great things and unsearchable, marvelous things without number" (Job 5:9). Wonder is at once the root and the purpose of my preaching.

Still Proclaiming Your Wonders is genuinely a sequel to *Sir, We Would Like To See Jesus: Homilies from a Hilltop* (Paulist, 1982). Like *Sir*, these sermons (with three exceptions) were delivered within the Eucharistic liturgy. Like *Sir*, most of the homilies (22 out of 34) were preached at Georgetown University. Like *Sir*, they follow a familiar pattern: a movement from God's Word in Scripture, through theological reflection on that Word in the context of contemporary experience, to evocation of a response from men and women whom the homily should help to see Jesus with their own eyes, hear his word with their own ears.

My stress on Scripture has induced me to include the introductory essay "The Word Forms the Preacher." A homilist's ceaseless

1

inspiration, my source material above and beyond all others, has to be God's privileged Word. Not simply as material to be learned and then used. More basically, the Word first fashions not the homily but the homilist. Shaped by the Word, I am a different person. Different person, therefore different homilist.

Once again I dare to hope that the following pages will prove not merely a springboard for harried homilists but more importantly "a spring of water welling up" to freshen life (cf. Jn 4:14) for all manner of Christians who are trying in trying times to "know [the Lord] more clearly, love him more dearly, follow him more nearly" (*Godspell*).

Walter J. Burghardt, S.J.

PROLOGUE

THE WORD FORMS THE PREACHER

Some years ago, two Catholic scholars found themselves at odds in print. The issue was Scripture—specifically, contemporary Catholic exegesis, the historico-critical method. The "concerned" Catholic expressed his displeasure with Catholic exegetes in the words of a distraught Mary Magdalene at the tomb of Jesus: "They have taken away my Lord, and I know not where they have laid him" (Jn 20:13). The unconcerned exegete retorted in the words of angels: "Why do you seek the living among the dead?" (Lk 24:5). "He has risen; he is not here" (Mk 16:6).

That confrontation is not impertinent here. My topic reads "The Word Forms the Preacher." Not a question: "Does the Word Form the Preacher?" A declarative sentence. Actually, a declarative that is more like a Greek optative, a mood expressive of wish or desire: "The Word Should Form the Preacher," or "Would That the Word Formed the Preacher!" A tough topic, for all its seeming self-evidentness. I propose to address the topic in three stages, moving from the less difficult to the more difficult. First, I shall ask why the Word should form the preacher. Second, I shall cast a glance over my shoulder, to ask how the Word formed a particularly impressive gaggle of preachers in the past. Third, I shall ask the most difficult question of all, the heart of the homiletic matter: How might the Word form the preacher today? In other words, I shall play, in turn, the theologian, the historian, and the prophet.

I

First, why should the Word form the preacher? Four succinct definitions will clarify what the question means—the way we operated in a tighter seminary theology. The "Word" I take to be the inspired text of Scripture, Old Testament and New. The "preacher" on whom I focus is the homilist, addressing a congregation in the context of Eucharistic liturgy. Not indeed exclusively (other religious situations may be beneficiaries of my bons mots) but primarily. To "form" is to give a particular shape to something or someone, to mold or fashion into a certain shape or condition. To form a preacher is to help shape what a homilist ought to be, how he ought to think and feel and express himself. The verb "should" is here an ought: not simply what is fitting or becoming or expedient, but what is necessary, indispensable, therefore involving moral obligation. My thesis, therefore: To preach effectively in the Eucharistic liturgy, the homilist must be molded in his being and his feeling, in his thinking and his speaking, by the inspired pages of Scripture.

But why? Why can't I mount the pulpit armed with the sword of the Spirit and a manual of orthodox theology, supplemented by pastoral experience and the irresistible attraction of my Brite smile? Because the homily is not just *any* sermon. "Its character," Vatican II insisted, "should be that of a proclamation of God's wonderful works in the history of salvation, that is, the mystery of Christ. . . ." That is why the homily "should draw its content mainly from scriptural and liturgical sources."[1] And so the Council urged the clergy to read Scripture diligently and study it carefully. Such "cultivation of Scripture is required (*necesse est*) lest any of them become 'an empty preacher of the word of God outwardly, who is not a listener to it inwardly,' since they must share the abundant wealth of the divine word with the faithful committed to them, especially in the sacred liturgy."[2]

In a nutshell: We are to preach, above all else, God's wonderful works, and these works are detailed in privileged fashion in the Old and New Testaments. Not all God's works, of course, are recorded there. After all, God did not cease working wonderfully in our midst after the Second Letter of Peter was completed early in the second century. "The world is" still "charged with the grandeur of God."[3] The fifth act in the drama of salvation (the "last age") is being played right now, and we are witnesses thereto, even actors therein; but the first four acts have been played: Eden, Israel, Calvary, and the newborn Church. And the record lies in a book that moves from creation to a final "Come, Lord Jesus!" (Rev 22:20)—a record that, inevitably couched in words of men, is unique in being the Word of God. No other source, no other reference book, can claim that distinction.[4]

No doubt, therefore, that Scripture must not simply season or salt our sermons but shape them. I would not dream of producing a modern *Hamlet* without being saturated by Shakespeare's hero, even though I am not bound to be faithful to the Bard's every genuine word. I can reinterpret a Chopin sonata, but to do so justifiably I had better know Chopin as well as I know myself. A fortiori for Scripture. At the close of my homily I should be able to say "This is the word of the Lord." With some trepidation indeed, some nuancing, and a lower-case w. How can I call this God's word if my sermon is not steeped in God's Word? Not only my sermon but myself.

Precisely how I do this I reserve to my third point. Right now I see no benefit in belaboring a first point which should elicit a speedy amen from every Christian preacher—not only the Bible-thumping TVer but also the sermonizer whose eyes are fixed not so much on yesterday as on the signs of *our* times. Our own signs—the hell of the Holocaust or the hell of nuclear war, the agonizing struggle for justice and the muted cries of the hungry—make no Christian sense unless their context is the age-old story of salvation, God's dealings with His people through every captivity and every exodus. No spoken word without the written Word.

II

Second, a look back into the distant past, to see how one rather well-defined group of preachers were formed by the Word. I mean the Fathers of the Church, those ecclesiastical writers of the first six or seven centuries who were distinguished for orthodoxy of doctrine and holiness of life, and have therefore been approved by the Church as witnesses to its faith.[5] These men saw themselves, in Campenhausen's words, "as trained, enlightened interpreters of the Bible, which contains God's saving revelation."[6] A popular current of contemporary thought would have us believe that these writers have little or nothing to offer the twentieth century in the realm of the Bible, that their passion for the allegorical and their poverty in the basic tools of biblical research have made them expendable in this area. A more balanced appraisal of the patristic contribution to the Christian understanding of the Bible might well begin with the praise of Pius XII in the encyclical *Divino afflante Spiritu*. Despite inferiority in secular learning and in knowledge of languages, the Fathers still had a God-given gift, "a delightful insight into the things of God and a remarkably keen discernment" which enabled them to penetrate deeply the depths of God's Word and bring to light what can help to clarify the doctrine of Christ and assist to sanctity.[7] In somewhat the same vein, but from a different perspective, the first-rate Scripture scholar Pierre Benoit wrote:

> . . . We are not merely Westerners; we are moderns, who have passed through the crisis of rationalism and are still imbued with its scientistic positivism. Despite us, in us rational truth has supplanted religious truth. Hence that itch for material precision, that passion for dwelling on the detail of some fact, the while we forget its value as sign—the only thing that ultimately matters. We "strain out the gnat and swallow the camel" (Mt 23:24). This insistence on the critical is useful, but in its subordinate place; it ought not be a myopia which hinders one's view of the horizon. "This must be done, but without leaving the other undone" (Mt 23:23). The sacred writers of old, who saw in everything the problem of God, grasped the inner meaning of history better than we, even though they were not as successful in mastering its exact details. And the Fathers of the Church, Greek and Latin though they were, possessed nevertheless that religious sense which made them go straight to the essential, without being troubled to the same extent by deficiencies that are secondary. It is this feeling for the faith that we must recapture if we too want to understand what the Bible is trying to tell us. Then it will be that many of the false problems will vanish. We shall find in the Bible the truth in its totality, because we shall be searching for it there alone where God put it.[8]

Now I am not advocating a return to the exegetical method of the Fathers, especially the allegorism of the Alexandrians; we have gone beyond it. I am not canonizing their interpretations; they are frequently wild, off the wall—as when they find Christ in every line of Scripture. I am not recommending large-scale priestly plagiarism; it is the rare paragraph that can be transferred bodily from the fourth century to the twentieth; our rhetoric, like our people and our problems, is not theirs. I do submit that, for our spirituality and our preaching (they go together, you know), we can with profit appropriate the Fathers' familiarity with Scripture, their love for Scripture, their search for Christ in Scripture, their refusal to cut Scripture up into a set of isolated texts heaven-sent to prove theses, their deep realization that Scripture is God's story of salvation, that there are depths to Scripture which even the most accomplished exegete will never completely fathom. Their value for the preacher is a three-pronged principle that bursts forth from the patristic pulpit: It is God's revelation that must be preached; we know this revelation, in unparalleled fashion, from Scripture; and so we should know Scripture intimately, love it dearly, preach it passionately. Their preaching, like their theology and their sense of tradition, can be summed up in four words: Scripture within the Church.

Take Augustine of Hippo.[9] An eloquent preacher who constantly astonished and delighted, though he had a weak voice and tired quickly. Most of his sermons were more spontaneous than they seem: delivered first, written down then or afterwards by someone else. His preparation was prayer or a short meditation. "What he really did was to improvise on the Bible texts that had just been read."[10] Nor was orderly construction his forte: "Augustine disregarded any need for logical construction and observed only that order which was dictated by circumstances and by his own heart."[11] He played perpetually on words, punned shamelessly; he was inordinately fond of assonance, alliteration, antitheses. He encouraged reactions from his audience, found applause stimulating, provocative: "What is there to cheer about? We are still battling with the problem and you have already started to cheer!"[12] He saw the sermon as not only education but entertainment: "You must not believe, brothers and sisters, that the Lord intended us to be entirely without theatrical spectacles of some kind. If there were none here, would you have come together in this place?"[13]

Now it is not improvisation or disorder that I am commending to you, unless you are Augustine reincarnate. I do resonate to his weaving of words, even to his paronomasia; I would love to be interrupted by applause; and I get immoderate pleasure when the people of God are amused by my pleasantries.

But something far more substantial in Augustine's sermons impresses me most. His preaching is essentially biblical in character; he is proclaiming biblical truth. "As soon as he touches a text it seems to open up like a flower. And when the text in its turn touches Augustine, it becomes . . . a stream of living water from the hidden places of Holy Scripture; for he lives so much in Holy Scripture that a single associational link suffices to call some unfamiliar word into life and bring out the sweetness of its meaning."[14] Read his homilies on each Psalm, on just about each verse of John. You may be amused or amazed at what he gets out of a Psalm or reads into the Gospel; you will be touched by the way Old Testament and New have shaped him. His exposition of the Sermon on the Mount, Pelikan concludes, "shows Augustine as a master of biblical preaching, a converted rhetor who had learned from the living Word that rhetoric could be a snare, but who brought his rhetorical gifts to the service of that Word."[15]

The Donatist Tyconius called the Bible an immeasurable forest of prophecy. Augustine "believed that this forest rustled with one single truth and that every leaf whispered a prophecy for him who knew how to listen. In all its treetops, he said, there rustled but the single word—the Word."[16] The Bible is at once full of riddles and very simple, accessible to all. And in Augustine's theory of knowledge, no man or woman really instructs another; the real teacher is God. And so he planted the word of God from God's Word and let God make the twig bear fruit, the leaf burst forth.

On the Greek side, take John Chrysostom. Chrysostom is not his name; it is a description that has replaced his name since the sixth century: "the man with the golden mouth." The 18 large volumes of his works in Migne (MG 47–64) are for the most part sermons. The remarkable purity of his language, the style the classical scholar Wilamowitz-Moellendorff called "the harmonious expression of an Attic soul," and his startlingly direct, down-to-earth applications can make us forget that most of his sermons are exegetical homilies on the Old and New Testaments. An amazing aggregation. You find 76 homilies on Genesis, sermons on 58 selected Psalms, 90 on Matthew, 88 on John, 59 on Acts. Almost half of his homilies are on Pauline epistles, for no one fired his eloquence more than Paul: 32 on Romans, 48 on 1 Corinthians and 33 on 2 Corinthians, a series on Galatians, 24 homilies on Ephesians, 15 on Philippians, 12 on Colossians, 11 on 1 Thessalonians and 5 on 2 Thessalonians, 18 on 1 Timothy and 10 on 2 Timothy, 6 on Titus, 3 on Philemon, 34 on Hebrews.[17] The homilies home in on the literal sense; they invariably extract a spiritual message; and they confront the congregation where the people actually live. Chrysostom can do all this because yesterday's Scripture and today's issues are part and parcel of him, are inextricably intertwined in the one man who is at once preacher and pastor, exegete and shepherd.

III

So far so good: Scripture should form the preacher, and Scripture has formed preachers. The most urgent question remains: How might Scripture form the preacher today? How do you go about it?

Let me begin with a proposition that at first glance is discouraging. A remarkably articulate Lutheran preacher, Joseph Sittler, published a little book almost two decades ago with the expressive title *The Anguish of Preaching*.[18] Speaking of the preacher as the appointed voice of a community that "came into existence speaking, confessing, praising, reporting," of a community that "continues" and that "continues doing those same things," Sittler goes on to say:

> Disciplines correlative to preaching can be taught, but preaching as an act of witness cannot be taught. Biblical introduction, training in languages, methods of exegesis, cultural and other historical data that illuminate the texts of the Scriptures—these matters can be refined and transmitted in teaching. But preaching itself, the creative symbiosis within which intersects [*sic*] numberless facts, experiences, insights, felt duties of pastoral obligation toward a specific congregation, the interior existence of the preacher himself, this particular man as he seeks for right utterance of an incommunicable and non-shareable quality of being and thought—this cannot be taught. It is, nevertheless, commanded—and not only by custom of the church.[19]

"Preaching as an act of witness cannot be taught." After a decade of being taught homiletics and four decades of homilizing, I tend to agree. I can indeed help you in ways that are not insignificant. I can alert you to useful commentaries such as Brown on John, Fitzmyer on Luke, McKenzie on Second Isaiah. I can urge you to deepen your understanding of theological themes highly pertinent to preaching: Read Dulles on the Church, Cooke on ministry and sacraments, Schillebeeckx and Sobrino on today's Christ, McCormick on bioethics in a brave new world. I can correct your composition, retool your rhetoric, propel you to project, perhaps even lessen your lisp. All these are important, especially in a context where the long-suffering laity are intolerant of the trivia we dish out, the constipation of thought amid a diarrhea of words, are surprised or scandalized by a dismal style and a vapid vocabulary unworthy of the Word we claim to proclaim, and are puzzled by our ability to declaim about the divine without a shred of feeling or emotion.

All true; and still it remains true that "preaching as an act of witness cannot be taught." For here we confront what Sittler called "the interior existence of the preacher himself, this particular man as he seeks for right utterance of an incommunicable and non-shareable quality of being and thought." Here, I suggest, it is the living Christ who is our teacher; more comprehensively, the Father through Christ in the Spirit.

At first blush, frightening; on second thought, encouraging. For it fits fascinatingly into my thesis: It is the Word that forms the preacher. Not exclusively, but in large measure and at the roots. Encouraging because it takes some of the pressure off our native oratorical skills and deficiencies. Preaching is not, in the first instance, a matter of posture and gesture, of assonance and resonance. It is primarily a question of the person—the person who precedes the preacher, the person who *is* the preacher. It is not first the homily that the Word must fashion; it is the homilist. Shaped by the Word, you are a different person. Different person, therefore different homilist.

But how? God's written Word must take hold of you as His spoken word took hold of Isaiah and Jeremiah, of Ezekiel and Hosea; as the spoken word of Christ mesmerized Matthew and Magdalene, captured Simon Peter and the Samaritan woman.

But how? Basically, the Word you study has to be the Word you pray, and the Word you pray the Word you live. You recall, I'm sure, how Luther's study of Scripture between 1513 and 1517—the Psalms and Romans, Galatians and Hebrews—transformed his theology.[20] But not his theology alone—his life and his preaching. And still he could recognize and regret how inadequate sheer scholarship soon proves itself. At the close of his Christmas sermon in 1522 he cried out despairingly:

O that God should desire that my interpretation and that of all teachers should disappear, and each Christian should come straight to the scripture alone and to the pure word of God! You see from this babbling of mine the immeasurable difference between the word of God and all human words, and how no man can adequately reach and explain a single word of God with all his words. It is an eternal word, and must be understood and contemplated with a quiet mind. . . . No one else can understand except a mind that contemplates in silence. For anyone who could achieve this without commentary or interpretation, my commentaries and those of everyone else would not only be of no use, but merely a hindrance. Go to the Bible itself, dear Christians, and let my expositions and those of all scholars be no more than a tool with which to build aright, so that we can understand, taste and abide in the simple and pure word of God; for God dwells alone in Zion.[21]

But even contemplation of God's Word was not enough for Luther's theology, not sufficient for his preaching. To become a theologian worthy of the name—and, Luther would surely add, a preacher worthy of that name—you must have *experience* of sin and grace, of life and death. "Consequently Luther's teaching on justification bears the marks of profound, often anguished, moments of personal involvement with deep feeling. Sin and guilt are terrifying in this world of thought, grace and forgiveness liberating and full of delight."[22]

I submit that Luther offers a rich model for the way the Word should shape "the interior existence of the preacher": quiet contemplation of the Word in the context of serious study and profound experience. A word on each of the three facets.

For most of us, there is no substitute for *study* of the Word. I know that my dear forebear Ignatius Loyola had a single illumination—of God One and Three, of the world's fashioning, and the bodying forth of the Son—that outstripped, by his own admission, all he learned or was given by God in 62 years. But *I* cannot count on such a self-manifestation of God. I must have recourse to the source God invented for all of us, the self-disclosure that is His written Word. It exists not to while away some disenchanted evening, but to transform me, to turn me inside out, to fashion a new creature. If that is so, then the more I know about it and the deeper I plunge into its depths, the more likely I am to experience its incomparable power.

It's a strange situation, isn't it? The Catholic preacher has at his beck and call the single most significant book in the history of humankind, the most revealing story of human existence, a book we profess to be God's Word. And yet, over 32 years I've seen swarms of seminarians study Scripture as simply another course to be passed: This is not where the action is. Unnumbered priests in parish ministry will not touch a commentary: It's just too tough; it doesn't speak to the people, to the ditchdigger and the "bag lady"; there's enough information in some prepackaged "homily hints."

I have news for you, bad news. For all their immediate and practical value, for all their ability to rescue the storm-tossed pastor, "homily hints" are not likely to reshape your spirit, to mold the core of your being. Granted, study alone will not so shape you; but organized, disciplined, methodical searching is a splendid beginning. If nothing else, it tells God and your people that you take Him seriously, take Him "at His Word."

Still, Luther was on target: Scholarly tomes and commentaries are "no more than a tool with which to build aright, so that we can understand, taste and abide in the simple and pure word of God." The Word we study calls for *contemplation:* It "must be contemplated with a quiet mind." The Bible is not Blackstone's *Commentaries* or Einstein's theory of relativity; it is a book to be prayed. Not only does it inform the intellect; it ought to form the whole person. This is impossible in a classroom; it demands a prie-dieu, forces you to your knees.

What I am commending to the preacher is a spirituality that is biblically based—and expressly so. Not simply the *study* of Old and New Testament spirituality, though this can base the broader life of the spirit. Rather, a reverent immersion in Scripture such that intelligence is subservient to love. We Christians do fairly well with the Gospels. My own spirituality continues to be shaped by the Spiritual Exercises of St. Ignatius, where three of the four Weeks are contemplations on a living, dying, rising Christ. Nor am I singular in this regard. Your inner life is surely fed more nutritiously by the story of Jesus than by any other aliment. This is the way it should be, and I can only slap your spiritual rump in macho encouragement: Keep it up, baby!

One problem here: Such contemplation is restrictive. To limit myself to the Gospels, or the Gospels and Chrysostom's beloved Paul, is like reading only the end of a mystery, the last chapter of an Agatha Christie. God's story and mine, God's love for the human family, is much broader. The Christian, particularly the Christian preacher, ought to be nourished by all that has gone before: by a God who walked with Adam in the cool of evening and with His people through the Red Sea; by a God who was Father and Savior and Lover long before His Son took our flesh; by singers of psalms and prophets of doom and deliverance; by a special people's journeying to God through faith and infidelity, through wisdom and purification.[23] Forget not the advice of Paul to Timothy: "As for you, continue in what you have learned and have firmly believed, knowing from whom you learned it and how from childhood you have been acquainted with the sacred writings [the books of the Old Testament] which are able to instruct you for salvation through faith in Christ Jesus. *All* Scripture [again, the Old Testament] is inspired by God and profitable for teaching, for reproof, for correction, and for training in righteousness, that the man of God may be complete, equipped for every good work" (2 Tim 3:14–17).

Good indeed, but not yet enough. The contemplation which complements study must itself be completed. How? By *experience.* I mean very specific experiences, analogous to Luther's experience of sin and grace, of life and death. Let me concretize this with one powerful example: Jeremiah. I borrow it from an essay in biblical spirituality by Carroll Stuhlmueller.[24]

It is the search for vocation in Jeremiah. What developed from that search is a theology of vocation that became the classical biblical model. The Suffering Servant (Isa 49), John the Baptist (Lk 1), Paul (Gal 1:15–16), and Jesus himself appealed in varied ways to Jeremiah's soul-searching attempt to appreciate the meaning of God's call. It is a theology that "exploded from his heart . . . seemingly without structure or order," less a theology than a ferment.

Throughout his long ministry Jeremiah was constantly questing for the meaning of his vocation. The first six years of his preaching (627/26–21 B.C.) were exciting. He was responding to an apostolic opportunity. On the one hand, Babylon's declaration of independence meant a resurgence of Babylonian deities and Babylonian religion; on the other hand, independence for Judah meant a fresh enthusiasm for the God of Israel. High were Jeremiah's hopes and ideals; the future was rich in possibility. Success came speedily; and such success, Jeremiah reasoned, surely proved that God had called him, demonstrated beyond doubt what his vocation should be.

Then ensued a series of reversals. In 621 young King Josiah and some cronies began to *impose* reform on the people. It was so contradictory to Jeremiah's "new covenant" written on the heart, expressing itself spontaneously in an interior knowledge of the Lord (Jer 31:31–34). Then even the dictatorial reform ground to a halt. Now commenced the second period of Jeremiah's life, the "long trek across the dreary plateau of failures." The reign of Jehoiakim, puppet of the Egyptians and then of the Babylonians, was the prophet's way of the cross. Time and again he disputed with God: "You are just, O Lord. . . . Why does the way of the wicked prosper?" (Jer 12:1). To be where God was to be found, he had to search into darkness. And God's answer, when it came, was discouraging: Things will get worse before they get better. Only as he walked deeper and deeper into the shadows of his faith, sustained only by the conviction that God must be there, did the very concept of his vocation come to be increasingly purified. Only at the end of his life could he tell with fair clarity what his calling meant. Only after repeated failure and frustration did he realize that his plans for God were not necessarily God's plan for him. His own dreams, dreams for God, had to crumble before he could lose himself totally in God. Stuhlmueller writes with insight:

> At the end of his life when he wrote chapter 1, Jeremiah said that his vocation was to be a prophet to the nations, a prophet to the Gentiles. Jeremiah never was a prophet to the nations. Jeremiah died with that hope which he left to the next generation, picked up by the Suffering Servant and by St. Paul. Jeremiah's vocation was to be the carrier of hopes to the next generation.[25]

The point of this seeming excursion into Jeremiah land? If I, this preacher, am to be formed or reformed to the depths of my existence by the Word, study of Scripture is insufficient, and not just any contemplation will do. Scripture must speak to my experience, my experience to it—an endless oscillation, rhythm, dialogue. Jeremiah is not merely a nifty story from an alien past. Jeremiah is not primarily a rich source for quotable quotes: "Before I formed you in the womb I knew you" (1:5); "I have loved you with an everlasting love" (31:3). Jeremiah is I; I am Jeremiah. Oh, not in every smallest detail; but surely at the level of their deep significance our experiences run parallel. All my life long I too must search for the more profound meaning of what I started out to do; only at the end will I be able to write that meaning.

Old Testament? It is perennially new, ceaselessly fresh—if I pray it. Need I add that contemplation of Christ, this kind of contemplation, contemplation-*cum*-experience, should prove even more formative of the Christian homilist, of the Christian person? If the Word that is Scripture is to take flesh in us, the Word that is Christ must be enfleshed in us. I suspect that, in the last analysis, my hope for you as homilists can be summed up in St. Paul's affecting cry to the Christians of Galatia: "My little children, with whom I am again in travail until Christ be formed in you!" (Gal 4:19). Until Christ be formed in you. . . .

ADVENT

1

ADVENT WITH JOHN THE BAPTIST
Second Sunday of Advent (A)

♦ Isaiah 11:1–10
♦ Romans 15:4–9
♦ Matthew 3:1–12

Advent, you hear constantly, is a month of waiting—waiting for Christ. It is a period of preparing—preparing for his coming. If you follow the Advent liturgies closely, you find that three persons play especially prominent parts: Isaiah, Mary, and John the Baptist. The prophet Isaiah shows us God readying His exiled people, through suffering, to be a people of hope, waiting in hope for a God who will come to rescue them in His own good time.[1] Mary waits uniquely, as no one in history has ever waited, because the Promised One, the one for whom she too is waiting, is resting within her, growing from her.[2] And there is John the Baptist (John the Baptizer, if you prefer), whose father, Zechariah, prophesied soon after John's birth: "And you, child, will be called the prophet of the Most High; for you will go before the Lord to prepare his ways" (Lk 1:76). Since I have already spoken of Advent with Isaiah and Advent with Mary, let me spend these moments on Advent with John, to see what he suggests about waiting, about preparing for the coming of our Savior.

Three New Testament passages about John are singularly suggestive for Advent. The first is today's Gospel: John comes "preaching in the wilderness of Judea, 'Repent, for the kingdom of heaven is at hand' " (Mt 3:1–2). The second is the Gospel you will hear next Sunday: John in prison sends his disciples to ask Jesus: "Are you he who is to come, or shall we look for another?" (Mt 11:3). The third is a Gospel you hear during the fourth week of Advent in the C cycle: Elizabeth, pregnant with John, exclaims when Mary comes to visit her: "Behold, when the voice of your greeting came

19

to my ears, the baby in my womb leaped for joy" (Lk 1:44). A word on each.

I

First, today's Gospel. Here the message sounds awfully grim. John comes to us arrayed in "a garment of camel's hair and a leather girdle" that are definitely not Calvin Klein, eating "locusts" not prepared by Pierre (Mt 3:4). His message? "Repent!" (v. 2). The Greek word means "change your mind," "change your thinking," "turn about," "return," "be converted." John is telling his fellow Jews to reform their lives, to return to the way of life demanded by the covenant between God and Israel, to be faithful to the promise of their fathers: "All that the Lord has spoken we will do, and we will be obedient" (Exod 24:7), to be faithful to the "new covenant" described in Jeremiah: "I will write [my law] upon their hearts; and I will be their God, and they shall be my people" (Jer 31:31, 33).

Now the Baptist's command is just as urgent today as it was then. If Christ is to come to us in any meaningful way, if Christmas is to be more than "Ho, ho, ho, and a bottle of rum," we Christians have to change our minds, our way of thinking, our way of living. I am not accusing any individual of any sin; a homilist is not a judge. I am recalling the first Letter of John: "If we say we have no sin, we deceive ourselves, and the truth is not in us" (1 Jn 1:8). I am afraid that, in our reaction to the guilt some old-fashioned Sister Ignatius supposedly inflicted on our tender psyche, sin itself has vanished from our vocabulary.

And yet, cast your eye across the earth. From Belfast to Beirut, from Africa to Afghanistan, men are massacring their own brothers and sisters—and not all the killers are pagans. In "Christian" countries death squads terrorize dissenters, thousands disappear without a trace, political prisoners waste away without trial, an Aquino is killed as he returns home, an archbishop is murdered in his cathedral. Whole nations groan in helpless slavery. Each day 120,000 innocents are aborted. Look at the pimps, the dealers in drugs, the cocaine kings, battered wives and burnt children. No sin?

Look closer to home. Do Hoyas lie less, lust less, hate less, cheat less, drink less, "throw up" less than, say, Terrapins?[3] Or is it only Protestants who sin, and Catholics are careful not to hurt anyone? No sin?

My brothers and sisters, I speak of sin not to make you wallow in guilt. I speak of sin because you and I are part of a covenant people; we have a sacred pact with God. God-in-flesh cut a new covenant with us in his blood: "This is my blood of the [new] covenant, which is poured out . . . for the forgiveness of sins" (Mt 26:28). We recall that covenant each time we transmute wheat and wine into Christ's body and blood. With this pact God has promised us His special love, His blessing, His protection; and we have promised to be faithful, to have no master save Christ, to be a people that is growing into his likeness. Sin is sacrilege because it mars the features of Christ in us, betrays the new covenant, shows us faithless to a God who never ceases to be faithful despite all our infidelities.

If you would prepare for Christ's coming, pray the Psalmist's prayer for healing:

> Have mercy on me, O God,
>   according to your steadfast love;
> according to your abundant mercy
>   blot out my transgressions.
> Create in me a clean heart, O God,
>   and put a new and steadfast spirit within me.
> Cast me not away from your presence,
>   and take not your holy Spirit from me.
>   (Ps 51:1, 10–11)

II

The second passage is the Gospel you will hear next Sunday (Mt 11:2–11). John the Baptist, in his prison cell, is puzzled. He has heard about "the deeds of the Christ" (v. 2), but he is still uncertain. Where is the fiery social reformer he has been led to expect? Where is Isaiah's "liberty [for] the captives, the opening of the prison [for] those who are bound" (Isa 61:1)? He does not see "the oppressed go free," "every yoke" broken (Isa 58:6). The Jews are still chafing under Roman domination; the poor still beg for bread; the society has not changed. Oh yes, Jesus has healed some sick, raised some dead, cast out some devils. But the real devils are still around: Roman soldiers, Pilate, Herod; poverty and sickness and inequality. And so he sends his own disciples to ask Jesus: "Are you he who is to come [the Messiah], or shall we look for another?" (v. 3). Are you the one I am supposed to proclaim, the long-awaited of the ages? I'm not sure.

John's puzzlement is a rough lesson for our Advent waiting. It is not always easy to recognize Christ. He comes in unexpected ways, ways you and I are not prepared for. If you were living in Palestine at Christ's first coming, and some prophet told you the Messiah would be coming soon, would you have looked for a baby wrapped in straw? Would you have looked for him on a cross? Would you have expected him to come to you looking like bread, tasting like bread?

It is still difficult to recognize Christ. He *should* speak to us through those who speak in his name. And we do hear his voice when they tell us that he is more than man, that he died for us and lives in us, that he is to be our joy days without end. But many find his voice less than trumpet-like, less than clear, when his spokesmen speak of the relations between a man and a woman, when they speak of war and peace between nations. He *should* transpire, come to light, on the face of his Church, but she is not yet St. Paul's Church "in splendor, without spot or wrinkle or any such thing, . . . holy and without blemish" (Eph 5:27); and so a good many ceaselessly look for him elsewhere. He *should* reveal himself in the crucified of this world; but how often do you find him there?

What I am suggesting is that Christian existence is an endless Advent. We are not simply in possession of a Christ who came to us once, is back in his heaven, and will come again at the end of the ages. No, Christ is here; but we have to search for him, look for him, often like the anguished beloved in the Song of Solomon: ". . . I sought him whom my soul loves; I sought him, but found him not; I called him, but he gave no answer" (Cant 3:1). Christian faith is not a guarantee against doubt, uncertainty, wavering, ambiguity. We walk in darkness; we grope; we cry out. If John the Baptist—no one greater than he "among those born of women" (Mt 11:11)—had to ask "Are you the Christ?", don't be surprised if your prison cell forces from your parched lips the same question: "Is it really you, Lord?"

III

The third passage is a Gospel you hear during the fourth week of Advent (Lk 1:39–45). You remember how, when the angel left Mary, left her with God in her womb, Mary "went with haste into the hill country" (v. 29). Why? Two reasons: to congratulate her cousin Elizabeth on her unexpected pregnancy and to help her through her final three months. As soon as Mary greeted Elizabeth, "the baby in [Elizabeth's] womb leaped for joy" (v. 44). Little John, locked six months in the womb of Elizabeth, sensed somehow the presence of his Lord locked in the womb of Mary; and he stirred, not as any child stirs within a mother's body—John stirred for *joy*.

What you have here is a striking symbol of a remarkable truth: A special sign of God's coming is joy. God's coming brings joy, and joy is a proof that God has come. I never tire of Nietzsche's caustic criticism of Christians: We do not look redeemed. We do not look as if the Son of God touched this earth with our flesh, died a bloody death for us, rose to fresh life for us, lives and acts in us. We seem to live half of one beatitude: "Blessed are they that mourn" (Mt 5:4). Blessed are the melancholy.

No, my friends. The promise of Christ "I will see you again and your hearts will rejoice, and your joy no one will take from you" (Jn 16:22) is not restricted to the disciples who shared his last supper. He pledges the same to you. He has come again; he is here; he does see you. The question is, do you see him? Oh, not face to face—not yet. But do you ever experience him? Not an ecstasy or a vision. Simply, do you know Christ? Not words about him, but Christ himself. When he nestles in your palm, on your tongue, do you sense his real presence? Does his living in you thrill you, give you goose-pimples? Do you ever feel what a Sister once sang so lyrically:

> It's this that makes
>   My spirit spin,
> My bones to quake,
>   My blood run thin,
> My flesh to melt
>   Inside my skin,*
> My very pulse
>   Create a din—
> It's this that makes
>   My spirit spin:
> That Heaven is
>   Not *up*, but *in!*[4]

This is not poetic fancy; it is Christian realism. That is why in next Sunday's liturgy you will pray to the Father with the whole Church: "May we, your people, who look forward to the birthday of Christ, experience the joy of salvation." Not simply believe you are saved. Experience . . . the joy . . . of salvation. If you do not, then repeat again and again the prayer that opened today's liturgy: "Remove the things that hinder us from receiving Christ with joy."

What is it, Christ-bearers, that keeps your spirit from spinning? What is it that keeps you from looking redeemed?

To sum it up, then: What is John the Baptist's Advent message? First, take a fresh look at the covenant Christ cut with you in his blood, your Christian commitment to mirror Christ day in and day out, and then repent: Re-form your life, change your thinking, excise whatever is less than Christlike in you. Second, recognize with St. Paul that "now we see in a mirror dimly" (1 Cor 13:12), realize that the face of Christ is not easy to discern, and then redouble your struggle to discover him—in the Word proclaimed and the Bread broken, in your God-filled heart and the empty eyes of the crucified all around you. Third, focus on the fact that God-in-flesh lies no longer in straw but in you, let this realization suffuse not your intellect alone but your whole being, and then let go—let the joy that *is* Christ thrill you beyond your power to control.

Spend Advent like this, and you will turn Christmas upside down: Christ will not come to you (he is already here), you will come to him. And that, my friends, is the way it ought to be.

Dahlgren Chapel
Georgetown University
and
Holy Trinity Church
Washington, D.C.
December 4, 1983

2

ADVENT WITH MARY
Second Sunday of Advent (C)

♦ Baruch 5:1–9
♦ Philippians 1:4–6, 8–11
♦ Luke 3:1–6

There is a danger to Advent. It tends to become impersonal, a season—like winter. We are still waiting for Christ to come, and till he comes we have a vacuum; there is no one else around. All we have is an Advent wreath with four candles.

In point of fact, three captivating persons dominate the Advent liturgy—three persons who prepare in different ways for the coming of the Savior. One is the prophet Isaiah. He hopes passionately for the prince of peace, represents Israel's yearning for the messianic king, but does not know where he is to be found. Israel is waiting for God to come in His own good time, a God who is readying His people even in exile to be redemptive, to bear suffering witness to Yahweh, to be a people of hope.[1] The second Advent figure is John the Baptist. He is the Messiah's messenger, his herald, his forerunner; but he is puzzled. He expects the Messiah to be a fiery social reformer, Elijah come to earth again; and he doesn't quite know what to make of the Jesus he sees. The third dominant figure is a soft-spoken lady in Nazareth. It is of her I would speak to you today. In three stages, with three questions: (1) What is the Advent liturgy all about? (2) How does the mother of Jesus fit into it? (3) What does the Mary of Advent say to us today?

I

First, what is the Advent liturgy all about? What are we doing these four weeks? Very simply, it is a period of expectation; we are

waiting. Waiting for what? We focus on two events. We put ourselves back into the situation of an expectant people, a people on
tiptoe for the first coming of the Messiah; and we rekindle our expectation of his final coming.

A people on tiptoe. That is why today's reading from Baruch,
Jeremiah's companion and secretary, is so appropriate. We put on
the shoes of a people in exile, thirsting for a God long in coming but
certain to come. They are told to "take courage . . . for He who
named you will comfort you" (Bar 4:30). They are summoned to
look out of their darkness to a new dawn:

> Arise, O Jerusalem, stand upon the height
>   and look toward the east,
> and see your children gathered from west and east,
>   at the word of the Holy One,
>   rejoicing that God has remembered them.
>
> (Bar 5:5)

It matches the matchless lines Luke quotes from Isaiah in today's
Gospel:

> Every valley shall be filled,
> and every mountain and hill shall be brought low,
> and the crooked shall be made straight,
> and the rough ways shall be made smooth;
> and all flesh shall see the salvation of God.
>
> (Lk 3:5–6; cf. Isa 40:4–5)

This waiting for the Promised One we recapture in Advent, we
relive it, we re-present it. But, as Christians, we know that this
aspect of the liturgy, Christ's first coming, is a fact of history; he has
already come. He came on a midnight clear, in infant powerlessness. What we actually await now is his second coming, "with great
power and glory" (Mk 13:26). That is why today's reading from St.
Paul is so appropriate: "I am sure that He who began a good work
in you will bring it to completion at the day of Jesus Christ" (Phil
1:6), the day when Christ will return and the present age will end.
This is the day of which we pray in each day's Mass: "Deliver us,
Lord, from every evil and grant us peace in our day. In your mercy
keep us free from sin and protect us from all anxiety as we wait in
joyful hope for the coming of our Savior, Jesus Christ." We wait in
joyful hope. In this liturgy, in every liturgy, we proclaim Christ's

death "till he comes again." Only then, in its full reality, will "all flesh see the salvation of God."

Advent, then, announces two advents. One advent is history, and the liturgy helps us relive it "on tiptoe of expectation" (Lk 3:15 NEB). The other advent is "future shock," and the liturgy fixes our eyes on it; for when he comes, we "shall see [Christ] as he is" (1 Jn 3:2).

II

But how does Mary fit into the Advent liturgy? Not only on next Wednesday's feast day. Not primarily because we celebrate her birthday on September 8, subtract nine months, and celebrate her conception on December 8. The reason goes much deeper. Mary is an Advent figure because the mother of Jesus is history's most remarkable model of a world's waiting. More strikingly than anyone else, she reveals in living color how the Christian should wait for Christ.

First, the way Mary waited for Christ's *first* coming. Not only like every other Jew waiting for the Promised One. Not only peering into a clouded future, hoping against hope, wondering, anxiously questing: "Are you he who is to come, or shall we look for another?" (Mt 11:3). No, Mary waited uniquely, as no other in history: He for whom she was waiting was nestling within her. Not simply in her thoughts, her dreams, her hopes, her yearning. In her flesh. His flesh was her flesh; her flesh was his. She was waiting only to see his face and to offer him to the world. Little wonder she burst into rapturous song: "My soul declares the greatness of the Lord, and my spirit finds delight in God my Savior, . . . for He who is mighty has done great things for me . . ." (Lk 1:46–49).

"On tiptoe of expectation" indeed, a singular sort of waiting, those nine intimate months: her Savior within her, her Savior growing from her, her Savior coming to manger straw through her.

Second, the way Mary waited for Christ's *second* coming. In a word, she was his disciple. Not only the first of Jesus' disciples, but the very model of what discipleship demands. Not that she was one of the Twelve; rather that she lived what the New Testament "disciple" means. To be a disciple means to follow—to follow only one Master. How? A constant theme in the Gospels: "Whoever does the will of God is my brother and sister and mother" (Mk 3:35). "My mother and my brothers, they are the ones who listen to the word of God and act on it" (Lk 8:21).

That, at its best, is Mary: she who hears God's word and does it. Such was Mary at the Gospel's beginning. At a decisive moment in salvation's story, God asked this teen-age Jewish girl to mother His Son. Her response, simple and total: "Let it happen to me according to your word" (Lk 1:38). As you say, so be it done. No wonder that in Luke Mary is the first to be praised in a phrase that will characterize the faithful down the ages: She is the woman "who has believed" (Lk 1:45). And this girl who believed, who said yes to God's word, acted on it. She did not lie down and act pregnant. "In those days," Luke tells us, "Mary arose and went with haste into the hill country" (Lk 1:39). Why? To be with a relative, Elizabeth; for Elizabeth was with child, and Elizabeth was old. Mary was carrying Christ not for herself but for a world in need. Quite fitting, therefore, that when Mary greeted her kinswoman, John the Baptist "leaped for joy" in Elizabeth's womb (Lk 1:44).

Such was Mary throughout her life. It is a slender but thrilling theme in Luke. Six times he takes the notion "hearing and doing God's word" and touches it somehow to the mother of Jesus.[2] Perhaps most impressively, she is "blessed" not primarily because she bore God's Son; rather because she is a prime example of "those who listen to the word of God and keep it," observe it, follow it (Lk 11:28). She is family to Jesus not so much because she is his physical mother; rather because she is of "those who listen to the word of God and act on it" (Lk 8:21).[3]

Luke knows, too, that to be Jesus' disciple is to follow a Lord who is on the way to Jerusalem and a cross; and so he recalls Simeon's prophecy to Mary in the temple: "a sword shall pierce you too" (Lk 2:35). It did. On Calvary—in line with Luke—the Evangelist John, who speaks harshly of Jesus' relatives "who never believed in him" (Jn 7:5), does not stress physical relationship. Mary's role is to be mother of the beloved disciple, and with her as mother the beloved disciple becomes Jesus' true brother. These two who believe in him, these two he "leaves . . . behind as the family of disciples who constitute truly a mother and a brother."[4]

And how did Mary act between the ascension of Jesus and the descent of the Spirit? Listen to Luke: The Eleven "with one accord devoted themselves to prayer, together with the women and Mary the mother of Jesus, and with his brothers" (Acts 1:14). The first to hear the gospel even before Jesus' birth, praised during his ministry because she heard the word of God and acted on it, Mary remains faithful after her Son's death—listening to the Lord, waiting for the Spirit.

III

A remarkable woman, no doubt; but what does Mary say to us today, these Advent weeks? Simply, she shows us how to wait for Christ. Not only for his second coming, "with great power and glory"; for his constant coming each day, in poverty and powerlessness that make his crib look like a castle.

This is not pious poetry; this is the word of God. Jesus comes to us in the hungry and thirsty, in the stranger and the naked, in the sick and the shackled (cf. Mt 25:35–40). Mary saw that even before her Son proclaimed it. Her Magnificat, her song of joy after Gabriel's glad tidings, is not an abstract theological thesis: "Bend the knee, my friends; for within me lies the God-man, consubstantial with the Father, consubstantial with us." Mary rejoices because God "has had regard for (has looked with loving care upon) the low estate (the humble station) of His slave woman" (Lk 1:48). The good news about Jesus, she sings, is that God "has scattered the proud . . . has put down the mighty from their thrones and exalted the lowly . . . has filled the hungry with good things and sent the rich away empty . . . has come to the aid of His servant Israel, mindful of His mercy" (Lk 1:51–54).

The problem is, God fills the hungry not with miraculous manna from heaven but through us. The hungers of the human family cry out to us: hunger for bread, for justice and peace, for understanding and love—hunger for God. Their cry is not only a human cry; it is God's word to us. We are Jesus' disciples, in the image of Mary, only if we listen to that word and act on it, as God gives us to act. I cannot prescribe for any of you; only God does that. I don't know what you are supposed to do about the living skeletons in Mother Teresa's Calcutta and the downtrodden in D.C., about the bombed-out in Lebanon and the MX in Wyoming, about the slums in El Salvador and the pimps and prostitutes in Times Square, about the schizoid psyches in St. Elizabeth's and the lonely old on your street. This alone I do say: God is not telling you to do nothing. You must give ear to a God who is speaking to you now, and act on what He says. For here is today's manger, the way Christ comes to you in helplessness. No longer a baby, but just as impotent.

This fresh kind of Advent—active awaiting, ears tuned to the

Spirit, eyes awake to Christ in a thousand Gethsemanes—this will cost you: "a sword shall pierce you too." Discipleship, like grace, does not come cheap. But for your comfort and strength, be aware that you wait, like Mary, with your Lord already within you. Don't envy our Lady to excess; for, as Jesus told you, if you love him and keep his word, his Father loves you and they come to you and make their home with you (cf. Jn 14:23). Christ deep in you and Christ all around you—your whole life can be a ceaseless Advent, a splendid prelude to his final coming. All you have to do is murmur with Mary "Whatever you say, Lord," and then do whatever he says. That's all. . . . That's all?

Shrine of the Immaculate Conception
Washington, D.C.
December 5, 1982

LENT

3

REPENT!
First Sunday of Lent (B)

♦ Genesis 9:8–15
♦ 1 Peter 3:18–22
♦ Mark 1:12–15

You know, we Christians have given Lent a bad name. The first Preface for Lent announces "this joyful season"; and still, for many of us, it's the season of gloom and giving up, of ashes and lashes. When it's gray outside and purple inside. When we feel guilty about not feeling guilty. When we wonder what to substitute for the old-time fast. When children give God the icing on their cake, oldsters the cream in their coffee, students the foam off their Michelob. When the risen Christian pretends that Christ is not yet risen. When the Church's cry is not "Rejoice!" but "Repent!" (Mk 1:15).

I am not about to change the cry the Church borrows from the lips of Jesus; I shall not shout "Don't repent!" What I want to do is accent the positive in "repent," translate the joyous sense of that fearsome word. First, a swift glance at biblical repentance; second, the Christian stress; third, a moving challenge from a young contemporary believer.

I

Repentance has a rich biblical history.[1] At times it means that you regret something; you are sorry for what you have done; you feel remorse and you do penance. David regrets that he has bedded Bathsheba and murdered her husband. The prodigal son confesses that he has lived riotously, wallowed in sex. Peter weeps because he has denied his Lord. All of these repented of something.

But the word carries a still more basic idea; "repent" has a more

33

positive thrust. That idea emerges from the Old Testament prophets. They knew the liturgies of repentance. The people fasted; they wore sackcloth and ashes; they shrieked and sobbed publicly; they cut themselves; they confessed their faults aloud; they recited the sins that scarred Israel's history.[2]

But the prophets were unhappy with this. These were external symbols of repentance; little or nothing was happening inside. The love of repentant Israel, we read in Hosea, "is like the dew that goes early away" (Hos 6:4). Real repentance is a change of mind and heart; repentance means new attitudes, fresh patterns of behavior. "Rend your hearts," says the Lord, "and not your garments" (Joel 2:13). To repent is to turn, to be converted. The sinner turns from sin to God, the lukewarm heats up. Not merely by sharing in community ritual; a man or woman is totally changed, has a new attitude towards Yahweh, abandons hardened habits. What God wants is not sacrifice but steadfast love, not so much burnt offerings as knowing God in love (cf. Hos 6:6).

Such profound repentance is powerfully symbolized in Hosea (chap. 2). Israel is like a faithless wife who has gone after all manner of lovers. But she changes. She not only rejects her past life; she returns to her husband, Yahweh. Her life from here on in is to be shaped of fidelity and love.

For Jesus, too, repentance is a total turning. He describes it as becoming like a child (Mt 18:3). You repudiate your past and begin a new life.

II

This brings us to the Christian stress. It stems, of course, from the biblical background; it involves turning to the Lord—but with several urgent emphases. For us, repentance means refusing to live in yesterday. As the dance you've just shared reveals,[3] yesterday is death and sin and fate; today is life and love and freedom.

Yesterday is death. Yesterday is the plaint of the Psalmist: "O Lord . . . in death there is no remembrance of thee; in Sheol [the place of the dead] who can give thee praise?" (Ps 6:4–5). Yesterday is Job begging God: "Let me alone, that I may find a little comfort before I go whence I shall not return, to the land of gloom and deep darkness" (Job 10:20–21). Yesterday is the powerful figure of Death you have just seen standing before the stone that sealed the tomb of Christ and pronouncing doom:

So
if a passer-by would ask
who rules this life,
point him to this stone
and tell him I am inside
disassembling the handiwork of God.[4]

If yesterday is death, today is life. For today is Christ risen from the rock, "his shroud a wedding garment, his feet between earth and air in dance."[5] Do you believe that? That Christ is alive, more gloriously alive than when he walked the rugged roads of Palestine, that "he dances still"?[6] Do you believe that, with Christ risen, death no longer has power over you, will hold you captive no more than a swift moment, that you too will dance around death, will rise to a life beyond your wildest dreams? Do you believe that you are already risen with Christ, because his life courses through you like another bloodstream?

Only if you do can Lent be life for you. For what is it to repent in Lent? I turn more and more completely to a living Christ. I adopt "the attitude which Christ Jesus had" (Phil 2:5), the Christ who gave up the glory of his yesterday and chose a cross. I refuse to imprison myself in the past, all the more deadly for being so comforting. I give up not some bauble or trinket, not body fat or the Pub, but that damnable concentration on myself where the days and nights rotate around *me*, around my delights and my worries, my dreams and my frustrations, my love life or lack of it, my heartburn or my hemorrhoids.

Today's Gospel is instructive here: not simply "Repent" but "Repent and believe in the Good News" (Mk 1:15). Believe in life—Christ's life and your life, life here and hereafter, life now and for ever. If you want to repent, live! Come alive!

Yesterday is sin. Yesterday is St. Paul's anguished cry: "I am carnal, sold under sin. I do not understand my own actions. For I do not do what I want, but I do the very thing I hate. . . . I know that nothing good dwells within me. . . . I can will what is right, but I cannot do it" (Rom 7:14–18). Yesterday is the frightening figure of Sin you have just seen dancing before Death: "I manure the dreams of the young and wait for a harvest of betrayal."[7]

If yesterday is sin, today is love. For love alone is the solution to sin. Not soap-opera love, not the deadly lust of "Dallas";[8] but the love that keeps all God's commandments, the love that is not crushed by a cross, the love that dies for the other, the love that is stronger than death. Such was the love of Christ, the crucified love that took away the Sin of the World. Such, increasingly, must be our love, if we are ever to break out of a self that stifles, smothers, suffocates, if we are not to tack without end on some unreal "Love Boat."⁹ If you want to repent, love! Love someone else!

Yesterday is fate. Yesterday is your horoscope, the position of the stars when you were born. Yesterday is the Stoic telling you your consolation lies in being swept along with the universe. Yesterday is theologians chirping merrily that some of you are predestined to be damned and there isn't a damn thing you can do about it. Yesterday is the hopeless figure of Fate you have just seen draining men and women "empty of struggle, their faces whitening into resignation."¹⁰

If yesterday is fate, today is freedom. Not only our power to make choices, the fundamental freedom to construct our human existence. More importantly, Jesus Christ is shaping you and me to the freedom that was supremely his. Not license to do whatever we want. Rather, freedom from a fourfold slavery: the sin that diminishes our humanness and keeps us from realizing ourselves; the thousand and one laws that strangle religion; the self that glues our eyes and hearts to this earth's values; the "night" of death into which (with Dylan Thomas) we do "not go gentle." If you want to repent, go free! Open yourself to God in free obedience, open yourself to others in uncompelled love!

III

Such, then, is the positive thrust of Lenten repentance. You shape or reshape your lives: from death to life, from sin to love, from fate to freedom. You live love freely. How do you manage it concretely? I have no magic formula, no infallible injection. For my third point, therefore, let me simply tell you how one person is trying to "re-form" her life—a young lady in her twenties. I met her only once, six years ago—by accident or providence, I know not. In any event, her recent letter runs like this:

> Over the years, since the time we met at St. Louis, while you were attending the Catholic-Lutheran Dialogue, I have journeyed long and far. Yet, as I reflect on our meeting and as I reflect on my own change and growth, I feel somewhat the same. I still have the same zeal to share the Gospel and still search out un-

trodden paths to share that News. I am finding more creative ways, more outlets to share this relationship of awesome love. . . .

Duane and I, after living for a year in West Palm Beach, Fla., and while working in a very wealthy wealthy parish, decided to journey to the Appalachian area, and live out the struggle of poverty [so] as to be bonded with and become one with the poor. My experience in campus and parish work left me starving for a broader base of ministry, unconfined by diocesan restrictions or university rules. I now venture out into hospitals, neighborhoods, wherever, and just allow the Spirit to flow. It's a wonderful time, free flowing, open, new, creative. I can now look back at limitations and closed doors and give thanks—for they were the push I needed toward creativity.

Duane . . . supports me in my quest and is such a loving, gentle man. No one ever told me that marriage gets better, that love deepens and freedom is unmeasurable. Why doesn't anyone tell us that? What a gift to have such an intimate relationship with one person. Who would ever know the worlds and vast things to discover in the heart of one another? Who would know—to Him be glory for ever.

I volunteer at a shelter for battered women—still struggling with a society which hurts women and imposes images and bodies on her. Still struggling with the desperate need women have to give spiritually yet aren't being fed by the usual vessels of church life. Still confused at the ministry of so many tied up in liturgy when neighborhoods house the lonely and the desperate woman of today. Searching for healing and for some kind of viability. . . . Anyway, I'm trying—struggling, and hoping. Reading and pondering Isaiah 43:18&19 these days ["Remember not the former things, nor consider the things of old. Behold, I am doing a new thing; now it springs forth, do you not perceive it? I will make a way in the wilderness and rivers in the desert."]—learning to trust more and watch and wait. . . .

Pray for us, Walter, we are very poor, trying to make it, heat our apartment, eat, and share the truth of our experience. I wait for miracles. Some day all of us will care enough about the other that no one will ever be hungry.

Now my friend's way is not the only way to repent, to change our minds and hearts, to live love freely. God speaks to us in ever so many different syllables. Still, her way responds splendidly to a passage from Isaiah that may set the tone for these forty days:

> Fasting like yours this day
>   will not make your voice to be heard on high.

Is such the fast that I choose,
  a day for a man to humble himself?
Is it to bow down his head like a rush,
  and to spread sackcloth and ashes under him?
Will you call this a fast,
  and a day acceptable to the Lord?
Is not this the fast that I choose:
  to loose the bonds of wickedness,
  to undo the thongs of the yoke,
to let the oppressed go free,
  and to break every yoke?
Is it not to share your bread with the hungry,
  and bring the homeless poor into your house;
when you see the naked, to cover him,
  and not to hide yourself from your own flesh?
Then shall your light break forth like the dawn,
  and your healing shall spring up speedily;
your righteousness shall go before you,
  the glory of the Lord shall be your rear guard.
Then you shall call, and the Lord will answer;
  you shall cry, and he will say, Here I am.
               (Isa 58:4–9)

Dahlgren Chapel
Georgetown University
February 28, 1982

4

THROUGH WHAT HE SUFFERED HE LEARNED TO OBEY
Fifth Sunday of Lent (B)

♦ Jeremiah 31:31–34
♦ Hebrews 5:7–9
♦ John 12:20–33

Today's readings are too rich for any one homily—even a homily with three points. They are incredibly rich because they reveal our redemption, sum up our salvation. Do you want to know what makes you alive in God, beloved of God? Let me begin with the Gospel as John proclaims it, then point up the pith and marrow of that message from the Letter to the Hebrews, and end up with an important insight from the prophet Jeremiah.

I

Today's Gospel is a "sleeper." Taken by itself, read out of context, it's not especially striking. It recalls several seemingly unrelated items. Some Gentiles ask Philip if they can see Jesus; Philip relays the request; John never finishes the story, doesn't make it clear whether they actually got to see Jesus. Instead, Jesus insists that we must die if we are to live. And he goes on to tell us that it is now the "hour" for him to be lifted up and for Satan to be cast out.

In point of fact, this is a perfect Gospel for this particular Sunday. Next Sunday, Passion/Palm Sunday, we will enter with increasing intensity into the mystery of Jesus' dying/rising. With this in mind, today's Gospel marks an end. It is the climax of Jesus' public ministry, the last act before he opens his passion. Note the dramatic events; they are intimately related.[1]

First, Gentiles, non-Jews, seek Jesus out for the first time. Not simply to "see" him, visit with him, have an audience with "the Man." For John, to "see" Jesus is to believe in him. Non-Jews want to believe in him. That is why John is not interested in the rest of the episode: Did they get to press his flesh? The important thing is why they came. John has been stressing (chapters 11–12) that Jesus will die not only for the Jews but "to gather together even the dispersed children of God" (Jn 11:52); that this king who rides into Jerusalem on a donkey is the universal king of the prophet Zechariah, the king on a donkey who "shall command peace to the Gentiles," whose "dominion shall be from sea to sea" (Zech 9:10); that of him the Pharisees complained with unconscious irony "Look, *the world* has run after him" (Jn 12:19). And now, here, God's all-embracing intent begins to be realized: Gentiles come to Jesus to believe in him. For John, the significance of the episode is its theology: God took flesh to touch every man, every woman, every child.

With that clear, Jesus can now say: "The hour has come" (Jn 12:23). What "hour"? Why, the hour of his passion. Only by his dying would we come to life. That is the point of the pithy parable: "I solemnly assure you, unless the grain of wheat falls to the earth and dies, it remains just a grain of wheat. But if it dies, it bears much fruit" (v. 24). Jesus must die. And the realization makes for anguish. In words that recall the agony in the garden, Jesus' "soul is troubled" (v. 27). Should he ask his Father to save him from death? No, "this hour" is the reason why he borrowed our flesh. Only if he is "lifted up from the earth" will he "draw all men and women" to himself (v. 32). Only if he is lifted up: lifted up on a cross, lifted up from the grave, lifted up to his Father.

For lack of time, today's Gospel reading omits the rest of John 12. Jesus asks his listeners to believe in him, for he is the light of the world: "Walk while you have the light, or the darkness will come over you" (v. 35). And then, in a striking symbolic gesture, Jesus "left them and went into hiding" (v. 36). The light goes out. As would happen to Judas: "As soon as he took the morsel" at the Last Supper, "he went out." And John adds: "It was night" (Jn 13:30). Judas was walking in darkness.

It is a marvelous chapter, this twelfth chapter of John. Immerse yourself in it this week; for next Sunday you begin John 13: "Jesus was aware that the hour had come for him to pass from this world to the Father. Having loved his own who were in the world, he now showed his love for them to the very end" (Jn 13:1)—to death and to the very limits of human loving. Next week you will experience dying at its depths, relive rising at its highest.

II

Enough, dear homilist! We now know a little more about John 12. "Non-Jews for Jesus" tell us he took flesh for all; they are a sign his "hour" has come; and for all its agony, it is only through his death that life will spring up, light illumine our darkness. But really, don't we already know that, believe it? This is catechism stuff, bolstered by biblical erudition. So what? Where is the food for our souls? We come for fresh bread, and you give us . . . old spinach warmed over.

A bit simple, but still reasonable. I think it a good thing to grasp more fully what the Word of God meant when it was written; but the more important question in our liturgy is: What does the Word of God say to us now?

For this, I suggest that you recall the anguished words of Jesus: "What should I say? 'Father, save me from this hour'? No, this is just the reason why I came to this hour" (Jn 12:27). Now flesh those sentences out with today's reading from Hebrews: "In the days of his flesh [in the Garden of Gethsemane], Jesus offered up prayers and supplications, with loud cries and tears, to Him who was able to save him from death [to his Father], and he was heard. . ." (Heb 5:7). He was heard? When he prayed to have the bitter cup of his passion taken away, he was heard? Yes, "through what he suffered he learned to obey" (v. 8); he experienced obedience. He was heard: In suffering he learned to say yes to his Father's will.

A mystery-laden remark—and yet it's the very core of Jesus' passion, the heart of our redemption. The crucifixion of Christ is not primarily a physical fact, the cruel death of an innocent man. It makes sense, it saves, only because the death is Jesus' free yes to his Father's mysterious will.

It's so hard to imagine. We see Jesus as Son of God whose divine will is identical with his Father's from eternity, whose own unchangeable will it was to take flesh and die for us. We find it difficult to reconcile with this a Son of Man who prays, sweats blood, cries like we cry, because he does not want to die, because his flesh and spirit rise up in rebellion against a bloody death. A man who was afraid—as fearful as a soldier in a foxhole, a child in a burning building, the swimmer in *Jaws* before a shark.

And yet he *was* afraid. He prayed: "Father, if possible, don't ask this of me! Don't do this to me!" And he cried. The Gospels tell us he cried over Jerusalem and over Lazarus, over his city and over his friend. Hebrews tells us he cried for himself, cried not to die.

And he was heard. He found in his Father the strength to obey, to say yes. In his passion he learned obedience. In St. Paul's words, "he humbled himself and became obedient unto death, even death on a cross" (Phil 2:8). It is a fascinating Greek word that Hebrews uses (*hypakouē*). It means that I listen, I give ear, I answer when someone calls; and so it comes to mean "obey." When someone calls, I say yes. In his suffering Jesus listened to his Father, answered when He called: Jesus said yes.

This obedience of Jesus is the salvation of us all. For, as Paul put it, one man's disobedience made sinners of us all, one man's obedience constitutes us upright before God (cf. Rom 5:19). From Bethlehem to Calvary, his life was "to do not my own will, but the will of Him who sent me" (Jn 6:38). It is splendidly summarized in another passage from Hebrews: "When Christ came into the world, he said [to his Father]: 'Sacrifices and offerings you have not desired, but a body you have prepared for me; in burnt offerings and sin offerings you have taken no pleasure. Then I said: Lo, I have come to do your will, O God. . . .' And by that will we have been sanctified through the offering of the body of Jesus Christ once for all" (Heb 10:5–7, 10). Jesus obeyed, and his obedience is our salvation.

III

But, kind homilist, you still haven't answered the question: What about us? Two points down, and you're still talking about Jesus, not about us. Not really; for the general principle "about us" is starkly stated in the first Epistle of Peter: "Christ suffered for you, leaving you an example, that you should follow in his steps" (1 Pet 2:21).

The "example" that concerns me today is not sheer suffering. It is indeed true that all our maladies, from terminal cancer to adolescent acne, should become our sharing in the suffering of Christ. Like St. Paul, we should be "always carrying in the body the death of Jesus" (2 Cor 4:10); I should complete "in my flesh what is lacking in Christ's afflictions for the sake of . . . the Church" (Col 1:24). This is basic to bearing gospel fruit; otherwise the grain of wheat that is you remains alone, fruitless.

All that is wonderfully and fearfully true. But even more significant is the link between suffering and obedience. It is not naked pain that redeems; what redeems is obedience. Not only the obedience of Jesus; his obedience is bootless without yours and mine.

The problem is, obedience is not a word that turns our culture on. It conjures up all that we associate with oppression, enslavement, absence of freedom: Hitler and Stalin, Iran's Khomeini and Poland's Jaruzelski, wives "subject to [their] husbands as to the Lord" (Eph 5:22)—perhaps even a pope calling his Jesuit light cavalry to heel.[2]

But Christian obedience is not slavery. Like biblical obedience, it is not forced submission, something I endure because I have no choice. It is my free adherence to God's plan for me and my world, a plan still cloaked in mystery but proposed to me in faith.[3] It is an uncompelled yes.

The principle itself is clear enough, beyond dispute: If God speaks to me, I ought to say yes—freely. Things get sticky because God rarely addresses me directly. Abraham heard God distinctly: "Leave your country . . ." (Gen 12:1). "Take your only son Isaac . . . and offer him as a burnt offering . . ." (Gen 22:2). I don't have that experience: "Walter, this is the Lord your God speaking." I don't get direct-dial long-distance calls from the risen Christ. God ordinarily speaks to me through the events that encircle my existence and the people who touch it, through the intelligence He has given me and the faith that graces me. And so He speaks to me through the oppression of the black and the rape of the poor; He speaks to me in the political process and through shepherds who, Scripture tells us, must "tend the flock of God that is [their] charge" (1 Pet 5:2).

It's sticky because so often it is not evident that *God* is speaking, not obvious what He is saying. Events can be ambiguous (Central America is not Poland) and popes make mistakes (don't ask me for examples). Must this leave us helpless, with each Catholic ultimately his or her own pope? By no means. Here, I suggest, today's reading from Jeremiah can lend us insight.

Jeremiah foretells "a new covenant" (Jer 31:31) that the Lord will make with Israel. Now what is really "new" in this covenant? Not the content: new laws, new prescriptions, new commandments. What is new is that the covenant will enter the *heart* of every member of the community: "I will write my law upon their hearts" (v. 33). Israel's commitment to God will be thoroughly interiorized. And this new heart, this new spirit, has three values above all else: knowing God, loving God, obeying God.[4]

As for Israel, so for us. No homilist can trace out for you the path your obedience will take: what God will ask of you and how He will ask it. There are only two predictions I dare make with fair confidence. First, you will hear God speaking and you will say yes to His address in the measure that your covenant—your commitment to Christ, to his Church, to his brothers and sisters—is interiorized, is written on your heart. God never stops speaking; but the cold mind, the locked heart, those for whom Jesus is a Sunday phenomenon, they will not hear his voice.

Second, a warning. The more deeply the covenant is etched in your heart, the more likely you are to learn obedience as Jesus did: through suffering. Lifted up, he will lift you to himself. A fearsome/gladsome prospect, for it involves you more and more in the dying/rising of Christ. To bear fruit, the grain of wheat must die. Easter and Good Friday are one paschal mystery.

Dahlgren Chapel
Georgetown University
March 28, 1982

5

BEHOLD, I AM DOING A NEW THING
Fifth Sunday of Lent (C)

♦ Isaiah 43:16–21
♦ Philippians 3:8–14
♦ John 8:1–11

One of my favorite films from the past has for title *Come Back, Little Sheba*. The male lead, Burt Lancaster, is a reformed alcoholic. His wife, Shirley Booth, is a devoted woman with a big heart; but she bores him endlessly by ceaselessly recalling the good old days. Remember when. . . ? Time and again she walks out on the porch calling for Little Sheba, the dog that has disappeared, the dog that is a symbol of those bygone days, a symbol of dashed hopes. And for twenty years these two good people live what Thoreau called "lives of quiet desperation."

I thought of that picture when first I read the Scripture passages that set the tone for today's liturgy. Each passage puts in relief the past and the future. All together, they form a powerful lesson for Lent. So, in tried and tested trinitarian fashion, let me develop my ideas in three stages: (1) Scripture; (2) the theology that Scripture reveals; (3) the spirituality that should emerge from both.

I

First, Scripture. What is it that Isaiah, Paul, and John say about past and future? Isaiah is at once stern and compassionate, sympathetic and demanding. The Jews are exiles in Babylon. Understandably, their memories take over. They look back nostalgically to their ancestors: the liberation from bondage in Egypt, the unforgettable Exodus, manna from heaven, entrance into a land flowing with milk and honey. But the Lord, for all His understanding, is not pleased,

45

not satisfied. He charges them: "Remember not the former things, nor consider the things of old. Behold, I am doing a new thing; now it springs forth; do you not perceive it?" (Isa 44:18–19). He wants them to look forward to a new and greater exodus, the return of Israel to Palestine. Their task is not to look back but forward; trust a God who is always faithful despite Israel's ceaseless infidelities; put idolatry behind them and serve the living God.

St. Paul knows his past, knows it well, knows it agonizingly, beyond his forgetting it. "I persecuted this Way [the Christian religion] to the death, binding and delivering to prison both men and women. . ." (Acts 22:4). "I not only shut up many of the saints in prison . . . but when they were put to death I cast my vote against them. And I . . . tried to make them blaspheme; and in raging fury against them, I persecuted them even to foreign cities" (Acts 26:10–11). He knows, too, the incredible graces God has given him: the light from heaven on the road to Damascus, his mission as apostle to the Gentiles, his elevation to the third heaven. And still he declares: "One thing I do: Forgetting what lies behind and straining forward to what lies ahead, I press on toward the goal for the prize of the upward call of God in Christ Jesus" (Phil 3:13–14).

So, too, for the adulteress in John. There is indeed a past; for she was "caught in the act of adultery" (Jn 8:4). Jesus does not minimize it; divine commandment forbade it. He condemns the sin, but not the sinner. The past is past; what concerns him is the future: "From now on, avoid this sin" (v. 11).

II

Such Scripture opens up a theology. I mean a way of viewing the relationship between God and His people, between God and us. To begin with, the salvation of woman and man, your redemption and mine, is not an event that takes place in outer space or simply in the recesses of the human heart. Salvation has a history; it is chained to times and places; it happens in and through living communities.

That is why the Hebrew people were justified in setting such great store by memory. I recall Rabbi Abraham Joshua Heschel's startling affirmation: Much of what the Bible demands can be summed up in a single word—remember! Ancient Israel was a community of faith vitalized by memory, a people that knew God by reflecting not on the mysteries of nature but on its own history. To actualize was to retain within time and space the memory and the mystery of God's saving presence. And Elie Wiesel, that remarkable Jewish storyteller who feels guilty because he survived the Holocaust, has reminded us that, for Jews, to forget is a crime against justice *and* memory: If you forget, you become the executioner's accomplice.

Similarly for St. Paul. Despite the language he uses, he could not really "forget" what lay behind. No advantage in such amnesia. In the book of Acts Paul is ceaselessly telling stories: how God dealt with Israel over the centuries, what God did for the world in Christ, the way God acted towards him, "the very least of all the saints" (Eph 3:8). Each of those stories was important for Paul. To forget any of them was to forget who he was, because to forget them was to forget his story, to forget where he came from and where he'd been. To forget his story was to forget his God.

So, too, for the woman caught in adultery. Despite Christ's "Neither do I condemn you" (Jn 8:11), neither she nor we can afford to forget her story. Not she, simply because it is her story. Not we, because her story is not an isolated event. The adulteress is all of us from Adam to Antichrist, in need of a Savior, in need of forgiveness. She is the story of salvation, of sin and mercy, of sin committed and sin forgiven.

The past, therefore, is not sheerly a specter to be exorcised from memory. It is part of the human story, of God's story; it is our story. And so we ought to know it, because we live off it. And yet, in this very past the Scriptures perceive a permanent peril: the temptation to live *in* the past.

Of course the Jews in exile could not forget their history. Remember how they wept by the waters of Babylon?

> If I forget you, O Jerusalem,
>   let my right hand wither!
> Let my tongue cleave to the roof of my mouth,
>   if I do not remember you,
> if I do not set Jerusalem
>   above my highest joy!
>
> (Ps 137:5–6)

The danger lay in living in the past—contrasting the exciting exodus from Egypt with the boredom of Babylon, God's obvious care then with His apparent indifference now, yearning for a yesterday that would wipe out today, despairing of God's saving act tomorrow.

Of course the Paul who wrote to the Philippians from prison could not forget the blinding flash on the Damascus road, "Who are you, Lord? 'I am Jesus. . .' " (Acts 9:5). The danger lay in living on the Damascus road, basking in the glory days—Gentile converts beyond counting, ecstasies for breakfast, "extraordinary miracles" from the touch of his handkerchief (Acts 19:11–12).[1]

A risk for the adulteress may well have been her sense of guilt. How can a God who prizes fidelity ever forgive my infidelity? How can I expect my husband to forgive me? Above all, can I ever forgive myself? This strange, unique, compassionate man has told me that he doesn't condemn me, that no other Jew in the area dares to condemn me. But how can I live with their leering looks, live with my husband, live with myself?

No, the past was not something to be lived *in*. The Jewish exiles were told to focus on the "new thing" that was about to spring forth. Paul realized that he had to fix his eyes on the story that lay ahead, the life with Christ that meant growing to the full stature of the Jesus he had persecuted. The woman taken in adultery was to begin a new life—not only "avoid this sin" but get to know and love the God-man who had refused to condemn her.

III

Which leads into my third point: the spirituality that should emerge for you from Scripture and theology. Briefly, your past is of high importance, because it is part of God's story and yours. It is for ever part of you; without it you would hardly be who you are. In a sense, you live *off* the past. And yet you dare not live *in* the past— precisely because it *is* past. Right here rests a triple peril that parallels the experience of the exiles, the Apostle, and the adulteress.

There is, first, a peril to the Christian community, a peril that rivals the experience of the Jewish community in Babylon. I mean a ceaseless yearning for the past: for the stately Latin of the fifties, the reverence of Gregorian chant, Communion on the tongue alone; for sisters with fluted wimples and priests in rumpled black; for the authority and obedience that marked us off from the Protestant "Here *I* stand"; for a clear Catholic morality without distraction from dissenters not in tune with the Sistine choir; for a Church above women's rights and gay dignity, above kisses of peace and protests outside the Pentagon.

Nothing wrong if it is only nostalgia, but disastrous if a Catholic tries to live there. Disastrous when, as for a young Catholic I know, Mass in English does not satisfy the Sunday obligation. Disastrous when meatless Friday is more Catholic than Communion in the hand. By all means, work restlessly to restore what radical reform has needlessly driven out, so much that is genuinely Catholic; for not every change has been inspired by the Spirit. And still, change is part and parcel of the Catholic condition: change in the way the Church thinks, in the way the Church lives, in the way the Church worships. We are ever in exile, a pilgrim people marching through a wilderness, groping for a God we cannot touch, mumbling and grumbling as loudly as the Israelites ever did, making all sorts of human mistakes.

The point is, this is still God's community of salvation; God still acts here. If you find it Babylon, then live in Babylon, not in some bygone utopia. And while you protest our fresh infidelities, give ear to the God who ceaselessly cries in all our Babylons: "Remember not the former things, nor consider the things of old. Behold, I am doing a new thing; now it springs forth; do you not perceive it?"

There is, second, a peril that recalls the prison situation of St. Paul. Whether it's turning 21 or 40 or 65, whether it's an enfeebling illness or a crumbier job or forced retirement, whether it's family problems or alcoholism or a nursing home—whatever the imprisoning situation, I can feel not only different but diminished. I am tempted to hark back to my glory days: Remember when? No, says Paul, let the past be past. Warm memories, of course; my own office has more honorary degrees than living plants. But I have to keep growing till I die; for the goal of Christian striving, oneness with a living Christ, is never perfected here below. The glory days are ahead: life with Christ in glory. And so I must "strain forward" as Paul did, "press on," keep dying with Christ so as to live more fully. In a word, tomorrow should be better than yesterday; for each day can be a new creation—if I fix my eyes not on a dead past but on a living Lord. A loving Lord.

There is, third, a peril that reflects the dilemma I have imagined for the adulteress: How do you live with guilt? Even apart from the Catholic horror stories—what Sister Mary Ignatius supposedly did to your psyche[2]—many a Christian seems unable to accept Christ's forgiveness, goes through life wallowing in guilt, afraid of hell, tormented by past offenses, impotent to make peace with his or her human frailty. Not for this did God become what we are; not for this did the Son of God die a beastly, bloody death. Christ "loved me," St. Paul insists, "and gave himself for me" (Gal 2:20). That love persists through all my infidelities. So fix your eyes not on yesterday's sin but on today's forgiveness and tomorrow's hope. Repent, yes; but remember, the repentance that saves is not ceaseless self-scourging but fresh self-giving, a new birth of love.

Only two weeks are left to Lent. If you are still searching for some self-denial, simply stop looking back. "Remember not the former things, nor consider the things of old." If you want really to rise with Christ, echo what he himself is singing to you: "Behold, I am doing a new thing; now it springs forth." Come to think of it, in the Christian story *you* are the "new thing." Why not spring forth?

Dahlgren Chapel,
Georgetown University
March 20, 1983

6

TRAGEDY OR TRIUMPH?
Passion/Palm Sunday (B)

♦ Isaiah 50:4–7
♦ Philippians 2:6–11
♦ Mark 14:1—15:47
or
15:1–39

Today's liturgy, my friends, is more important than you may realize. Important not only for the way you celebrate liturgy; important for the way you celebrate life. So let me (1) set up the problem, (2) submit one solution, and (3) suggest what this might mean for your everyday Christian living.

I

First, the problem. This morning you and I enter the most significant eight days in the Church's calendar. And how we see the liturgy today will pretty well determine how we act the rest of the week—perhaps the rest of our lives.

What are we doing in this particular liturgy? On the face of it, contradictory things. We call it Palm Sunday, and we call it Passion Sunday. In the procession we honor a "triumphant King," shout adoring hosannas, wave palm branches, join the Jews of Jerusalem in their joy over Jesus. In the Mass we suddenly stop all that. No glorious Gloria. We thank the Father for this "model of humility." We sing "My God, my God, why have you abandoned me?" Isaiah tells of a Servant who "did not cover [his] face from insult and spit" (Isa 50:6). Paul proclaims that Christ "emptied himself, to take up the status of a slave" (Phil 2:7). A pain-full Gospel closes with Jesus lifeless "in a tomb" (Mk 15:46).

You have a tension here, a paradox if not a contradiction. Palms bending in adoration and reeds striking a thorn-crowned

51

head. A king and a convict. Hosannas and mockery. Triumph and tragedy. And all this in one liturgy. It doesn't make sense. Or does it?

II

So much for the problem, the puzzle of Passion/Palm Sunday. Does it have a solution? Indeed it does, but only on condition that we surrender a deep-seated misunderstanding about Lent. As I grew up, there was a sharp dividing line between Lent and Easter. Lent meant that we lived again in memory the dying of Jesus, so that on Easter we might relive his rising. Six weeks of suffering for him and sadness for us, then all of a sudden he and we were alive again. Forty days in a barren desert, and then the flowers came out. Swallow the laughter, hold off on the jelly beans, because Christ was moving to his cross. We were looking forward to Easter dawn, when he would rise from the dead and we would rise with him, alleluia!

I have said it before, and I say it again: This is liturgical nonsense.[1] Lent is no more a preparation for the rising of Jesus than Advent was a preparation for his birth. Jesus will not rise next Sunday, no more than he graced a crib last Christmas. This is to stress the history at the expense of the mystery. There is indeed a history: Jesus did move from a desert to a garden to a cross to a rock from which he rose. And in Lent we try to relive that movement. But not as if Jesus is not yet risen, as if we must wait for Easter to relive his resurrection.

The point is, Passion Sunday, like all of Lent, gets its liturgical meaning from Easter. And what is Easter? Easter is what we call the paschal mystery. What is the paschal mystery? An inseparable twosome, a duality: the dying-and-rising of Jesus. The fact is, he has already died and risen; we dare not pretend he has not. Lent is not the dying of Jesus, Easter his rising. The whole of Lent is a progressively more intense initiation into the twin reality of Jesus dead and risen.

Today, Passion/Palm Sunday, this whole week, we enter with growing intensity into the *whole* paschal mystery. Not palms *or* passion; both. Not triumph *or* tragedy; triumph *in* tragedy. Not a dying *or* a rising Christ; a dying-rising Christ. The paschal mystery is *one* mystery: life in and through death.

Passion Sunday, then, is not a prelude to the Resurrection. The tragedy of Calvary is not a promise of triumph at Easter. The cross is itself a triumph; the cross is victory. In Christ's death there is life. That is why the Church puts palms and thorns together. The King is triumphant not simply on Easter; he is triumphant on Calvary. Dying-rising is one complex reality, the mystery of Christ. Today I rejoice, for in his dying the world comes alive.

III

But this is not a lecture on liturgy. From liturgy we should leap to life. Liturgy is not an escape from living, a quiet hour away from the muck and grime of the week. Liturgy should shape our Christian existence.

Passion/Palm Sunday is a splendid example. Here we uncover the core of Christian living. Not simply uncover it; we get the strength to live it. I mean the essential Christian reality: For us, to live is to share in the dying-rising of Christ. Not in two stages: dying here, rising hereafter. Not sharing his Calvary in this vale of tears, till we can cast off this burden of flesh and share his Easter in eternity. No, as with Jesus, so with us: Our dying-rising is a twin, inseparable reality. In our dying is our rising—now.

It began with your baptism. On this St. Paul is emphatic, ecstatic: "Do you not know that all of us who have been baptized into Christ were baptized into his death? We were buried therefore by baptism into death, so that as Christ was raised from the dead by the glory of the Father, we too might walk in newness of life" (Rom 6:3–4). Newness of life—now. Not after death; now. At this moment the life of Christ courses through you like another bloodstream. That is why you can cry out with Paul: "I have been crucified with Christ; it is no longer I who live, but Christ who lives in me; and the life I now live in the flesh I live by faith in the Son of God, who loved me and gave himself for me" (Gal 2:20). In Christ you are "a new creation" (2 Cor 5:17).

But your dying-rising is not simply a matter of sacraments—from baptism through reconciliation and Eucharist to your final anointing. You are indeed risen with Christ, but not fully risen. With Paul, "we who have the first fruits of the Spirit groan inside ourselves as we wait for . . . the redemption of our bodies" (Rom 8:23). And so we must ceaselessly reproduce the journey of Jesus to Jerusalem, not only in the liturgy but in our flesh and bones and in the wrenching of our spirit. In this life we rise to new life only by dying, ceaselessly dying.

Dying to what? Basically, to sin and to self. Dying to sin is never ended. For dying to sin is not merely turning from evil; dying to sin is turning to Christ, and turning to Christ is a constant conversion. If sin is rejection, dying to sin is openness: openness to God's presence poured out on you through saguaro cactus and red rock, the warm breeze that caresses your skin, the eyes that meet yours in friendship and love, the awesome presence of the Holy One tabernacled in your lovely chapel and in the shelter of your hearts. It's a splendidly positive way of dying to sin. Turn to the Lord all around you, turn to the Lord within you.

More difficult perhaps is dying to self. Here I'm not thinking of sin. I'm thinking of that very human problem, how do you let go of where you've been? How do you let go of yesterday, of the past that is so much part of you? Not forget it; let go of it. Whether it's turning 21, 40, or 65, whether it's losing your health or your hair, your looks or your lustiness, your money or your memory, a person you love or a possession you prize; whether it's being fired or retired, divorced or disabled; whether it's a change of life or a change of pace; whether it's as fleeting as applause or as abiding as grace— you have to move on. Wherever you've been, you dare not live there. Essential to your Christian journey is the journeying of Christ: He "did not treat like a miser's booty his right to be like God, but emptied himself of it, to take up the status of a slave" (Phil 2:6– 7). And to let go of yesterday is to die a little. But only by dying will you rise to fresh life. Only by letting go of yesterday will you open yourself to tomorrow, to being surprised by the Spirit.

My brothers and sisters in Christ: If you want to celebrate both liturgy and life these eight days, I have three suggestions: (1) Don't divorce passion and palms, Good Friday and Easter. They are inseparable. *In* Christ's death there is life. (2) Act today, and all week, like risen Christians. You have already risen with Christ. Then rejoice . . . today! (3) Let Linus' blanket go. Let all your dying be a new living. Not without pain; but let the pain be permeated with Easter promise. There is no dying that does not bear within it the seeds of fresh life. Let go!

Franciscan Renewal Center
Scottsdale, Arizona
April 4, 1982

7

A CAMEL ON THE ROOF?
Passion/Palm Sunday (C)

◆ Isaiah 50:4–7
◆ Philippians 2:6–11
◆ Luke 22:14—23:56

Some months ago I ran across a story that intrigued my imagination. It was reproduced from a collection of lives of saints. Not Catholic saints—the saints of Islam. The central figure in the story is Ebrahim ibn Adam, king of Balkh (now, I believe, a district in North Afghanistan). Ebrahim was a wealthy man, but at the same time very sincere, very concerned, in matters religious—what we might call the search for God. One night the king was roused from sleep by a fearful stumping on the roof above his bed. Alarmed, he shouted: "Who's there?" "A friend," came the reply from the roof. "I've lost my camel." Perturbed by such stupidity, Ebrahim screamed: "You fool! Are you looking for a camel on the roof?" "You fool!" the voice answered. "Are you looking for God in silk clothing, and lying on a golden bed?" These simple words, we are told, filled the king with terror; he rose from his sleep to become a remarkable saint.

The camel on the roof raises a pertinent question this Sunday of passion and palms. In fact, the camel on the roof is a profound prelude to the whole of Holy Week. It compels us to ask ourselves: Where are you looking for your God? Which raises a prior question: Where is our God to be found? And a final question: Where do we go from here? A few moments on each.

I

First, where is our God to be found? If your philosophy is scholastic and your theology Catholic, you will answer: everywhere. He lives in all the world. He is everywhere, in every nook and cranny of His universe. Look up—at the sun or the stars or the trailing clouds; He is there. Look down—into the hollows of the earth; He is there. Look out—at the desert or the city; He is there. Look in—to the depths of your soul and the marrow of your bones; He is there. Look about you—wherever your eye falls, He is there. He *is* everywhere because He is *active* everywhere, because without Him the sun could not shine nor the raindrop fall; without Him the cactus could not grow nor the heart beat; without Him you could not know Him or love Him.

All this is true, and there is a wild richness here. But Passion/Palm Sunday stresses something terribly different; it tells you that your God is to be found where no one in his or her right mind would expect to find Him. It tells you that He is to be found in our flesh, in "the form of a slave" (Phil 2:7). It tells you that this Son of God is to be found not in silk clothing but in swaddling cloths, not on a golden bed but in a feeding trough. It tells you to look in a garden called Gethsemane, the "oil press" where the God-man's "sweat became like great drops of blood falling down upon the ground" (Lk 22:44), where God-with-us begged God the Father "Don't let me die!" (cf. v. 42). It tells you to find your God in a prisoner mocked, blindfolded, and beaten; kept captive while a convicted murderer went free; crucified between two criminals while "darkness lay over the whole earth" (Lk 23:44). It tells you to find your God in a man who "breathed his last" (v. 46) in an agony of flesh and spirit few human beings have ever tasted.

The liturgy of Passion/Palm Sunday tells you to read the story told by Luke with the eyes of Paul, tells you to make your own the lyrical early hymn you heard in the second reading. Jesus Christ,

> though he was in the form of God
> [pre-existent and divine],
> did not count equality with God
> a thing to be clutched,
> but emptied himself of it,
> to take on the form of a slave
> and become like men.
> And having assumed human form,
> he still further humbled himself
> with an obedience that meant death,
> even death on a cross.
> That is why God has so highly exalted him
> and given him the name which is above every name,

that at the name of Jesus every knee should bow,
in heaven and on earth and under the earth,
and every tongue confess,
to the glory of God the Father,
that Jesus Christ is Lord!

(Phil 2:6–11)

For those who have eyes to see, where does Passion/Palm Sunday locate our Lord? In humiliation and obedience, beneath bone and blood. Simply, pinned to a cross, hung on a tree.

II

If our Scripture and our liturgy find our God on a cross, this raises a challenge: Where, in point of fact, do you and I look for Him? Rarely do we resemble the man looking for his lost camel on a roof. I am not denying that God is everywhere. I am simply suggesting that we rarely look for Him in the *un*likely places where He has promised to be. Read the Old Testament book of Exodus, the liberation of Israel from Egypt, and the book of Numbers, Israel's wandering in the wilderness. Oh yes, the people of Israel found God when He drowned the hosts of Pharaoh in the sea of reeds. They sang ecstatically:

I will sing to the Lord,
   for He has triumphed gloriously;
the horse and his rider
   He has thrown into the sea.
The Lord is my strength and my song,
   and He has become my salvation;
this is my God, and I will praise Him,
   my father's God, and I will exalt Him.

(Exod 15:1–2)

But it was difficult for them to find Yahweh in the wilderness. When Moses delayed his return from the God of Sinai, they fashioned a new god out of their gold. They loved their God when first He rained manna upon them; but they got fed up with the manna, and wept for the meat and fish they had gotten free in Egypt, "the cucumbers, the melons, the leeks, the onions, and the garlic" (Num 11:4–5). Yahweh brought them to a land flowing with milk and honey, but they murmured because they were afraid of being killed—so much so that the Lord said: "How long will this people despise me? And how long will they not believe in me, in spite of all the signs which I have wrought among them?" (Num 14:11).

Take the Gospels. Peter could find his Lord on the mount of transfiguration; but when Jesus told the disciples that he had to "suffer many things . . . and be killed" (Mt 16:21), Peter "began to rebuke him, saying: 'God forbid, Lord! This shall never happen to you' " (v. 22). And surely you remember the two disciples on the road to Emmaus after Christ's crucifixion: "We had hoped that he was the one to redeem Israel" (Lk 24:21). We *had* hoped. . . .

Much the same thing has happened time and again in the history of the Church. In the fifth century a powerful patriarch named Nestorius proclaimed: "A born God, a dead God, a buried God I cannot adore."[1] Just another confused theologian, you may say; but Nestorius was raising a question that has tormented good Christians through the ages: Was that writhing, blood-raw convict who cried to his Father "Why have you abandoned me?" (Mt 27:46) really God's only Son?

Even today, many a Christian can live comfortably only with Easter Sunday; Good Friday is too much. Perhaps I should ask myself: Is it only on Easter that the exclamation of doubting Thomas bursts from my lips: "My Lord and my God!" (Jn 20:28)? You know, even now, at this moment, the risen Christ somehow still carries the wounds of his passion—glorified indeed, but still the scars of Calvary. To be a Christian, I suspect, is to look for a camel on a roof.

III

Which leads to my third question: Where do we go from here? How do we move all this from the abstract to the concrete, from theology to life, from the first century to the twentieth, from Jerusalem to Scottsdale? After all, Jesus is no longer on a cross, even when I find him there in history. Granted I reproduce his dying in my baptism and in my personal Calvary, he no longer suffers, he dies no more. "Christ *has* died; Christ is risen." We once transported the London Bridge to Arizona. Can we transport the bleeding body of Jesus?

Yes, indeed; for he told us how: "In so far as you did it to one of the least of these my brothers and sisters, you did it to me" (Mt 25:40). The Jesuit poet Gerard Manley Hopkins sang lyrically how "Christ plays in ten thousand places,/ Lovely in limbs, and lovely in

eyes not his/ To the Father through the features of men's faces."[2]
Now it's not very hard to find Christ, to discover God's image, on
lovely faces (Brooke Shields?), on loving faces (Mother Teresa?), on
strong faces (John Paul II?), on friendly faces (Alan Alda?), on
proud faces (Thomas More?), on free faces (Oscar Romero?), on
faces that age gracefully (Katie Hepburn?). Indeed Christ is there.
And yet, he told us to look for him especially in "the least" of his
brothers and sisters, those who seem insignificant, those who are in
trouble or forgotten. We are to find him, therefore, in stomachs
swollen by starvation, on lips parched with thirst, in hands arthritic
with age, on faces torn with terror, in eyes empty in hopelessness,
flesh eaten by cancer, bodies raging behind prison bars, strangers
threatening our turf, a face with a different color.

Here, my friends, is today's Calvary. No longer limited to Jerusalem; the cross casts its shadow over the face of the earth.
Whether it's twelve million Russians imprisoned in the Gulag Ar-
chipelago or thousands of Cambodian refugees tenting Thailand
with their malnutrition and malaria, whether it's Latin America with
seven out of ten in abject poverty or Appalachia powerless under
the new colonials, whether it's Afghans raped by the Soviet war machine or women and children blasted to bits in the north of Ireland,
here and everywhere Christ is crucified again in his children.

But I need not board a plane to find my thorn-crowned God; *I*
need not even fly to Phoenix! He meets me day after day in Washington, D.C. I pass so close to the very people Jesus specifically cited:
the hungry and the thirsty, the naked and the stranger, the sick and
the shackled. I pass so close to them, and so often I pass them by, as
the Gospel priest passed by the poor fellow felled by thieves. I face
so many others who in our society fall under "the least." I mean the
black and the Hispanic, asking only for the dignity that is their
birthright, asking to be recognized as images of God. I mean the elderly lady or gentleman who wants only my ear—that ear I reserve
for "the beautiful people" or the National Symphony or (God save
the mark!) Howard Cosell. I mean the young student who is
"down," has no personality to speak of, needs someone to "dump"
on; I too easily plead other commitments. I mean all those who are
afraid or alone, ridden with guilt or with acne, torn between security
and risk, in so many ways hovering between heaven and hell.

Early this month Pope John Paul II launched his Central
American pilgrimage in Costa Rica, on the tarmac of San José's in-
ternational airport. I come, he said, "to share the pain" of Central
America, to provide a voice for "the tears or deaths of children, the

anguish of the elderly, of the mother who loses her children, of the long lines of orphans, of those many thousands of refugees, exiles or displaced persons searching for a home, of the poor with neither home nor work."[3]

No need for you to join John Paul in Costa Rica or El Salvador. The passion of Christ is being played out right here—in Arizona, in Phoenix and Scottsdale, on red reservations and white streets, among Mexicans legal and illegal, perhaps in your own home. Christ is there, not by some vague, eerie presence, but in each and every person. Reach out to someone—to anyone in agony of flesh or spirit. Share that person's pain; for that pain is the passion of Christ, if you can believe St. Paul (cf. Col 1:24). Please God, on that Calvary where another Christ hangs, in your divine "foolishness" (1 Cor 1:25) you will discover, or rediscover, your God. Believe me, it beats looking for a camel on a roof!

Franciscan Renewal Center
Scottsdale, Arizona
March 27, 1983

8

THE LORD'S SUPPER, YOUR SUPPER
Holy Thursday 1

> ◆ Exodus 12:1–8, 11–14
> ◆ 1 Corinthians 11:23–26
> ◆ John 13:1–15

Tonight is not a time for much preaching; it is a time for much praying. A time to immerse ourselves in mystery—the mystery of "God-
head here in hiding, whom [we] do adore."[1] To immerse our whole
selves—mind and imagination, heart and senses. To see and listen,
then finally to touch and taste. To savor a unique presence of a
unique Lord. Let me, then, not so much preach at you as pray with
you, marvel with you, as we relive a singular supper, an evening to
remember. . . .

Today a breath-taking event is taking place across the face of
the earth. Jesus Christ, hiding all that is divine in him, hiding all that
is human, pillows himself on the tongue of a Polish miner and in the
palm of an Irish colleen; touches the flesh of a Philippine farmer
and a French financier; graces the stone altar of a Russian cathedral
and the crude wood of a Peruvian chapel; comes to organ music in
Baltimore's Basilica and in stillness to a hospital bed in Phoenix.
From the rising of the sun to its setting, from North Pole to South,
a priest is holding a host before eyes rapt in adoration: "This is the
Lamb of God. . . . Happy are those who are called to his supper."
And the ends of the earth ring with one changeless response: "Lord,
I am not worthy. . . ."

Why? Why this endless supper, this solemn ritual that circles
the globe? The answer lies in Jesus and in ourselves.

61

I

First, Jesus. To begin with, it's a touchingly human thing he did that startling Thursday. With passionate desire, he tells his apostles, he has yearned to share this supper with them before he suffers (cf. Lk 22:15). These are his special friends, and the next day he will die. As far as he can foresee, he will never again eat with them this side of heaven.

Now if that were all he did—share a supper—it would be moving enough. But this is not just a last meal; this is the paschal meal. Jesus' last meal with his special family is the sacred Passover of the Jews. This is the meal that by God's command each Jewish family celebrated each year, to commemorate the exodus from Egypt, the passage over the Red Sea, the escape from Pharaoh. Jesus did what each Jewish family faithful to traditional faith does today in the Seder, when it raises its cups and proclaims:

> Therefore it is our duty to thank, praise, laud, glorify, uplift, extol, bless, exalt, and adore Him who did all these miracles for our fathers and for ourselves. He has brought us forth from slavery to freedom, from sorrow to joy, from mourning to festive day, from darkness to a great light, and from subjection to redemption.

This would be touching enough—that Jesus should share the sacred meal of Jewish faith with his intimate family, his first followers, his disciples. But there is more. With this supper he strikes a new covenant, a pact not restricted to any one tribe or nation, a relationship open to all who will believe in him. But notice how he strikes this covenant: by bread and wine that he transforms into his body and blood, into himself, into the total Christ, Son of Man and Son of God; in the flesh that is to be flayed with whips and nailed to a cross on the morrow, the blood that is to be poured out over his body. This covenant, struck at the supper, will be ratified in blood— not the blood of sheep or goats, but his own blood. It is summed up splendidly in one deathless sentence: "This cup is the new covenant in my blood, which will be shed for you" (Lk 22:20).

That would be wondrous enough: the blood of God's Son poured out for every man and woman from Adam to Antichrist. But there is more, unbelievably more: "Take this and eat it. . . . Drink of this, all of you. . ." (Mt 26:26–27). Here is the new Paschal Lamb, the Lamb of God who takes away the sins of the world. The disciples are to feed on him. Here is fulfilled his earlier promise: "The man or woman who feeds on my flesh and drinks my blood has life eternal, and I will raise him/her up on the last day" (Jn 6:54).

It is hard to take any more; and yet there is more. The covenant, I said, is not only with the first disciples; it is with every human being. All humanity is called to discipleship, to live the covenant, to eat Jesus' flesh and drink his blood. This he could have announced by simply saying so. But no—love is never content with naked words. He adds the final touch, the last stroke of love: "Do this in remembrance of me" (Lk 22:19). Do what? Till the end of time, all over the earth, take into your quivering hands a lifeless loaf and turn it into my body; take between your trembling fingers a cup of wine and make it blush to blood. The Last Supper is only the first supper! And as often as you "eat this bread and drink this cup," Paul insists, "you proclaim the death of the Lord until he comes" (1 Cor 11:26). Each Eucharist trumpets two tremendous truths: By his death Jesus gave us life, and this Jesus who died for us is the Lord.

A meal with "family," a Passover meal, a fresh covenant in the blood of God's Son, a new Lamb to be eaten, a Eucharist to be relived and re-presented everywhere till time is no more—all this takes us from Jesus to ourselves.

II

To begin with, Jesus' "last supper" reminds us that *every* meal has something of the sacred about it. We've lost the age-old sense of that. Over the centuries, in myriad cultures, to break bread together was the privilege of a family. To be a guest at table was to be invited into the family. To share bread was to share love.

It is in this context that we must set the most sacred meal in Christian existence, the most sacred meal you and I share, the Supper of the Lord. We do as he did, in remembrance of him. We transform bread and wine into his flesh and blood, and we eat and drink it. But this we must do as a community. The new and everlasting covenant Christ struck was not a private pact with individuals: with the Apostle Peter or John Paul II, with Mother Teresa or Father Mulcahy—not even with Walter Burghardt! Oh yes, each of us is embraced in the covenant, but only because we are embraced within a people, the people God has chosen for His own.

That is why, when we come together to re-enact the covenant, to ratify it again by a Supper that re-presents the Last Supper, we come together as a family. As far as possible, there is only one Supper this day in any Christian community, to symbolize a solemn fact: We are one family. We eat together.

This was always true, but not always obvious. As I grew up, the Eucharistic stress was indeed on communion—but primarily on my individual communion with Christ, a sort of me-and-Jesus spirituality. I was surrounded, of course, by others—sometimes ten, sometimes a thousand. And I prayed for them, as (I hope) they prayed for me. But I was warned not to be distracted: by a squalling baby or an outlandish hat, by a familiar face or a fantastic body. Distractions were to be confessed: "I looked around in church; I talked in church." Nothing, no one, was to come between Jesus and me.

The principle was valid enough, but the emphasis was overdone. Vatican II tried to redress the balance, help us activate what was hidden in theory. If we are a community, we should celebrate as a community—celebrate our Passover as a community—aware not only of Jesus but of one another, coming to know one another in the very mystery itself. And so we try to break down barriers to communion. Altar rails disappear, priest faces people, people say "Peace" or "Howdy" to one another, shake hands, embrace. Not all the methods work, not for everybody. In the early Church, at least one community was told to "cool" the kiss of peace; the more "progressive" Christians were enjoying it far too lustily. And you may, without sin, find hugging me repulsive! But the significant thing is what the Church is trying to do: help a covenant people live the covenant, recover the sense of one family. The Church, in an early definition, is "the 'we' of Christians." Remember, Christ gave his body and blood, at the Supper and on Calvary, to fashion one body—the Body of Christ—linked in unique love. If that love is ever to break out like the love of Christ, it should begin and crest here—in this our family.

One further link between the first Supper and ours. Four words in the Roman rite summarize what Christ did at the Supper when he fashioned the Eucharist to be the instrument of his new covenant: He took, he blessed, he broke, he gave.[2]

1) He "took" a loaf of bread. Not high Mediterranean cuisine, but ordinary food. A staple of life indeed, but quite common. It reminds us how Yahweh chose for His people a motley mob of unruly, runaway slaves, culturally undistinguished, often rebellious, frequently unfaithful, unpredictable, unreliable. As Deuteronomy told them, "It was not because you were the greatest of all peoples that Yahweh set His heart on you and chose you (for you were the small-

est of all peoples), but it was because Yahweh loved you that Yahweh rescued you from a state of slavery . . ." (Deut 7:7–8).

And so for you and me. God chose you and me to be His servants, to be part of His people, to be Christians. *He* chose us; we did not choose Him. And He chose us not because we deserved it (What indeed recommends us?)—simply because He wanted to, because such was His mysterious will, His mystery-laden love. All He asks is, not that I understand His will, but that I accept it with faith, with trust, with love.

2) He "blessed" the bread. What incredible creative power in that blessing! What had been, a split second before, a common loaf is now, instantaneously, transfigured into the incarnate Son of God. It is this blessing, God's word, that transformed those restless Hebrew tribes into God's people. And the same blessing, pronounced over you in baptism, changed you from sinful clay into a child of God, a brother or sister of Christ, an heir of heaven. That blessing hovers over your whole life. In penance it turns you from enemy to friend; in the Eucharist it links you to the Father through the sacramental flesh of His Son. Each day is a fresh creation, a ceaseless miracle of grace.

3) He "broke" the bread. Jesus divided the bread so that there might be enough for all. In a sense deeper still, the body of Christ had to be broken if it was to bring life to the world. "Unless the grain of wheat falls to the ground and dies, it remains alone—just a grain of wheat" (Jn 12:24), cannot produce images of itself. You remember how God had to discipline His own people time and again, from the exile in Egypt to the captivity in Babylon and beyond, to bring them to a deeper awareness of Him, of themselves, of others. He had to "break" them. So too with us. To make us fit instruments in His service, God has to "break" us, destroy the false self in us. Paradoxically, I am least myself when I make the world revolve around me—my successes and my failures, my hurts and my frustrations, my arthritic hips and my ingrown toenail. The "I" has to be transformed. And so God remolds me in the fire of suffering. Not for its own sake; sheer suffering is neither good nor bad. Rather to reshape me in the image of His Son, the "Son of God [who] learned obedience through what he suffered [and so] has become, for all who heed him, the cause of eternal salvation" (Heb 5:8–9).

4) He "gave" the bread. He gave what he had blessed, what had once been mere bread and wine, now become himself, gave it to his friends and through them to all of us, for the world's redemption. It is strikingly symbolized on the cross, when Jesus flung his arms

wide to embrace the world—and at the same time his arms were empty, for he had given us . . . everything. He had given us himself—in the sacrament of his flesh.

Similarly, a gracious God poured life and love incessantly on the Hebrew people, till at the end He had only His only Son to give.

You too, chosen and blessed and broken, are given to a whole little world for its life. At each Mass, in this Supper, all of you, priestly people that you are, offer with an ordained priest the body of Christ—and on the same paten you offer yourselves. For you no longer belong to yourselves. The profound meaning of your Christian priesthood lies in this: You are "given"—given to others for their life. God changes into Christ not only bread and wine; He changes *you* into Christ—for the life of the world.

The point is, for you too the Eucharistic meal makes sense only if it is linked to a passion, to redemption—your own and others'. The Eucharist is not your private party. It will bear the fruit for which Christ was lifted up only if you become eucharists for the life of the world, only if you too become "really present" to someone's Calvary, only if your presence is so filled with Christ's life that the eyes of the desperate light up with hope, the bellies of the starving are fed with bread, the hearts of the loveless beat with love, if someone who has no reason for living discovers it in Christ—through you, taken and blessed, broken and given.

At that moment you will share, as never before, the Supper of the Lord. Then it will become *your* Supper.

Franciscan Renewal Center
Scottsdale, Arizona
April 8, 1982

9

I HAVE GIVEN YOU AN EXAMPLE
Holy Thursday 2

♦ Exodus 12:1–8, 11–14
♦ 1 Corinthians 11:23–26
♦ John 13:1–15

In the flow of the world's history, there have been many impressive meals. They move from the very simple to the highly elaborate, from the gruesome to the sacred. There was the first supper we know, where the *pièce de résistance* was a single apple shared by one man and one woman; and there are those endless state banquets where royalty toasts royalty over partridge and cherries jubilee. There is the Greek tragedy where King Atreus, pretending peace with his enemy Thyestes, served up three of Thyestes' sons for the main course; and there is the Passover of the Jews, moving memorial of their deliverance from the bondage of Egypt.

This evening we gather to commemorate and memorialize, to re-enact and re-present, what is for Christians the most significant supper of all time. I suggest that, before we partake of it, we muse on its meaning. I mean its meaning precisely as a challenge to love: a challenge to Jesus' love and a challenge to our love.

I

When Christ our Lord sat down to his last supper, three problems confronted him.[1] You know what a problem is. Very simply, a problem means two facts in conflict. On the eve of his crucifixion three problems confronted Christ, three challenges to his love.

The first problem was this: He had to go, and he wanted to stay.

He had to leave us: it was his Father's will. "The Son of Man goes," he said, "as it has been determined" (Lk 22:22). "It is to your advantage that I go away; for if I do not go away, the [Holy Spirit] will not come to you; but if I go, I will send Him to you" (Jn 16:7). He had to leave us; and yet he wanted to stay with us. His happiness lay in sharing our joys and sorrows, "delighting in the children of men" (Prov 8:31). And never had he loved his own so intensely as in that hour: "Keenly have I yearned to eat this passover with you before I suffer" (Lk 22:15). There you have it: the bitter anguish of two loves—two loves in conflict. Which will yield? The Father's will? Impossible: "The things that are pleasing to Him I do always" (Jn 8:29). His love for men and women, will that have to yield?

With all the power of his divine intellect, with all the tenderness of his human heart, Christ cuts through the problem with a solution that almost shocks us—a solution that did shock the good folk of Capernaum. Neither love will have to yield. He will go, and he will stay; he will leave us, and he will remain with us. He will take from his disciples, he will take from us—because the Father wills it—the sensible charm of his presence. No longer will men and women see his face, hear the music and the thunder of his voice; no longer will they sense the fascination of his smile or be touched by his tears. In that sense he will go: the sensible charm of his presence. And still he will stay: Till the end of time he will leave with us the truth of that presence.

Listen to his words: "This is my body. . . . This is my blood" (Mt 26:26, 28). It looks like bread, it feels like bread, it tastes like bread; but it is not bread—it is his body. As long as *this* remains *this,* as long as what looks like bread continues to look like bread, so long will he remain: his real body, his real blood, and everything inseparable from it—his soul, his divineness.

The first problem? He had to go, and he wanted to stay. The solution? He did go, and he did stay. He took from us the God-man as Palestine saw him with the eyes of the body; he left with us the same God-man, whom you and I see with the eyes of our faith. The solution is simply the Real Presence: He is *present* in this blessed sacrament, and his presence is *real.*

The second problem. Once again we have two facts that clash. The first fact is the urgency of love. To love is to give; to love perfectly is to give till there is nothing left to give. Jesus knew it: "Greater love than this no man has, that a man lay down his life for his friends" (Jn 15:13). Death is the final effort of love, its masterpiece, its triumph. To give till you can give no more, that is love's finest hour, that is love's incredible joy. And so Christ our Lord, whose love for us was beyond human knowing, would gladly have died a thousand deaths for us, would gladly have died daily.

That is the first fact, the urgency of love. The second fact, the fact that clashes with the first, is the tragedy of love. Love cannot die daily, love cannot really die a thousand times. A man, a woman, can die no more than once for the object of their love. "It is appointed for men and women to die once" (Heb 9:27). Oh yes, God can suspend that law by a miracle. After all, Jesus raised the daughter of Jairus to life, the widow's son, the rotting corpse of Lazarus. They died twice. But that is not for the ordinary run of humankind; that was not for Jesus. His Father wants him to taste death once. As St. Paul put it, "Christ, being raised from the dead, will never die again" (Rom 6:9).

How does he solve that problem? As before, so now, he cuts through the problem with a solution that almost shocks us—a solution that has shocked thousands through the ages. Of course he can die but once; because the Father so wishes, he will taste but once the bitter joy of bloody death, of blood-red sacrifice. But what a revenge he invents for that deep-seated, unsatisfied desire to die each day for us! "Jesus took bread, blessed it, broke it, and gave it to his disciples: 'This is my body.' Taking a cup, he gave thanks and gave it to them: 'This is my blood' " (Mt 26:26–28). And he added those eternally significant words: "Do this in remembrance of me" (Lk 22:19). To his priests down the ages, till time be no more: Do this: Take within your spotless hands a lifeless loaf and breathe into it the Bread of Life. Do this: Take between your trembling fingers a cup of wine and bathe it with my blood.

The solution to the second problem is, simply, the Mass. In each Mass a human being, lending his lips to his Lord, whispers: "This is my body." And with those awesome syllables he brings down on an altar the same Victim who died once for all on Calvary; he offers that same Victim to the Father for the sins of the world. In each Mass God gives us Calvary all over again. Not that Jesus dies again; that he cannot do. But the Christ who rests on that altar is the same Christ, wounds and all, who died once for all on the cross.

The third problem. Once again we have two facts that clash. The first fact is the very nature of love. The dream of love is union—but perfect union, unending union, sensible and sensed, face to face and heart to heart. And, at the Supper, such was the disposition of the heart of Christ. "I have loved you with an everlasting love" (Jer 31:3). He wanted perfect, inseparable oneness with his own, with us—not only in spirit, not merely in poetry, but heart beating against heart.

That is the first fact, the dream of love, love's yearning for union. But, in conflict with the dream of love, we find the law of Providence. This total self-giving is something reserved for heaven. A union between man and God that is perfect and unending—why, that *is* heaven, and Providence will not permit even Jesus to put heaven on earth.

The problem, then, is this: How will love follow its natural bent, its yearning for union, without going counter to the law? How satisfy that yearning for a union he cannot yet give? The solution is shockingly simple. When he takes bread into his healing hands, he murmurs, not simply "This is my body," but "Take and eat" (Mt 26:26). So, too, for the wine. Not simply "This is my blood," but "Drink of this" (Mt 26:27). It is the realization of the remarkable promise made in Capernaum: "Truly, truly, I say to you, unless you eat the flesh of the Son of Man and drink his blood, you have no life in you. He who eats my flesh and drinks my blood has life everlasting, and I will raise him up on the last day. For my flesh is food indeed, and my blood is drink indeed. . . . He who eats me will live because of me" (Jn 6:53–57).

The solution is Communion. Providence is obeyed and love is satisfied. He gives himself, but beneath a veil. He unites himself to us, but without making himself felt. The union is a passing thing, but it is real—and it can be a daily thing, if only you wish it. It is not heaven, but it is awfully close.

Three challenges to his love; three incredible responses. He had to go, and he wanted to stay; so he went, and he stayed: the *Real Presence.* He would have preferred a daily death, and yet he could die but once; so the Victim of Calvary returns to us each day, still our Victim, still our Sacrifice: the Sacrifice of the *Mass.* He wanted perfect union, and perfect union is impossible this side of heaven; so he gave us the next best thing, *Communion*—his own heart next to our own beating hearts. Little wonder that the Christian sings with St. Thomas Aquinas:

> See, Lord, at thy service low lies here a heart
> Lost, all lost in wonder at the God thou art.[2]

II

So much for the challenge to *Christ's* love; he accepted it, wrestled with it, solved it. His reaction is no longer in question. But what of the challenges to *our* love? Where are they? And how do we respond to them?

Let's begin with our paschal supper, this very meal. A meal, at its best, is not simply a stomach-stuffer. A meal is a way of sharing presence. That is why eating alone is a bit of a contradiction—unless you're sick or in a foul mood, on a singular retreat or a solitary by vow. A wide range of human hungers is shared—not only physical but psychological, emotional, spiritual. Even in silence. To pass food is, in symbol, to pass yourself; to accept food is to accept presence, to accept the other. A true meal is one where you give yourself to those who surround you. Like Jesus: "This is my body." This is me! To make that crystal-clear, Jesus washed the feet of all who shared his supper: "If I, your Lord and Teacher, have washed your feet, you also ought to wash one another's feet. For I have given you an example, that you should do as I have done to you" (Jn 13:14–15).

But where do we begin? Right here, where we meet to eat—together. Not hundreds of private parties; not alone. No, one supper for one family. In this chapel, all around us, are brothers and sisters with hungers—just about every hunger in the human book. In sharing the same food, the one Jesus Christ, you are promising to be present to them. If not to all, surely to some one of them. You know how *you* hurt. What makes you think you are unique, alone on a cross for one? There is no one in this room who does not hurt. From adolescent acne to lonely old age, from loss of a loved one through death or divorce to loss of looks or hearing, the hurt is here. Not because this is some way-out Casa, but because you are men and women, fashioned of fragile flesh and sensitive spirit, needing to be loved.

To share the Eucharist here is to share real presence. Not only Christ's but your own—the real presence of each Christ to another Christ, communion in the same cup, the cup Christ drank. Not only while you worship here, pressed together like Christian sardines, but especially when you go your separate ways, back to your normal routine. Only, don't let it be normal! Never again take these people here for granted—not your nearest and dearest, not the strangest stranger. When you share this Bread with them, there are no strangers—only other Christs with their own wounds, only members of the one body.

Here, however, in this chapel, our real presence only *begins*. A basic challenge to the human family is how we deal with distance, with separation, with absence. New forms of communication, satellites in space, have touched us to the whole world: Bombay and Beirut, Nepal and Northern Ireland, are only a TV button away. Paradoxically, this merely increases our sense of distance, our experience of apartness, our feeling of frustration. We can see the blood on battered bodies, can hear the howls of hunger, but it is all so far away. How do we who feed on the flesh of Christ make ourselves present to the absent?

We had best be realistic. Only the few can fly to refugee camps in Thailand, build cement-block homes for slum dwellers in Nicaragua, teach school in Appalachia, nourish *Los niños* in Mexico. How do the rest of us become eucharists for the life of the world?

Simply, right where we are, where we live. For this we have a prime precedent in the God-man. Jesus himself did not move past Palestine. He did not cast his eyes on the far horizon, look to see what he could do for Lebanon. He helped people as they crossed his path: the bridal pair short of wine at Cana, the Jews worshiping in Nazareth's synagogue, a leper along the Jericho road, a bleeding woman in a mob scene, Peter's mother-in-law on a visit, the sorrowing women on his way of the cross. Even the dear Twelve, his special friends, he seemed to choose as he found them: fishermen casting their nets, a tax collector in the customs house. Not unthinking or at random. He took the initiative (as God always does), went out on the dusty ways, but without playing favorites—save for sinners.

And so for you and me. The distance, for most of us, is not geographical. Parish priest or corporation president, doctor or lawyer, nurse or politician, teacher or preacher, banker or broker, father or mother—our people can occupy the same space and still be as far away as the Lebanese or Japanese. We create our own distances.

The other day, right out of the blue, I indulged in a fantastic fantasy: "A Day in the Life of Jesus." It begins with breakfast. While his mother is preparing his bagels and cream cheese, Jesus is reading the Jerusalem *Post*—comics first, then the sports pages. A few grunts in response to Mary's tries at conversation, then he bolts a bagel, grabs another on the flight from table, a hurried peck on the cheek with his mouth full—and off he goes to meet the Twelve outside the Sheraton Sinai.

All day long they run across people; people are his job. But the "kitchen cabinet," Peter, James, and John, have their instructions. "Keep the scribes and Pharisees away; they're as bad as *Post* reporters, always trying to catch me in a contradiction. Watch out for that woman who hemorrhages; she'll get blood all over my new tunic. Remember, I don't like Samaritans; they don't like us, and they're just not our kind of folk. If you accept an invitation to dinner, make sure it's with a respectable host like Simon; tax collectors and adulterers give me a bad name. And, for the Lord's sake, don't promise any more cures on the Sabbath; I've had enough trouble with the local officials. When that centurion asks about his sick kid, tell him in a nice way that I'm tied up; better say 'overcommitted.' By all means, get an SRO crowd for my next sermon, but don't let them touch our boat; and make sure they go home by sundown, else we'll have to send Judas with all our money to the nearest Deli. By the way, John and James, if your mother comes around once more asking seats for you on the dais in my kingdom, I'm going to tell her flat-out to 'buzz off.' And Peter: I know I agreed to eat at your house tonight. But your mother-in-law has this high fever; she'll want me to sit by her all evening, soothe her burning brow with my cool hand, give her one of those endless blessings. We'll never get to the Manischewitz."

Fantasy? Yes—about Christ. No more than a modest satire about many Christians. I thought it was real funny—till I changed the title to "A Day in the Life of Walter Burghardt." Then, as we youngsters used to say in a simpler age, it was as funny as a rubber crutch.

Good friends: In a few moments I shall wash the feet of twelve disciples of Christ. It ought not be, for you, a spectator sport. I shall be each of you. In my symbolic act, you should be washing one another's feet. In that washing you should be telling a little world that, like your Master, you too are a servant; like each pope, servant of the servants of God. You will supplement that charged symbol at the Consecration, when you borrow the words of Jesus and whisper them to uncounted, oft-unknown others: "This is my body, which will be given for you." You will consummate the symbol in Communion, when each of you cradles in your hand or pillows on your tongue the selfsame Life that binds all of you in one body, the Body of Christ.

Foot-washing and Eucharist, my friends, go together—not only at the Last Supper but in our lives. "I have given you an example. . . ."

Franciscan Renewal Center
Scottsdale, Arizona
March 31, 1983

EASTER

10

MY LORD AND MY GOD?
Second Sunday of Easter (C)

♦ Acts 5:12–16
♦ Revelation 1:9–13, 17–19
♦ John 20:19–31

Each year the Church celebrates "doubting Thomas" day. It's a rough day for the apostle. Not only does the poor fellow miss out on Jesus' first appearance to his beloved Eleven.[1] He tells the excited Ten that they must have dreamed it; the only way he will believe Jesus risen is to put his fingers into the wounds of Calvary. A week later the Lord embarrasses him with just that invitation: Trace my wounds. To top all that, Thomas blurts out a confession hardly justified by the evidence: "My Lord and my God!" (Jn 20:28).

I suggest that there is more to this Gospel than meets the eye. This is not simply a fascinating story of belief and disbelief, a reproach to those of you who believe only what you can see. It tells all of us something highly important (1) about Jesus, (2) about Thomas, and (3) about ourselves.

I

First, this appearance of the risen Jesus, like all his appearances, tells us something of supreme importance about Jesus himself. You know, there are many remarkable features to what we call the Incarnation. That the Son of God took our flesh as his own from a teen-age virgin; that the Son of God grew up much as you and I do, save for sin and drugs; that the God-man ate and drank, got tired and slept; that his flesh was slapped and spat upon, whipped like a dog and nailed to a tree; that this flesh was raised by God the

Father from the grave—and all this for me; this is gospel indeed, "good news" beyond our wildest imagining.

But the appearances add one more truth still more exciting, of unparalleled significance for our human and Christian living. The appearances of Jesus—to Magdalene at the tomb and to the two disciples on the road to Emmaus, to the Eleven and "to more than five hundred brethren at one time" (1 Cor 15:6)—tell us that the Son of God has chosen to remain human forever.[2] Jesus did not just revert to what he had been before Bethlehem, "in the form of God" (Phil 2:6). Till time is no more, and through eternity, God's own Son will be clothed in our flesh. Right now, he wears our humanity.

True, there are differences. Jesus' risen flesh does not have the limitations of our earthbound bodies. Doors cannot keep him out; space disappears before him; he doesn't have to eat; his flesh will not age. That is because his flesh has been freed from all that usually hems a human body in. He is totally free. And still it is the flesh that grew from Mary and stopped breathing on a cross. It still bears the marks of his passion. It is simply permeated, shot through, with God's life.

But what a tribute, what a remarkable compliment, to our humanity! The Son of God wanted the flesh he took from us to be his forever. A compliment, yes; but a burden as well. It lays on us the task of shaping our humanity in Jesus' own likeness, of gradually liberating our flesh and spirit from so much that is less than human, so that one day, as St. Paul put it, "Just as we have borne the image of the man of dust [Adam], we shall also bear the image of the man of heaven [Jesus]" (1 Cor 15:49). As his flesh rose in glorious freedom, so shall yours and mine.

II

Second, today's Gospel tells us something significant about Thomas. He is indeed a somewhat obstinate fellow. Earlier in John's Gospel we sense much the same attitude. Jesus has told his disciples plainly "Lazarus is dead." And he adds: "for your sake I am glad that I was not there, so that you may come to have faith" (Jn 11:14–15). The startling fact that Jesus, miles away, knows a friend is dead doesn't impress Thomas in the least. And when Jesus says "Let us go to [Lazarus]" (v. 15), he doesn't understand that Jesus is going "to awake him out of [death's] sleep" (v. 11). He can only urge his fellows, with a flash of bravado, "Let us also go, that we may die with him" (v. 16). Courageous, but dense, thickheaded. Education apparently made as bloody an entrance in Judea as it does in Ithaca!

And now, here is Thomas refusing to believe his peers, demanding to probe the very wounds of Jesus. Still, don't be too tough on Thomas: He moves impressively from disbelief to genuine faith. When Jesus appears and, with perhaps a touch of sarcasm, offers him the very proof he has asked, Thomas does not take him up on it. There is simply no reason to suspect that his fingers actually traced the wounds in Jesus' hands and side. The Gospel does not say he did; the Evangelist implies that he did not;[3] every instinct in us argues against it. Without touching, Thomas cried "My Lord and my God!"

But you will retort, so what? Thomas still had his proof: Jesus risen was standing in front of him. Thomas could see his hands; what need to touch them? He had as much proof as the rest of the disciples a week before. Eyeball to eyeball, who wouldn't believe? Wouldn't you?

Careful! Seeing is *not* believing. Thomas' cry goes beyond the evidence. He has seen the risen Christ, yes. But still a chasm yawns between seeing someone risen from the dead and exclaiming "My Lord and my God!" After all, Thomas did not shout like that when he saw Lazarus stride from the tomb; he did not call Lazarus his Lord and his God.

What more was needed? A gift of God over and above the physical presence of Christ. "No one," St. Paul insists, "can say 'Jesus is Lord' except by the Holy Spirit" (1 Cor 12:3). Nor can one say "Jesus is God" save by the Holy Spirit. Here is the supreme profession of faith in Christ to be found in the Gospels. You hear him called Rabbi, Messiah, Prophet, King of Israel, Son of God. Now you hear Thomas address him in the same language Israel used to address Yahweh: "my God and my Lord" (Ps 35:23). No, not on the evidence of your senses, not from sight or touch, can you say to Christ "You are my Lord and my God." At that critical moment Jesus could have said to Thomas what he said on a similar occasion to Peter: "Blessed are you. . . . For it was not flesh and blood that revealed this to you; it was my Father in heaven" (Mt 16:17).

A gift indeed, this grace to believe, utterly undeserved. But faith is never forced, not even on an apostle. For all the power of God's self-revealing, Thomas could still have said "I will not believe" (Jn 20:25). Breath-taking in his outburst is not only *what* he said;

breath-taking is how he said it: in complete freedom. Like Mary before the angel, Thomas before Christ could have said no. Like
Mary, Thomas said yes.

III

By this time you should be impatient. It's gratifying to realize
that Jesus is still a man and will always be a man, vibrant in flesh and
spirit. It's nice to know that Thomas wasn't just a crusty, pigheaded
apostle who would believe only what he could see. But how does today's Gospel touch you—touch you today? Does it have anything to
say about Christian life at Cornell?

In one sense, I do not know—simply because I do not know *you*.
On the other hand, the Gospel speaks to every single one of you, to
every Christian, when Jesus says to Thomas: "Have you believed because you have seen me?[4] Blessed are those who have not seen and
yet believe" (Jn 20:29).

But notice: Jesus is not contrasting a faith that is good and a
faith that is bad. He is not saying that Thomas' faith ("My Lord and
my God!") is not good, or is less good, because he has seen Jesus.
Two kinds of believers are regarded as blessed here: those who have
seen Christ and those who have not. Thomas and his fellow disciples
were actually in the same boat: All had seen the risen Christ, and all
had believed. And that was good. But when the Evangelist was writing his Gospel two generations later, the vast majority of Christians
had not seen Christ. He makes it clear that they too are blessed, fortunate, happy; they are not inferior to those who did see the risen
Lord; they too share in the joy heralded by Jesus' resurrection.
Whether one has seen Christ or not is relatively unimportant; what
is of supreme importance is to believe.

You and I live, obviously, in an era that does not see the risen
Christ. He does not show us the print of the nails, the trace of the
lance. If the Lord Jesus were to appear in Sage Chapel and say to
you "Examine my hands, put your hand into my side," I suspect,
with tongue in cheek, that even the most skeptical among you might
exclaim "My Lord!" if not "My God!" But such is not our situation.
Not that Christ is removed from us, remote from us; far from it. He
is present in the preached word and in the broken Bread. He is
present, as he promised, "where two or three are gathered in [his]
name" (Mt 18:20). If you love him, he told you, he and his Father
make their home with you (cf. Jn 14:23). The trouble is, we cannot

see him, cannot touch him, as we can see or touch so many others we love. And that makes for problems; it tests your faith. If you are anything like me, you will experience his absence: There will be times, terrifying or just empty, when Jesus does not seem to be here—seems indeed to have brushed the dust of Cornell from his feet. Little wonder that Jesus called you blessed. You are in fact quite fortunate, highly favored: Never having seen the risen Christ, you still exclaim, on bended knee, "My Lord and my God!"

But the Christian story does not end with that exclamation. Matthew's Gospel lays a frightening warning on the lips of Jesus: "Not everyone who says to me 'Lord, Lord' shall enter the kingdom of heaven, but he who does the will of my Father . . ." (Mt 7:21). Not everyone who confesses "My Lord and my God!" will be saved. For all its unparalleled importance, sheer faith is not enough. On this the Letter of James is rude, uncompromising: "What does it profit, my brothers and sisters, if a man says he has faith but has not works? Can his faith save him? If a brother or sister is ill-clad and in lack of daily food, and one of you says to them, 'Go in peace, be warmed and filled,' without giving them the things needed for the body, what does it profit? So faith by itself, if it has no works, is dead" (Jas 2:14–17).

This is not the place to revive the Reformation controversy on faith and works. But this much should be said: James is not the "Catholic" preaching salvation through works, Paul the "Protestant" preserving the sufficiency of faith. Both proclaim, in different language, that a faith which is not lived will not save you—save that Paul would not call that "faith."

A living faith, however, is a loving faith, a total commitment to Christ that forces me out of my small self, out to the hundred hungers of the human family. We were told by God's Son that our love for others would be the sacrament, the visible sign, that he is among us; this is how the world would recognize him. To some extent it does. That once cantankerous journalist Malcolm Muggeridge tells movingly how he put Mother Teresa on a train in Calcutta: "When the train began to move, and I walked away, I felt as though I were leaving behind me all the beauty and all the joy in the universe. Something of God's love has rubbed off on Mother Teresa."[5] Brazil's archbishop of the poor, Helder Câmara, has called forth from a Methodist missionary a tribute that should be true of all Christians: "Being with him, watching him, listening to him, one is less and less aware of him and increasingly aware of the reality to which he points—a God who cares about the little people of the earth."[6]

Decade after decade in our own country, Dorothy Day opened "houses of hospitality" for the hungry, the heavy-burdened, the down-and-out. At her funeral, former yippee Abbie Hoffman remarked: "She is the nearest thing this Jewish boy is ever going to get to a saint." And in the overflow outside the church, "a drifter who gave his name as Lazarus" said "with tears oozing down his seamed cheeks: 'That fine lady gave me love.' "[7] And there are the untold thousands across the world—some of them right here—hearts without headlines, whose daily lives are sacraments of God's love, whose living faith brings a ray of hope to those who, unloved, stumble about in darkness.

And still it is true that, by and large, the world does not recognize Christ because the world does not see him in the lives of those who claim to believe in him. Whole cities could live on the garbage from our dumps, on the clothes we wear once, on the luxuries we have made necessities. Black and white are threatened with bloody combat because we have been, still are, as color-conscious as our unbelieving neighbors. We too rape the earth, pillage it, refuse it the reverent care required of responsible stewards. There is no evidence that we Christians drink less, lust less, hate less than the men and women who reject the risen Christ. I am afraid many of us who claim to be Christlike are rather what St. Paul called the pagans of his day: "faithless, ruthless, pitiless" (Rom 1:31).

On the other hand, I am ceaselessly moved, thrilled, humbled by the profound spirituality and social concern of many college students—and this in the midst of a pleasure-loving culture and a drug-addicted, so-called "mercenary" generation. At Georgetown, where I hang my theological hat, many have an intense prayer life, know and love Jesus as a real person, joy in genuine liturgy. A good number move out to the poor and downtrodden, the helpless and hopeless, from mid-city Washington through Appalachia to Central America.

I suspect that a similar dedication dots Cornell's campus. And still I am afraid. If sociologist Robert Bellah is right and the rugged individualist is newly rampant in our nation, responsible only to himself or herself, your faith will be terribly tried in the years that loom ahead. For you cannot lift the Easter cry "My Lord and my God!" and live for yourself alone; it is a Christian contradiction.

Despite my fear, however, my hope for you is strong and confident; for my hope in your regard rests where Christian hope must always rest—not in ourselves but in the Christ who died for us, in the Christ who rose for us, in the Christ who lives for us. Because you believe in the Christ you have never seen, you may well learn to love and serve the Christs you see each day. They are sitting all around you.

Sage Chapel
Cornell University
April 10, 1983

11

HOW THEY HAD COME TO KNOW HIM
Third Sunday of Easter (B)

◆ Acts 3:13–15, 17–19
◆ 1 John 2:1–5
◆ Luke 24:35–48

Today's readings intrigue me. Each contains a sentence or two that has to do with . . . knowing. Peter tells the people: "[When you put to death the Author of life,] I know that you acted out of *ignorance*, just as your leaders did" (Acts 3:17). The first Letter of John claims: "By this we may be sure that we *know* [Jesus], if we keep his commandments. Whoever says 'I know him' and does not keep his commandments is a liar . . . " (1 Jn 2:3–4). In Luke "the [two] disciples recounted what had happened on the road to Emmaus and how they had come to *know* [Jesus] in the breaking of the bread" (Lk 24:35). And a bit later: "[Jesus] opened the minds [of the disciples] to *understand* the Scriptures" (v. 45). Let's reflect on each reading.

I

The words of Peter are more revealing than they seem at first sight. Whoever of you crucified the Christ, you "acted out of ignorance." It reminds us of Jesus' prayer from the cross: "Father, forgive them; for they know not what they do" (Lk 23:34). They did not know who Jesus really was. Had they known, they would not have killed him.

I am not concerned here with the guilt of Jesus' executioners. Only God knows the secret of their hearts, and on the cross Jesus excused them because they were ignorant. What interests me is the tragedy that can come from not knowing Jesus. At one point ignorance crucified him. But perhaps more tragic still is what ignorance of Jesus does not to him but to the ignorant—to us.

Let me tell you a story, and I want you to pretend you've never heard it before. Once upon a time there was a world of men and women in a dreadful mess. They had lost their God and they had no way of finding Him. So He decided to find them. He sent His only Son among them. Not in blazing majesty; this Son borrowed from them their flesh and blood, their fears and tears, everything save their sin. Not only did he live with them—infant and adolescent, young adult and mature man; he died for them, strung up on two slabs of wood, like a common criminal. Through his dying, that world of men and women came to life again. God was theirs once more, not afar off in outer space, but in their hearts and on their altars.

By and large, the people were grateful to the crucified one; their guilt feelings were gone and they felt fairly safe from the fires of hell. But they didn't think about him very much, only talked to him now and again—mostly on Sundays, or as a last resort, when they had problems they couldn't solve by themselves—problems too tough even for their priests. There was too much else to do, too many other people and things they had to get to know—corporation executives, college professors, the boy or girl next door, history and economics, Bruce Springsteen. It got so bad that a concerned Christian wrote this terrifying bit of verse about a large manufacturing city in England:

> When Jesus came to Golgotha,
>   They hanged him on a tree.
> They drove great nails through hands & feet,
>   And made their Calvary.
> They crowned him with a crown of thorns;
>   Red were his wounds and deep.
> For those were crude and cruel days,
>   And human flesh was cheap.
>
> When Jesus came to Birmingham,
>   They simply passed him by;
> They never hurt a hair of him;
>   They only let him die.
> For men had grown more tender;
>   They would not cause him pain.
> They only passed him down the street,
>   And left him in the rain.

Still Jesus cried: "Forgive them,
    For they know not what they do!"
And still it rained a winter rain,
    That drenched him through and through.
The crowds went home and left the streets
    Without a soul to see,
And Jesus crouched against a wall,
    And cried for Calvary.[1]

When we realize who Jesus is, it strikes us how frightful a loss it is not to know him. Not simply his biography, the way I know Caesar or Shakespeare, Plato or FDR, Jane Fonda or Florence Nightingale. Not know about him; know him. My brother . . . my life . . . my God.

II

Which leads to my second point and our second reading. What does it mean to know Jesus? The first Letter of John declares: "By this we may be sure that we know him, if we keep his commandments" (1 Jn 2:3). What was the writer concerned about? A number of people who claimed to know God but did not take seriously the ethical demands that genuine religion makes on us.[2] No, he replies. If you want to test how well you know God, look to your obedience: How seriously do you take what He asks of you?

But this leaves unanswered the basic question: In the Christian scheme of things, what does it mean to "know" God, to "know" Jesus? A basic question, because the fourth Gospel has Jesus declaring: "Now this is eternal life, that they know you, the one true God, and the one whom you sent, Jesus Christ" (Jn 17:3). What kind of knowledge is this, that in knowing I am alive, alive now and hereafter, alive with God's life?

Our Western ways of thinking do not help much. For most of us, to know is to grasp reality with the intellect, and then affirm it in a judgment. "God is good." "Light travels 186,282 miles per second." "Cigarette smoking is dangerous to your health." And so we favor proof over poetry, reasoning over imagining, objective science over subjective art. Not so the Hebrew. The Israelite knew with the heart.[3] "I will give them a heart to know me, that I am the Lord" (Jer 24:7). To know Yahweh was to experience Him: to recognize Him in His words and deeds—from the parting of the Red Sea to the simple "Samuel, Samuel" (1 Sam 3:4), from the covenant on

Sinai to the "still small voice" to Elijah (1 Kgs 19:12). To experience Him was to respond to Him: "Your servant hears" (1 Sam 3:10). To respond by doing justice, by defending the poor and the needy. " 'Is not this to know me?' says the Lord" (Jer 22:16).

This sort of knowledge—knowledge by experience—runs through the Gospel and Letters of John. But in an original way. For John, knowledge and love grow together; each enriches the other. To know is to accept the love I experience. "Beloved, let us love one another; for love is of God, and he/she who loves is born of God and knows God. He/she who does not love does not know God; for God is love" (1 Jn 4:7–8). This is not naked knowledge, new information for the mind. To know Jesus, the first Letter lets us know, is to be "in him," to "abide in him" (1 Jn 2:5, 6). It is his presence in us, our presence in him. *This* is eternal life.

This kind of knowing I find constantly in the spiritual writers of the early Church. Take just one, Gregory, fourth-century bishop of Nyssa in Cappadocia. For him, the life of the mind is to know God. And there is but one way, ultimately, to know Him, and that is to be like Him, to get to be in His image. Oh yes, Gregory admits that we can know God from the things He has made, that we can rise to the Creator from His creation. But this is a knowledge that even the wise of this world can achieve. To really know God is to share in His holiness—that knowledge which is union, which is love. And how participate in God's holiness? By following Him, through faith, eyes closed, wherever He leads. By opening our hearts always to a further and deeper submissiveness. By divesting ourselves of every favor already received through unceasing yearning for what is always beyond. In a word, by the "ecstasy" which is a going out of oneself. To know God, then, is not a question of clearer and clearer vision; it means sinking ever deeper into God's unknown.[4]

III

Which leads to my third point and our third reading. If to know Jesus is to experience him, if to know God is to share in His holiness, does God's word offer practical advice on how to go about it? Today's Gospel sounds a resounding yes. On two levels; for Jesus' disciples came to know him when he broke bread with them, and they came to know him when he opened the Scriptures to them. A word on each; for so it should be with you and me, with every disciple of the Lord. We should experience him at the table of his word and at the table of his body.

At the table of his word. Here the Second Vatican Council has a startling sentence: Christ "is present in his word, since it is he himself who speaks when the holy Scriptures are read in the Church."[5] We are so used to the Eucharist as Christ's "real presence" that we hesitate to speak of his presence in the proclaimed word. And yet he is present there—as really present as in the blessed Bread, though in a different way. He is present, first, because what we hear is God's word. The words we hear may indeed be Isaiah's or John's, but they were inspired by God and often they bear a message from God.[6] But the liturgy is not a Scripture class. We are not simply uncovering a timeless message, intended for all believers everywhere. God and His Christ are addressing you and me at this moment in our lives. We listen to Acts 3, not primarily to hear Peter remind us that ignorant men crucified Christ 1950 years ago. We listen to Christ challenging our own ignorance. In what ways do I, in my ignorance of Christ, crucify him again? We listen to the Letter of John, not to argue the relationship between knowledge of Christ and obedience to Him. He is challenging our love, asking if we are ready, like him, to learn obedience through suffering (Heb 5:8). More accurately, I don't know what he is saying to you; I know only that he is speaking to you. But to hear him, you dare not be passive, listen to the lessons like an Arena play, wonder whoever chose this dreadful lector. You must listen to the Lord the way young adults listen to Bob Dylan, peace people to Joan Baez, collegians to Carly Simon or James Taylor, Hoyas to Coach Thompson. Then will you know him at the table of his word, for heart will be speaking to heart.

At the table of his body. Here we bow low before mystery. And yet this experience of touching is a unique adventure in knowing. You may remember that the Hebrews used the verb "know" to designate the most intimate sexual relations between a man and a woman: "Adam knew Eve his wife, and she conceived and bore Cain" (Gen 4:1). And we still speak of "carnal knowledge." In such touching is profound knowing. I suggest that an incomparable moment of "carnal knowledge" should come when my fingers enfold the flesh of Christ, and the cup of his blood moistens my lips, when I touch in unique fashion the risen humanity of Christ and through this contact with his life-giving body share in his awesome divinity. No wonder the early Christian theologians sang so lyrically that at Communion I am one body with Christ, we are one body in Christ.

To know him in the breaking of the Bread calls not for theology, only for the adoration of Aquinas:

> Godhead here in hiding, whom I do adore
> Masked by these bare shadows, shape and nothing more,
> See, Lord, at thy service low lies here a heart
> Lost, all lost in wonder at the God thou art.[7]

Oh yes, there are other ways of knowing Christ. Teilhard de Chardin insisted that Christ can be found in the fascinating, demanding, intense, brutal world in which we live. At the Front in World War I, "He saw the Mass taking place everywhere about him. All that was growing and flowering was seen to form an immense host to be consecrated; all the suffering and death of the war was seen as the wine being painfully prepared for its consecration. In the turmoil of events Teilhard discovered a great communion with God was possible, a communion with God through matter."[8] In each place, in every event, in any person we can come to know Christ. For the present moment, let us be quietly content, intensely content, to savor him where we are: at the table of his word and at the table of his body.

Dahlgren Chapel
Georgetown University
April 25, 1982

12

RISEN CHRIST, RISEN CHRISTIAN
Third Sunday of Easter (C)

♦ Acts 5:27–32, 40–41
♦ Revelation 5:11–14
♦ John 21:1–14

Ever since Easter dawned once again, I've been restless. The rest-lessness increased in intensity as I focused on today's readings. They are indeed stirring passages. In the face of death, Peter and his fel-low apostles insist that they will continue to preach Jesus crucified and risen: "We are witnesses to these things" (Acts 5:32). Exiled to Patmos' rocky isle, John has a vision of the Lamb that was slain, hailed by "every creature in heaven and on earth, under the earth and in the sea" (Rev 5:13). By the Sea of Tiberias, a Christ newly alive invites seven of his disciples to breakfast on bread and fish; and none of them dares, or needs, to ask him who he is: "They knew it was the Lord" (Jn 21:12).

All of this is grist for a good homily; and still I stayed restless. In the dead of one night I discovered why. I had to rediscover my Easter faith. It was not enough to join the apostles before the council and proclaim that Jesus is Lord, not enough to shout with myriads of angels "Worthy is the Lamb who was slain, to receive power and wealth and wisdom and might and honor and glory and blessing!" (Rev 5:12). I had to get behind all this. I needed to breakfast with Jesus at the shore, squat near the charcoal fire, ask him to tell me what all this means. First, what does it mean that *Christ* is risen? Sec-ond, what does it mean to be a risen *Christian?* Here is what I heard.

I

What does "risen Christ" say to me? To begin with the basic, it tells me that his soul and his body, torn violently asunder on Good Friday afternoon, came together gently on Sunday morn, came together to shape the selfsame Jesus. The Jesus who broke bread at the lake with the seven is the same Jesus who took flesh from teen-age Mary, the same Jesus who learned carpentry from Joseph and taught "theology" to doctors in the Temple, the same Jesus who walked the dusty roads of Galilee and raised the widow's only son from the dead, the same Jesus who changed wheat and wine into his body and blood and the next day was pinned cruelly to a cross. The Jesus who rose is the Jesus who died.[1]

But this is only the beginning, the sheer physical fact: He . . . really . . . rose. The Resurrection draws its profound meaning from two slender monosyllables: for me. An astonishing aspect of Jesus is that everything he did, he did for me. He borrowed my flesh . . . for me; he lived his hidden and public life . . . for me; he gasped out his last painful breath . . . for me; he sprang from the tomb . . . for me; he returned in glory to the Father . . . for me.

But what can this possibly mean—Jesus lived, died, and rose to life *for me?* I find the crux of the matter in John: "God sent the Son into the world, not to condemn the world, but that the world might be saved through him" (Jn 3:17). Not some impersonal, abstract world, but every man and woman born of woman and man—you and I. Coloring each conception from Cain to Antichrist is Sin with a capital S.

Now this is not a lecture on original sin, on Adam and Eve and the first rotten apple. Suffice it to say here that each human being comes into this world disadvantaged, underprivileged. At birth we are not one, the way we should be one, with the God for whom we were fashioned. And because Sin distances us from God, it sunders us from our sisters and brothers, estranges us from our mothering earth, even splits us deep within.[2] As Paul put it, "My own actions bewilder me. What I do is not what I want to do; I do the very thing I hate. . . . In my inmost self I delight in God's law; but I see in my lower self another law at war with the law of my conscience, enslaving me to the law of sin which my lower self contains" (Rom 7:15–23). To abolish the law of sin within me, to destroy the death that sin seeds in me, the Son of God died and rose again. He rose not for himself alone; he rose "the first fruits of those who have fallen asleep. . . . For as in Adam all die, so also in Christ shall all be made alive" (1 Cor 15:20–22). He rose for me.

Why me? No persuasive reason; no reason that would hold up in court. He "loved me," Paul proclaims (Gal 3:20). Not that something lovable in my irresistible personality called out to him; it is *his* love that makes me lovable. God "chose us in [Christ] before the foundation of the world . . . destined us in love to be His sons and daughters through Jesus Christ. . ." (Eph 1:4–5). Why me? The why is buried deep in the mystery that is God—a God who not only loves but *is* Love.

What does "risen Christ" say to me? It tells me that he is alive and that he is alive for me. He *is* alive. Not merely in my memory. Were the whole world to forget him, he would still be alive. Vibrantly, thrillingly alive. Far more alive than you and I. Alive not only in his eternal Godness—Son of God without beginning or end. Alive in the flesh that Magdalene clung to (Jn 20:17), the wounds Thomas was invited to examine (Jn 20:27). This flesh, these wounds, are his now and for ever. And they are his for me. On this the Letter to the Hebrews is eloquent: "Christ has entered, not into a sanctuary made with hands . . . but into heaven itself, now to appear in the presence of God on our behalf" (Heb 9:24). That flesh, the living Christ, is a ceaseless, wordless plea to the Father: "Father, forgive them; for they know not what they do" (Lk 23:34). "Father, I desire that they also, whom you have given me, may be with me where I am, to behold my glory which you have given me in your love for me before the foundation of the world" (Jn 17:24).

Here is the heart of Easter: Jesus alive . . . alive for me.

II

This leads quite naturally into my second question: What does "risen Christian" say to me? To begin with, it tells me what St. Paul told the Christians of Colossae: "If you have been raised with Christ, seek the things that are above, where Christ is, seated at the right hand of God" (Col 3:1). You and I have indeed been raised with Christ. Paul insisted on this in the full maturity of his thought. "Do you not know," he asked the Christians in Rome, "that all of us who have been baptized into Christ Jesus were baptized into his death? We were buried therefore with him by baptism into death, so that as Christ was raised from the dead by the glory of the Father, we too might walk in newness of life" (Rom 6:3–4).

Rapturous rhetoric, these "things that are above," this "new-ness of life." But what is Paul talking about? He is telling me that my baptism has introduced me "into Christ," identifies me in a singular way with the Lord Jesus in his passion, death, and resurrection. In consequence, right at this moment I am living my life in union with the risen Christ. "I have been crucified with Christ," Paul cries. "It is no longer I who live, but Christ who lives in me; and the life I now live in the flesh I live by faith in the Son of God, who loved me and gave himself for me" (Gal 2:20).

Not pretty poetry; this is Christian reality in the raw. The risen Christ who lives in me makes possible a risen life now, a human life above the human. I mean a risen faith, a risen hope, a risen love. I mean a faith akin to Abraham's: Abraham who left country, kin, and father's house, "went out not knowing where he was to go" (Heb 11:8; cf. Gen 12:1); Abraham who was ready to slay his only son, the son God had promised would continue his line. A faith like Mary's: Mary who, in Augustine's succinct insight, "conceived [Christ] by believing."[3] I mean a hope that looks for salvation not from man or woman but from God, expects perfection not from Radio Shack but from divine grace. A hope such as has sustained martyrs from Stephen stoned in Jerusalem for preaching Jesus of Nazareth, to Dietrich Bonhoeffer, Lutheran pastor hanged in a concentration camp for conspiring to overthrow Hitler. The kind of hope we find in Mother Teresa, who walks ever in the shadow of death and fears no evil because God is with her. I mean a love that is centered above all in a living God. A love as impetuous as Peter's: "Lord, I am ready to go with you to prison and to death" (Lk 22:33). A love so total that it responds to the commandment Jesus borrowed from the Old Testament: "You shall love the Lord your God with all your heart, and with all your soul, and with all your mind [and with all your might]" (Mt 22:37; cf. Deut 6:5).

This is "newness of life"; these are "the things that are above." And all this faith, all this hope, all this love in a context of joy, the kind of joy only the risen Christ gives, the kind of joy he said no human being can take from me (cf. Jn 16:22)—no human being save myself. And all this in the setting of Eucharist, the nearest thing to heaven on earth: the risen Jesus cradled in my fingers, pillowed on my tongue, nestling in my body. Little wonder I feel the way Mary must have felt when the flesh of God's Son stirred within her.

Yes, "if you have been raised with Christ, seek the things that are above." And yet, glorious as all this is, spine-tingling, it is not enough. At the risk of offending St. Paul, let me add: "If you have been raised with Christ, seek the things that are below." Not "the things on earth" he censured, "what is earthly in you: immorality, impurity, passion, evil desire, and covetousness . . . anger, wrath, malice, slander, and foul talk from your mouth" (Col 3:2, 5–8). But to be raised with Christ means, paradoxically, that the risen Christian still lives, for now, on Calvary. Till I am finally raised with Christ, till he changes my "lowly body to be like his glorious body" (Phil 3:21), I continue to walk my own way of the cross, and I stand beneath countless crosses to which other Christs are fixed with their own nails.

A rare confession: I have never delighted in my crosses, have never really enjoyed carrying my cross daily. Pain, as long as it remains pain, never quite stops hurting. And I just don't like to hurt—whether it's a blistering book review or my hiatal hernia. I find only one way to ease the weight of my own cross, and that is the way of Simon of Cyrene: Carry another's cross, help another Christ struggle to Calvary.

Now this is not simply sound psychology: Get your mind off yourself, visit someone with a bigger tumor! This is risen religion. This is St. Paul's "one body" of Christ with many members (cf. 1 Cor 12:12 ff.): "If one member suffers, all suffer together" (v. 26). We who worship within these walls are not 300 bodies crucified on 300 Calvaries: "We, though many, are one body in Christ, and individually members one of another" (Rom 12:5). More than that, we here are a microcosm, the Church in miniature, the human family on a tiny scale.

Here, then, gathered round the table on which the risen Christ will rest, here is a splendid spot to begin seeking things that are below. Here we minister to each other, awesomely aware that each of us is a *wounded* healer—risen indeed with Christ, but still frightfully flawed, needing another's touch, another's "Peace!" In healing touch with one another, we can move out from these warm walls, these wine-red seats that cushion our gethsemanes. Move out not to Lima or Lesotho, not dreamily to Mother Teresa's Calcutta or Father Ritter's Times Square, but to the acres on which we dance so lightly. For me, there are the red-brick buildings to my right, rooms that house 63 of my brothers. Two of them died this winter: One's movement to death was torturous, the other's unexpectedly swift. Where was I in their dying, where in their living? Several hundred yards away stands a hospital with several hundred beds, each a beam off Calvary's wood. When did I last walk that way of the cross? And in-between these two complexes are thousands of youthful Christ figures, all the high spirits and low, all the manics and depressives, all the sin and sanctity, all the love and lust, all the chapel-visiting and pub-crawling that create a college campus. In this maelstrom, what part do I play, what figure do I project? The self-righteous Pharisee or the compassionate Christ? Or . . . just nothing?

The risen Christ destroyed distance. He made himself present: to devoted Magdalene and doubting Thomas, to two disheartened disciples on the way to Emmaus and seven hungry apostles for a sea-food breakfast. And the risen Christian? Too often our distances are not geographic—Cameroon or Kalamazoo; our distances are of our own making, our own choosing. Too often we seek out people the way we select a beer: good body and lots of froth.

At Communion time we shall sing a Shaker song that speaks powerfully *of* Christ and powerfully *to* the Christian. Sometimes called "The Lord of the Dance," sometimes "I Danced in the Morning," it reads like this:

> I danced in the morning when the world was begun,
> And I danced in the moon and the stars and the sun,
> And I came down from heaven and I danced on the earth;
> At Bethlehem I had my birth.
>
> I danced for the scribe and the Pharisee,
> But they wouldn't dance and they wouldn't follow me.
> I danced for the fishermen, for James and John;
> They came with me and the dance went on.
>
> I danced on the Sabbath and I cured the lame;
> The holy people said it was a shame.
> They whipped and they stripped and they hung me high,
> And left me there on a cross to die.
>
> I danced on a Friday when the sky turned black;
> It's hard to dance with the devil on your back.
> They buried my body and they thought I'd gone,
> But I am the Dance and I still go on.
>
> They cut me down and I leap up high;
> I am the life that'll never, never die.
> I'll live in you if you live in me:
> I am the Lord of the Dance, said he.

And the continuing refrain:

> Dance, then, wherever you may be;
> I am the Lord of the Dance, said he.
> And I'll lead you all wherever you may be,
> And I'll lead you all in the dance, said he.[4]

It is a risk-laden dance, this risen dance; for it opens your dance card to all manner of dancers; some of them will dance on your toes. But it has a built-in joy no man or woman can take from you, if . . . if you let the Lord of the Dance "lead you wherever you may be."

Dahlgren Chapel
Georgetown University
April 17, 1983

13

THEY'LL KNOW WE ARE CHRISTIANS. . . .
Seventh Sunday of Easter (C)

- ◆ Acts 7:55–60
- ◆ Revelation 22:12–14, 16–17, 20
- ◆ John 17:20–26

The four Gospels are packed with challenges. "Love one another as I have loved you" (Jn 15:12). "Love your enemies" (Mt 5:44). "If you have faith . . . you will say to this mountain, 'Move from here to there,' and it will move" (Mt 17:20). "If anyone would be first, he must be last of all and servant of all" (Mk 9:35). "If I, your Lord and Teacher, have washed your feet, you also ought to wash one another's feet" (Jn 13:14). "When you give a banquet, invite the poor, the maimed, the lame, the blind" (Lk 14:13). "If any man would come after me, let him . . . take up his cross daily" (Lk 9:23). "If you would be perfect . . . sell what you possess and give to the poor" (Mt 19:21). "He who has two coats, let him share with him who has none; and he who has food, let him do likewise" (Lk 3:11). "Forgive, and you will be forgiven" (Lk 6:37). "Whoever would save his life will lose it; and whoever loses his life for my sake and the gospel's will save it" (Mk 9:35).

Tough challenges indeed. And yet I doubt that any one of those is more challenging, more difficult, more necessary than the challenge Jesus hurls at us in today's Gospel. To clarify why I say this, let's see (1) what the challenge actually is, (2) why it is so all-fired important, and (3) what we risen Christians ought to do about it.

I

First then, what precisely is the challenge? To grasp it, you must re-create the scene, recapture the scenario. The moment is majestic, the air hushed. It is Jesus' final supper with his select friends, the last meal before his execution. He is closing his farewell address. He has reassured the troubled disciples that they will not be separated from him, has promised the Paraclete as a form of his continuing presence. He has stressed the Father's love for him and his own love for them: "No longer do I call you servants. . . . Rather, I have called you my beloved. . ." (Jn 15:15). He has commanded them to love one another just as he has loved them, warned them that because they abide in him the world will hate them: "the man who puts you to death will think that he is serving God!" (Jn 16:2). But alongside of suffering he has guaranteed them a joy no man or woman can tear from them, a joy that will come from knowing and understanding Jesus in his Spirit. He has told them on a note of triumph: "I have said this to you so that in me you may find peace. In the world you find suffering, but have courage: I have conquered the world" (Jn 16:33).

At that point comes the climax of the farewell discourse: Jesus turns to his Father in prayer. He asks for the glory that was his before the world existed: This will mean life for his followers. He prays for his special disciples: They will encounter the world's hostility. And finally, in our Gospel passage today, he prays for those who will believe through the preaching of the disciples: He prays for us (Jn 17:20-26):

> I do not pray for these only [the disciples], but also for those who believe in me through their word, that they may all be one, just as you, Father, in me and I in you, that they also may be [one] in us, so that the world may believe that you sent me. I have even given them the glory which you have given me, that they may be one, just as we are one, I in them and you in me, that they may become perfectly one, so that the world may come to know that you sent me and that you have loved them even as you have loved me. . . . To them I made known your name, and I will continue to make it known, so that the love with which you have loved me may be in them, and I in them.

A breath-taking prayer, startling, thrilling. Jesus prays that those who believe, those who confess him Son of God and commit themselves to him in love, may be one. Not in some shadowy sense, the way all Americans are one. Not simply in ideals and purposes, the way all Jesuits are one. We are to be "perfectly one." How perfectly? The model for our oneness is the unique oneness that unites God the Father and God the Son. What unites them is that the

Father gives life to the Son (cf. Jn 6:57). Similarly, we Christians are to be one with one another and with the Father and the Son because we receive of that divine life, we share it: Father and Son live within us.

The challenge, therefore, is clear enough: We who count Christ our Lord and Savior are to be one—with him and among our-selves—a oneness that mirrors on earth what goes on in heaven, what goes on in God.

II

Thrilling indeed, but why tense up about it? Why call it a chal-lenge? It's already a reality; it's a fact. We *do* share God's life, and in sharing it we *are* one with God and with one another. It comes to high expression in the Eucharist: "Because the bread is one," Paul tells the Corinthians, "we, though many, are one body; for we all partake of the one bread" (1 Cor 10:17). And in one of our bouncier hymns we trumpet "We are one in the Spirit, we are one in the Lord." We *are* one. Why all the sweat? Why a three-point homily?

For one strong reason—the reason Jesus himself gave why we should be perfectly one: "so that the world may come to know that you sent me." If Jesus' prayer is to be realized, it is not enough for Christians to be "one in the Spirit," one in mind and heart. That is terribly important, of course; it is essential; without it there is no genuine Christian oneness. And still it is not enough. Our oneness in the Lord, the love Jesus prayed would be in us, must be visible, audible, palpable. People should be able to see it, hear it, touch it. If it doesn't show, who will ever know?

But why should our love show, why should people know? Sim-ply because the Son of God claimed that precisely this oneness of ours in love would constitute a challenge to the world, a challenge to recognize God in Jesus. Jesus himself offered such a challenge when he insisted to the Jews that he was one with the Father: "Even if you do not believe me, believe [my] works, that you may know and understand that the Father is in me and I am in the Father" (Jn 10:38). Ever since then, Christians are part and parcel of that unity: "you, Father, in me and I in you, that they also may be [one] in us, so that the world may believe. . . ." It's a concrete application of our Lord's command to his disciples from the Mount: "You are the light of the world. A city set on a hill cannot be hid. Nor do people light a lamp and put it under a bushel, but on the lampstand, and it shines for all in the house. Let your light so shine before men and women that they may see your good works and give glory to your Father who is in heaven" (Mt 5:14–16).

At the Last Supper the same Christ exhorts you: Let your love, your oneness with God and one another, so shine before men and women that they may come to believe in me.

III

This raises the practical issue, a probing third point: What ought we risen Christians do about this? In a sense, the answer is obvious: Love! Love your neighbor as you love yourself; love one another as Christ has loved you. The problem with such pious phrases was cutely and acutely put by dear little Linus: "I love mankind; it's people I can't stand."

Pretend, for a moment, that you're an unbeliever looking through a one-way window out on a world of Christians. At the north end of a tight little island off the Irish Sea, you see committed Catholics and passionate Protestants killing one another with appalling abandon. Not too far north of where Jesus was born, Christians and Moslems are enjoying one of their periodic blood baths. In Central and South America, powerful Catholics are moving to Mass in their Sunday finery, while millions of their brothers and sisters are crying mutely for bread, thousands more are disappearing without a trace, and an archbishop is murdered in his cathedral. You look at the rotting corpses of children: Of the 122 million children born in 1980, the International Year of the Child, 12 million are dead—one in every ten—almost all from a needless, heedless poverty. You see your own country, that prides itself on being Christian, aborting children like wisdom teeth. You see Catholic parishes hopelessly divided, from contraception to the kiss of peace, from Communion in the hand to women proclaiming God's word from the pulpit. You see the disciples of Christ clawing one another like cats on a hot tin roof. Anyone wanna be a Christian?

A deceptive lens, I know; it's much too sweeping. Give you a macro lens and you can spy so much more that is truly expressive of Jesus. You see 500 Georgetown students moving out to maximum-security prisons and junior high schools, to soup kitchens and shelters for the homeless, playing big brother and sister to the retarded and the rejected. You see hundreds of Catholic hospitals, where thousands of caring Christians wash the wounds of Christ; homes

for the helpless and abandoned of all ages, where the one commod-
ity that never runs out is love. You see the love within human families—the family that has been called "a little church," "the Church
in miniature." You see Mother Teresa settling several of her sisters
in Washington. An extremely high-ranking District official asks her
skeptically: "And how are you going to feed ten thousand hungry?"
Her reply? "One by one."

The love is there; you can touch it. But the brutal question remains: Why doesn't it attract the outsider, startle the unbeliever,
convince the skeptic that Jesus is alive, that Jesus is Lord? If you
want to be theologically nasty, you can say that the world is blind,
that its sinfulness darkens its vision, keeps it from spying the light
of Christ glowing so lustrously on our lampstands. But after four
decades of priesting, I find this answer unconvincing. There are
just too many good people out there, men and women who are living graced lives and still are not "turned on" by the Christ in us.
Even the "hardened sinners" are rarely so hard of heart that Christian goodness can make no impression, merely bounces off their unchristian chests.

All right then, preacher, what *is* the answer? Very simply: If the
problem does not lie with those out there, then the problem lies with
us in here. Not enough of us live Christ fully enough. Too many of
us are in some measure faithless, hopeless, loveless.

I believe, with this finely-honed intellect, that God's only Son
died for me. Do I, in return, live for him? Is it patent to the pagan
that, as with St. Paul, "the life I now live in the flesh I live by faith in
the Son of God" (Gal 2:20)? My hope, I piously proclaim, is in the
Lord. But is my confidence in God and His grace as strong, as en-
thusiastic, as infectious, as my reliance on Atari or Apple, on rugged
individualism or the MX? Is it patent to the pagan that, for me as
for Peter, "there is salvation in no one else" save Jesus (Acts 4:12),
that "though I walk through the valley of the shadow of death, I fear
no evil, for thou [God] art with me" (Ps 23:4)? I profess to love God
above every creature, to love my sisters and brothers as deeply as I
love myself. Is it patent to the pagan that I really rank God above
power and pride, above sex and self, above wealth and status and
comfort? Is it patent to the pagan that, literally for Christ's sake, my
heart goes out not only to beauty but to the beast, to pauper as well
as prince, to anyone who needs my love?

We keep saying it is a form of pride to want to be different, better than others. But is it too much to expect that I who have been
gifted with God's revelation of Himself in Christ, I who have the

Spirit of Christ indwelling in me, I who share Christ's presence in the gathered assembly and the proclaimed word, I who feed on the very body and blood of Christ—is it too much to expect that Christ will transpire in me, come to light in me? If love makes every bride beautiful, why should not love make every Christian glow? If it doesn't, may we not suspect that the love itself is dull and lusterless, not resplendent enough for a church that is the bride of Christ?

The same hymn that rhapsodizes "We are one in the Spirit, we are one in the Lord" has for title and last line "They'll know we are Christians by our love." Will they?

Dahlgren Chapel
Georgetown University
May 15, 1983

ORDINARY TIME

14

WHAT ARE YOU LOOKING FOR?
Second Sunday of the Year (B)

- ◆ 1 Samuel 3:3–10, 19
- ◆ 1 Corinthians 6:13–15, 17–20
- ◆ John 1:35–42

In the Church's liturgical year that opened with Advent, we have moved through several significant stages. We have relived the world's waiting for its Savior; we have commemorated the unique coming of God in our flesh; we have recaptured the message of the Magi that the God-man meant his salvation for Gentile as well as Jew; and we have seen him begin his public ministry with a baptism from John and the descent of the Holy Spirit upon him, the Father's public testimony to him and his mission.

Today we move a step further: The God-man who came for all of us begins to gather disciples. It is an extraordinary episode, this Gospel of today, splendidly important not only for the original disciples but for each disciple today. And so, in typical fashion, three questions: (1) What does John's Gospel tell us about that first selection of disciples? (2) How should we men and women of today see the meaning of discipleship? (3) The question of Jesus to his disciples-to-be: "What are you looking for?" (Jn 1:38).

I

First then, what does the passage from John tell us about that first-round drafting of disciples? An important word in this episode is the verb "follow."[1] The two disciples of John the Baptist—Andrew and perhaps John the son of Zebedee—heard the Baptist say "Behold, the Lamb of God!" (Jn 1:36) and "they followed Jesus" (v. 37). Now this may sound like no more than walking in the same direc-

105

tion. But remember, in the Gospels the word "follow" is the distinctive word for a disciple. One after another, the disciples of the Baptist were following Jesus, were becoming his disciples.

Note, however, how they became disciples. First, it was Jesus who took the initiative, the first step. It was he who turned and spoke to them. This is what Jesus would state explicitly later in John's Gospel: "It is not you who chose me. No, I chose you" (Jn 15:16).

Second, note the question Jesus addressed to them: "What are you looking for?" (Jn 1:38). This is not for John the trite, stereotyped question you ask if you hear footsteps behind you: "What d'ya want?" With John's bent for the theological, this is a religious question. Why is it, Jesus asks, that you are turning to me? Why are you turning to "the Lamb of God"?

Third, their answer has to be understood on the same theological level: "Teacher, where do you live? Where do you stay?" (v. 38). That verb—live, stay, remain, abide, dwell, lodge—occurs 40 times in John's Gospel. It is particularly expressive of his theology of indwelling presence. What binds God the Father, His Son Jesus, and the Christian believer together is that we remain in one another: Father in Son, Son in Father, they in us, we in them. And so, very likely, what John has the disciples asking is not only where Jesus has his mattress but where he has his life.

Fourth, Jesus responds: "Come and see" (v. 39). Two pregnant words. Throughout John's Gospel, "coming" to Jesus is used to describe faith (cf. Jn 5:40; 6:35, 37, 45; 7:37). And for John, to see Jesus with real perception is to believe in him. It is an experience that will be consummated when the disciples see his glory.

Fifth, "the disciples went to see where he was staying and they stayed on with him that day" (Jn 1:39). This was the beginning of their discipleship. They went to Jesus to see where he was staying, responded to his invitation to believe, discovered what his life was like, and they "stayed on," began to live in him, and he in them.

Sixth, after he had stayed with Jesus, gotten a deeper insight into who Jesus was, Andrew "found his brother" Peter and "brought him to Jesus" (vv. 41, 42).

II

Which brings me to my second point: How should we men and women of today see the meaning of discipleship? The answer seems obvious: We should see discipleship as John portrayed it. Believe in Jesus, abide in him, bring others to him. A nice package, isn't it? Not much sweat; makes you feel pretty good; gives you time for "fun and games."

The problem is, the description is not complete. In those early days neither Andrew nor Peter realized what discipleship involved; they had to grow in understanding; Jesus did not tell them every-thing in the beginning. Only after his resurrection would Peter hear from Jesus: "Truly, I assure you, when you were a young man, you used to fasten your own belt and set off for wherever you wished. But when you grow old, you will stretch out your hands, and an-other will fasten a belt around you and take you where you do not wish to go" (Jn 21:18) . And John adds in parentheses: "This [Jesus] said to show by what death [Peter] was to glorify God" (v. 19). After the manner of his Master, Peter would stretch out his hands on a cross.[2] Then would he realize what Jesus had said earlier on: If you want to follow me, take up your cross (Mt 16:24; Mk 8:34); you have to drink the cup I drink (Mk 10:38).

Not to bore you with abstractions, let me talk about a modern disciple. I mean a German Lutheran pastor, Dietrich Bonhoeffer, hanged at 39 in a concentration camp in '45. The charge: conspiring to overthrow Hitler. The charge was true. It was leveled against a German who returned to Germany from New York in '39 because "I will have no right to participate in the reconstruction of Christian life in Germany after the war if I do not share the trials of this time with my people."[3] A Christian who agonized over Christian com-plicity with Hitler on war and the Jews. A churchman who could no longer endure the Church's silence "when she should have cried out because the blood of the innocent was crying aloud to heaven."[4] A theologian who wrote from prison that only by "living unreservedly in [this] life's duties, problems, successes and failures, experiences and perplexities . . . [does one become] a man and a Christian."[5] A prisoner who even gave thought to suicide, "not because of con-sciousness of guilt but because basically I am already dead."[6] A star-tlingly free spirit who believed that his living and dying were but "stations on the road to freedom."[7] A disciple who experienced what he had called so poignantly "the cost of discipleship."[8]

The cost of discipleship. Bonhoeffer's phrase has become a commonplace. But the reality is terribly real. Bonhoeffer made a powerful distinction between "cheap grace" and "costly grace." Cheap grace, he thundered, is the Church's "deadly enemy." It is the fallacy that, since Christ has paid up for us in advance, we can get everything for nothing. "Cheap grace is grace without disciple-ship, grace without the cross, grace without Jesus Christ, living and incarnate." Costly grace "is *costly* because it calls us to follow, and it is *grace* because it calls us to follow *Jesus Christ.*" It is costly because it costs you your life.[9]

I don't mean that, like Peter, every Christian must suffer a vi-olent death. There are degrees of discipleship. But there is no dis-cipleship, no following of Jesus, that does not include his cross. You are not a disciple if you live with Jesus only in Bethlehem and Naz-areth, but not in Gethsemane and on Calvary.

It's not a matter of looking around for ways to suffer—how to shut out joy and laughter. It's not masochism—delight in being abused. It's simply sharing fully in human existence, in the life of man and woman today. Bonhoeffer put it strongly when he re-minded us that the Christ we are to reflect, to follow, is the "one who enters a world of sin and death, who takes upon himself all the sor-rows of humanity, who meekly bears God's wrath and judgement against sinners, and obeys his will with unswerving devotion in suf-fering and death, the Man born to poverty, the friend of publicans and sinners, the Man of sorrows, rejected of man and forsaken by God. Here is God made man, here is man in the new image of God."[10]

To be a Christian, to follow Christ, to be his disciple, somehow you have to lose your life in order to find it (Mt 16:25). Christianity preaches not only a crucified God, but crucified men and women.

III

A cold Sunday indeed. It's not yet Lent, and already I'm preaching the cross. Only because the cross is not a season, like win-ter; the cross is in your Christian skin. Which suggests my third point, the question Jesus put to his disciples-to-be: "What are you looking for?" Why have you turned to Jesus? Why do you turn to him now?

Frankly, I don't know; only you actually know. Some Christians turn to Jesus because they were turned to him as children; it's "all in the family."[11] Some turn to Jesus because he's a security blanket; with him around, you don't have to look under the bed. Some turn to him because he's a problem solver; he gives you answers, espe-cially in tough exams. Some turn to him when they need a miracle;

he's the God of the impossible, heaven's own "incredible hulk"—or "wonder woman."[12]

But the genuine disciples of Jesus turn to him simply because they have been called, because Jesus has whispered "Follow me." Oh, they may well have been suckled on Christian milk; they may find their security in Jesus; they know he can give answers and pull rabbits out of human hats. But none of these explains why they believe in him, abide in him, bring others to him. None of these explains why they are ready to suffer with him. The only good reason is, Jesus has called.

He has called *you*. I'm not going to argue the point. It's not only Mother Teresa and the Archbishop of Warsaw who are called. The basic Christian call is baptism. There, by God's gracious turning, you first turned to Jesus—perhaps with a protesting howl. But turning to Jesus is not a one-shot affair. Conversion is a ceaseless process, like growing. You should be constantly turning to Jesus, looking for something. For what? Above all, for a person. Unless Jesus is real to you, as real as your closest friend, you will be at best a lukewarm disciple. It is the prayer of Ignatius Loyola, the song of *Godspell:* Let me know you more clearly, love you more dearly, follow you more nearly.

But that is not a logical process—know, then love, then follow. Like Andrew and Peter, you will come to know Jesus only if you "come and see," only if you say yes to him: yes to joy, yes to sorrow, yes to your brothers and sisters, yes to Christian living. Only if, like the boy Samuel in our first reading, the boy who "did not yet know the Lord" (1 Sam 3:7), you respond: "Speak, Lord, for your servant is listening" (v. 10). It is faith's leap in the dark, after the model of Mary, the perfect disciple. Not knowing all she was called to, knowing only that it was God who called, she murmured a total yes: "Let it happen to me according to your word" (Lk 1:38). Follow Jesus and you will know him; live like him and you will love him; abide in him and you will die with him. Yes, die with him. Can you think of a better way to go?

Dear friends: Twenty-five years ago, that remarkable monk Thomas Merton exclaimed ecstatically how glorious a destination it is to be a member of the human race.[13] How glorious to be a man or a woman! Yes indeed. But it is still more glorious for a man or a woman to be a disciple of Jesus. You may have gotten that title without knowing it; you surely got it without deserving it. The question is, are you living it? It's a full-time job. Not that you are always thinking *of* him, but that you are always thinking *like* him. Reproducing not what he did but the love with which he did it. Crucified not with nails, only with the anguish of the "little ones" for whom he died. Completing in your flesh, as St. Paul put it, "what is lacking in Christ's afflictions" for the sake of the Christian body (Col 1:24).

What are you looking for? The question stems not from me but from Jesus. From your answer you should learn a good deal about yourself—how convinced and passionate a disciple you are. For the question in another form is the question Jesus put to his disciple Peter after several years of discipleship: "Do you love me?" (Jn 21:17).

Dahlgren Chapel
Georgetown University
January 17, 1982

15

TELL ME, WHAT HURTS ME?
Sixth Sunday of the Year (C)

◆ Jeremiah 17:5–8
◆ 1 Corinthians 15:12, 16–20
◆ Luke 6:17, 20–26

Today's Gospel is a sizzler. Especially if your bankbook is full of credits, your stomach filled with food, your mouth full of laughter, and everybody loves you. And still, I shall not preach on Luke's beatitudes and woes. Not from cowardice. Simply because I told you all about them two years ago, and if your memory has dimmed you can read it in *Sir, We Would Like To See Jesus,* pages 93–98, now available in paperback at $8.95. What I propose to do is try to get inside the Jesus who pronounces "blessed" those who are poor or hungry, in tears or hated. This may (1) tell us something important about Jesus and (2) say something imperative to us.

I

First, Jesus. A remarkable Hasidic rabbi, Levi Yitzhak of Berdichev in the Ukraine, used to say that he had discovered the meaning of love from a drunken peasant. The rabbi was visiting the owner of a tavern in the Polish countryside. As he walked in, he saw two peasants at a table. Both were gloriously in their cups. Arms around each other, they were protesting how much each loved the other. Suddenly Ivan said to Peter: "Peter, tell me, what hurts me?" Bleary-eyed, Peter looked at Ivan: "How do I know what hurts you?" Ivan's answer was swift: "If you don't know what hurts me, how can you say you love me?"

Do you know what made Jesus so loving a person, the greatest lover in history? He knew what hurts us. He knew then and he knows now.

What hurts the human heart Jesus knew, precisely as a man, as human. It shows up all through his public life: with the woman caught in adultery, in danger of stoning; the sinful woman who touches him, to the scandal of his host; the Samaritan woman at the well, to the amazement of his disciples; the women of Jerusalem who weep for him on the way of the cross. It shows up in all those passages that describe Jesus as having "compassion"—a Greek verb that has to do with our inward parts, our entrails, our bowels, our heart—a word that is a wedding of mercy and affection and sympathy and fellow feeling. This powerful verb is used over the sick who reach out to Jesus, a crowd that is hungry, a mother whose only son has died, a king's servant dreadfully in debt, a boy cruelly tormented by an evil spirit, two blind men sitting by the roadside, a leper begging to be made clean, a man left half-dead by robbers, the prodigal son.

To all of these the Lord reached out, for each his heart was torn. Not a sweet, sickly, syrupy, sentimental feeling; he felt what they were feeling. Not because he was all-knowing God, but because he was all-human man. He was so exquisitely human that he was attuned to all that was human. Not indeed to adultery but to the adulteress, not to leprosy but to each leper, not to a dead Lazarus but to his sorrowing sisters. In fact, this *was* his humanness: He vibrated to, resonated to, the loves and hates, the hopes and fears, the joys and sadness of each person who touched his life.

This is the Jesus who says "Blessed are you poor . . . you that hunger . . . you that weep. . . . Blessed are you when people hate you. . . ." He knew what hurt them. How did he get that way? In large measure, by experiencing it. He did not discover poverty by reading unemployment figures in Jerusalem's gazette; he had no home, he told us, "nowhere to lay his head" (Mt 8:20). No one had to tell him what hunger tastes like; he went without food for forty days in the desert. Tears were not what other people shed; he wept over Jerusalem and over Lazarus, over his city and his friend. He did not hear about hatred from his disciples; his own townspeople tried to throw him over a cliff, and his own people finally had him nailed to a cross.

Over and above that, Jesus went out to where these people were. He did not wait in Nazareth's synagogue for the hungry and the sorrowing to make an appointment. He went looking for them—on foot and by boat. One sentence in Matthew is typical: "Jesus went about all their cities and villages, teaching in their synagogues, preaching the gospel of the kingdom, and curing every kind of disease and infirmity" (Mt 9:35). And one story in Mark gets to the heart of the matter, to the heart of Jesus. A woman whose life has been bleeding away for twelve years pushes through a tremendous crowd, comes up behind Jesus, touches his garment. She feels in her body that she has been healed. Jesus is aware that power has gone forth from him. What does he do? He doesn't take pride or pleasure in it, like a Washington Redskin doing a victory dance in the end zone. He quickly asks: "Who touched my garments?" The disciples are amazed, almost amused: "You see the crowd pressing around you, and yet you say 'Who touched me?' " But he keeps looking around, till the woman comes in fear and trembling and tells him the whole truth. And Jesus explains to her what has happened: "Your faith has made you well; go in peace. . . ." He is not curing a disease; he is healing a person. And so he wants eyes to meet; he wants to see a face; he wants to explain what has really happened in the depths of her heart, her faith in him that brought healing. So far she has only "heard the reports" about him; he wants her to *know him* (cf. Mk 5:25–34).

Even more marvelously, Jesus not only knew what hurt his fellow Jews; he knows what hurts you and me. This is not pious poetry. The risen Jesus is not a vague figure in outer space. His resurrection did not remove him from us; it simply made it possible for him to touch not only Decapolis but the District of Columbia, not only Magdalene but me. It is the same Jesus, you know—save that we do not see his gentle smile, do not hear the music or thunder of his voice, cannot touch the hem of his garment. Your Christian living makes no sense unless you believe that at this moment Jesus knows what hurts you. Not only knows but knowing seeks you out—whatever your kind of poverty or hunger, however you weep, wherever you feel unloved. His plea to his people is his promise to us: "Come to me, all you who are weary and burdened, and I will give you rest" (Mt 11:28). It's another profound Christian paradox: Jesus does indeed seek you out, but you have to "come to" him. With the Canaanite woman in Matthew, you have to bend the knee before him and cry out "Lord, help me!" (Mt 15:25).

II

Yes, Jesus knows what hurts us, and so we can turn to him with confidence. The problem is not with Christ; the problem is with Christians. There is a danger in the beatitudes. It is all too easy for me to repeat the words of Jesus: "Blessed are you poor, for yours is the kingdom of God. Blessed are you that hunger now, for you shall be satisfied. Blessed are you that weep now, for you shall laugh. Blessed are you when people hate you. . . . Rejoice in that day, and leap for joy, for behold, your reward is great in heaven . . ." (Lk 6:20–23). It is the ever-present peril in any religion like ours: If things are rough for you down here, my friend, forget it, hang in there, keep a stiff upper lip. Beyond this vale of tears there's another life, where virtue will be rewarded, where the good guys will have all the fun and the bad guys will be roasted.

This I do not deny, but it is only half the story. The same Jesus who told the poor and the hungry, the distressed and the despised, that they were special to him, told us that we shall inherit his kingdom, rate eternal life, only if we reach out to them. With gifts indeed: bread for the swollen belly and water for parched lips, a warm bed for the homeless and clean clothes for the ragged, a word of comfort for the sick and the chained (cf. Mt 25:34–36). But even that, good as it is, is not good enough—not Christlike enough, not human enough. I have to care, I have to love. Unless you love, the seventeenth-century apostle of charity St. Vincent de Paul used to warn his followers, unless you love, the poor will resent the bread they have to take from you.

Loving the outcast, loving the unloved—all but impossible, unless you know what hurts them. Not from the Washington *Post* or the Department of Labor. Here, I fear, there is no substitute for experience. I talk with a young Georgetown grad who has sweated a year with the poorest of the poor in Nicaragua. He has lived their hurts, those hurts are his, he is different deep within. I talk with a G.U. girl who spends hours in downtown D.C. with drug addicts, battered women, prostitutes. Now college life has a different look about it; even the Pub—not bad, just a little sad. I talk with Dahlgren choir members who sing liturgy at the D.C. jail. They have touched what it feels like to live without windows, wear the same old blue jumpsuits, have nothing to do that delights you, languish for months before coming to trial, give birth to your baby behind bars and have the infant torn from you. Now words of the Mass that slipped so easily from their lips take on meaning: "May the Lord accept this sacrifice at our hands to the praise and glory of His name, for our good, and for the good of *all His Church.*" The good of *all* God's people . . . the prisoners they *know.* Listen to one prisoner's letter (and he's not there for stealing Godiva chocolates):

> I want to take time to thank you and the beautiful Georgetown University choir for coming out and being a part of the services here. I shall always cherish that experience because of the love I felt when I walked into that room. And I anxiously look forward to seeing and singing with all of you again in the future. May the Lord richly bless and keep each and every one of you.

"The love I felt when I walked into that room." It reminds me of a memorable sentence in St. Augustine: "There is nothing that invites love more than to be beforehand in loving; and that heart is over-hard which, even though it were unwilling to bestow love, would be unwilling to return it."[1] Love gives birth to love.

Believe me, I am not laying a guilt trip on the Dahlgren community. If I were, my own face would have much more egg on it than yours. I am not missioning you to Latin America or 14th Street or the D.C. jail. These are simply examples; they illustrate how we can experience what hurts our brothers and sisters. What kind of experience God is actually calling any of you to, I consider privileged communication.

Still, Lent is coming up fast—this very Wednesday. You will be moving from ashes to crucifixion, reliving the dying that gave you life. If you are looking for a way to share Jesus' passion, share his compassion. The world you walk, however small, is heavy with hurt—some of it obvious to the naked eye, much of it cooped up inside skin. Why not make Lent a search for others' hurt? Oh, not a door-to-door questionnaire: "Tell me where you hurt, my dear." That might be counterproductive: "Get lost!" The search is more subtle, more complex, more Christlike. Ask God for increased sensitivity to needs and moods. Don't be put off by a forbidding face; we all look like that at times. Forget the jungle jingle "Do unto others before they do it unto you." Bear with those who bore you. Above all, listen; be present to another with your whole self, heart and marrow. For that, you don't need a hatful of answers; only the scatterbrain spouts the antidote to every hurt from acne to heartbreak.

Dear friends, many of you love to pray the lovely prayer of St. Francis of Assisi: "Lord, make me an instrument of your peace.

Where there is hatred, let me sow love; where there is injury, pardon; where there is doubt, faith; where there is despair, hope; where there is darkness, light; and where there is sadness, joy." Here's your chance, without leaving the States or even the District. Tremendous crowds surround you, as they did Jesus. Every so often someone in the crowd will pluck up courage, touch the sheer edge of you. But you won't feel it unless Jesus' insistent question becomes your own persistent quest: "Who touched me?" You won't sense it unless, like Jesus, you are open to it, unless you *want* to be touched, unless you have the courage to touch the compassion of Christ to another.

So, why not supplement *Jane Fonda's Workout Book* with the Lord's Lenten Special? You have to "stay the course": forty days stretching out your total self to those who hurt. Do that and you just might turn the Gospel woes into beatitudes: Blessed are you rich and full, blessed are you who laugh and are loved; for you have enriched others and filled their hungers, have brought laughter to their lips and love to their lives. Blessed are you!

Dahlgren Chapel
Georgetown University
February 13, 1983

16

SHE'S A SINNER!
Eleventh Sunday of the Year (C)

♦ 2 Samuel 12:7–10, 13
♦ Galatians 2:16, 19–21
♦ Luke 7:36–50

The obvious topic for today's homily is . . . forgiveness. The readings beg for it. King David commits adultery with beautiful Bathsheba, has her husband murdered in battle, is confronted by the prophet Nathan ("You are the man" [2 Sam 12:7]), confesses his sin, and is forgiven by a stern but merciful Lord. St. Paul insists that we have been justified by faith; through a crucified Christ our sins have been forgiven. The lovely Gospel scene teaches unforgettably how forgiveness leads to love, how love expresses a sinner's gratitude for forgiveness.[1]

Obvious indeed, and still I shall not focus on forgiveness. I gave you "my all" on forgiveness three years ago, on the parable of the prodigal. It merits repeating, of course, but the homily is in print and some of you have the book.[2] Let me rather concentrate on a related theme, a theme that leaps out of the same Gospel, a theme that is summarized in a single Gospel sentence. As often, so now, three stages to my development: (1) the Gospel sentence itself, (2) its translation into a living theology, (3) its particular pertinence for you and me.

I

First, the Gospel sentence. Luke's scenario is a masterpiece. A Pharisee named Simon is entertaining Jesus at dinner. Not just an informal, last-minute, come-as-you-are, cold-cuts buffet; this is a banquet for a "teacher" (Lk 7:40) who just might be the finest of the

117

prophets. All of a sudden, enter a woman, unannounced, uninvited. Not some stranger; this woman is well known in the city. Known not as patroness of the arts; her reputation is built on sinning. What sort of sin? Luke doesn't satisfy our curiosity. If you think her profession was the oldest, some Bible experts will agree with you. But Luke himself does not specify.

At any rate, in she comes. Not "bold as brass." She stands behind Jesus, who is reclining at the table—stands at his feet. And she cries. Not only that: With her tears she wets his feet. She loosens her hair, lets it fall around her, uses it to towel his feet. More than that: She kisses his feet, then anoints them with perfume from an alabaster flask.

Host Simon is surprised. Not so much that a sinful woman should dare to crash his party—though that is bad form enough. His surprise is his guest; his problem is Jesus. He begins to doubt about the whole dinner. Here is the man of the hour, the man all Galilee is talking about. Some say he is "the prophet," the man like Moses whom the Lord had promised to raise up (cf. Deut 18:15). Now a prophet should sense the character of the men and women with whom he is dealing. And so our crucial sentence: Simon thinks to himself, "If this man were really a prophet, he would know who this is, what manner of woman is touching him: She's a sinner!" (Lk 7:39).

Quite a dilemma, isn't it? If Jesus doesn't know who the woman is, he's not a prophet. If he does know, yet lets her touch him, he's still not a prophet: A prophet doesn't allow such intimacies—not from a sinner.

II

All of which leads into point number two: How do we translate Simon's banquet, Simon's question, into a living theology? To get to the heart of the matter, try not to be too hard on "simple Simon." No reason to think he was an evil man; he was simply ignorant. He did not know who Jesus really was—no more than did the rest of Galilee. Had he known, he would have sensed that the sinful woman bathing the feet of Jesus with her tears was not a rude intrusion; she symbolized the whole reason for his existence.

You see, the Son of God took our flesh not to make contact with angels, with cherubim and seraphim. He took flesh to be with *us*. And not because we were nice "guys and dolls" who deserved a visit from our Creator. He took our flesh because that flesh was sinful, because it had been infected by all the world's evil ever since Eden; because there was no way for us to reach God unless God reached out to us. And from the moment the God-man touched our earth, he literally reached out to us. Not only to the breasts of his mother and the arms of his foster father, but to a dead twelve-year-old girl and Peter's fevered mother-in-law, to the blind and the deaf, to lepers and an epileptic, to Peter sinking in the sea and children his disciples tried to keep from him. He even let Judas betray him with a kiss.

He was reaching out to a sin-scarred humanity. When the Pharisees and their scribes grumbled to his disciples "Why does he eat with toll collectors and sinners?" it was Jesus who answered: "It is not the healthy who have need of a physician, but the sick. I have come not to invite the upright to reform, but sinners" (Mk 2:16–17; Lk 5:30–32).

Here a warning. When Jesus speaks of "sinners" on the one hand and the "just" or "upright" on the other, he is not saying that these "righteous" folk are utterly without sin. They are "righteous" in the sense that they do all the law commands. Take the elder brother of the prodigal son: "[Father,] these many years I have served you, and never once have I disobeyed a command of yours" (Lk 15:29). But look inside his heart: anger at his father, resentment towards his brother. Look how he separates himself from the party: "He refused to go in" (v. 28). Or they are "upright" in their own eyes, not in God's—like the Pharisee praying in the temple: "God, I thank you that I am not like the rest of humankind—robbers, evildoers, adulterers—or even like this toll collector. I fast twice a week, I give tithes of all that I get." He was not lying—and still you have Jesus' sobering remark: "I tell you, [the toll collector] went down to his house justified ['right with God'] rather than [the Pharisee]" (Lk 18:11, 14). Why? Because, for all his good works, the Pharisee did not cast himself, in contrition, on God's mercy, did not cry out with the toll collector "God, be merciful to me, the sinner!" (v. 13).

These too were sinners—just a higher class, more respectable, not so obvious—and a lot harder to reach. Still, Jesus reached out to these as well. He dined in Simon's house not because Simon had a richer cuisine than the mother of James and John—a fatted calf or quail-under-glass. He ate with Simon because he was reaching out to him too, reaching out to his kind of people. He could sup with a simon-pure Pharisee and be hugged by a notorious sinner for the same basic reason: He was the point of contact between sinful humanity and a forgiving God. "I came," he claimed, "that they may have life, and have it in abundance" (Jn 10:10), have life in profusion. All of them.

III

My third point: What particular pertinence does Simon's banquet, Simon's question, have for you and me? One reaction might well be joy, even ecstasy. Full-throated, you could sing "Amazing Grace":

> Amazing grace! how sweet the sound,
> That saved a wretch like me!
> I once was lost, but now am found,
> Was blind, but now I see.[3]

A legitimate reaction, deeply Christian. But right now I find still more pertinent a widespread approach to Jesus that is dreadfully limited and can be perilously unchristian. In any age or situation we tend to shape Jesus to our own image, make him over to our needs. In a foxhole Jesus is a rescue squad; in a dentist's chair, a painkiller; on exam day, a problem solver; in an affluent society, a clean-shaven middle-of-the-roader; for a Central American guerilla, a bearded revolutionary; in Red Square, opium for the people. If we think of Jesus as the friend of sinners, the sinners are likely to be our own kind of people.

Rather than lose myself in abstractions, in generalizations, I commend to you a powerful short story by Flannery O'Connor, that remarkable Catholic writer who died of lupus before she reached forty. The story is titled "Revelation."[4] In a doctor's waiting room sits Mrs. Turpin, proud to be a small landowner, proud of her good disposition, proud of her goodness and sense of decency. But she is not really at ease. She is bothered by the "white trash" in the room, feels threatened by their laziness and their self-possession, must needs rehearse her moral and social superiorities. She feels akin only to a well-dressed, gray-haired lady. Towards Mary Grace, scowling daughter of the stylish lady, Mrs. Turpin feels defensive. She pities the teen-age girl for her acne, gives her a friendly smile, but Mary Grace only scowls the harder.

> Sometimes at night when she couldn't go to sleep, Mrs. Turpin would occupy herself with the question of who she would

have chosen to be if she couldn't have been herself. If Jesus had said to her before he made her, "There's only two places available for you. You can either be a nigger or white-trash," what would she have said? "Please, Jesus, please," she would have said, "just let me wait until there's another place available," and he would have said, "No, you have to go right now and I have only those two places so make up your mind." She would have wiggled and squirmed and begged and pleaded but it would have been no use and finally she would have said, "All right, make me a nigger then—but that don't mean a trashy one." And he would have made her a neat clean respectable Negro woman, herself but black.[5]

At one point Mrs. Turpin says with feeling: "If it's one thing I am, it's grateful. When I think who all I could have been besides myself and what all I got, a little of everything, and a good disposition besides, I just feel like shouting, 'Thank you, Jesus, for making everything the way it is! It could have been different!' " For one thing, someone else could have gotten her husband. At the thought of this, she is "flooded with gratitude and a terrible pang of joy" runs through her. She cries aloud: "Oh thank you, Jesus, Jesus, thank you!"[6]

At this point Mary Grace hits Mrs. Turpin with the book she has been reading (*Human Development*) and tries to strangle her. When things settle down, Mrs. Turpin asks the girl hoarsely: "What you got to say to me?" And she holds her breath, "waiting, as for a revelation." Mary Grace's gaze locks with hers as she whispers: "Go back to hell where you came from, you old wart hog."[7]

Back home, glowering down at her hogs, feeling rejected by God, Mrs. Turpin begins to attack Him. Jesus is now her enemy; he is no longer a reassuring echo of her self-righteousness. She commands him to justify his treatment of her. "What do you send me a message like that for? How am I a hog and me both? How am I saved and from hell too? Why me? It's no trash around here, black or white, that I haven't given to. And break my back to the bone every day working. And do for the church. How am I a hog? If you like trash better, go get yourself some trash then. You could have made me trash. Or a nigger. If trash is what you wanted why didn't you make me trash?" A last assault: "Go on, call me a hog . . . a wart hog from hell." A final surge of fury and she roars: "Who do you think you are?"[8]

She feels so alone, so vulnerable, in a universe too vast to be controlled by her self-serving piety. Cut off from real love, from genuine humility, her feelings for Jesus have been egocentric and sentimental. She has loved a God fashioned in her own image to satisfy her needs. This image can no longer be sustained. She must admit her fearful littleness, acknowledge her dependence on a God who is infinitely more than she is, who cannot be coerced by the cleanliness and grudging charities of His creatures. She is ready for her revelation.[9]

Lifting her head from the pig parlor that seemed to hold "the very heart of mystery," Mrs. Turpin sees "a vast swinging bridge extending upward from the earth through a field of living fire. Upon it a vast horde of souls [are] rumbling toward heaven": white trash, niggers, freaks, lunatics—and finally a tribe of people like herself "marching behind the others with great dignity, accountable as they had always been for good order and common sense and respectable behavior. They alone were on key. Yet she could see by their shocked and altered faces that even their virtues were being burned away."[10] The story ends with Mrs. Turpin making her slow way to the house, hearing not the invisible cricket choruses around her, only "the voices of the souls climbing upward into the starry field and shouting hallelujah."[11]

While struggling to end this homily on a striking note, I was brought up short. I put myself in Simon's place, but today. I'm hosting the toast of the town, the risen Jesus. It's a banquet, not at the Tombs but at the 1789, and all "the beautiful people" are there. We're just into the reindeer with lingenberry sauce. Suddenly, in comes a woman, unannounced, uninvited—a woman known in the District as a "lady of the night." She puts her arms around Jesus, thanks him with tears for the grace of repentance; a new life is hers, the life of Christ. What thoughts are going through *my* head?

Dahlgren Chapel
Georgetown University
June 12, 1983

17

ALL WE CAN DO. . . .
Twenty-fifth Sunday of the Year (B)

◆ Wisdom 2:12, 17–20
◆ James 3:16—4:3
◆ Mark 9:30–37

On August 11 a small, wrinkled woman, dressed simply in an Indian sari, came to a mental hospital in West Beirut. The building had been badly battered by shells and rockets; there was no water, little food. Thirty-seven children, most of them mentally retarded and paraplegic, were dangerously weak. Said a Red Cross official: "She saw the problem, fell to her knees and prayed for a few seconds, and then she was rattling off a list of supplies she needed: nappies [diapers], plastic pants, chamber pots. We didn't expect a saint to be so efficient." From a scary hell she took the children to the safety of her own Sisters in East Beirut. "All we can do is to give them tender, loving care. They are in God's hands."[1]

The news photo of Mother Teresa cradling a naked retarded child has never been far from my memory this past month, as I meditated on a sentence in today's Gospel: "Whoever receives one such child in my name receives me" (Mk 9:37). But that sentence occurs in the context of another sentence: "If anyone would be first, he/she must be last of all and servant of all" (v. 35). And so I want to talk to you about the Christian as servant, as servant of all. This in three stages: (1) a quick look into Scripture; (2) what this means on broad lines for Christian living; (3) what it says to you at this moment in your movement to God.

I

First, a swift glance at Scripture. The word Mark uses in our Gospel passage to express "servant" is the word from which our English "deacon" descends. It has a fascinating history in the New Testament. It is used of the waiters who serve the water-made-wine at Cana's marriage feast (Jn 2:5, 9). Matthew uses it of the king's servants in the parable of the marriage feast (Mt 22:13). It is St. Paul's way of describing himself: He is servant of the gospel (Col 1:23; Eph 3:7), servant of the Church (Col 1:25), servant of the new covenant in the Spirit (2 Cor 3:6), servant of God through much affliction (2 Cor 6:4). John uses it of Jesus' adherents in general; they are his "deacons," his servants: "Where I am, there shall my servant be also" (Jn 12:26). The first Letter of Peter claims that all Christians should employ, literally "deacon," the many-splendored charisms they have from God for the advantage of one another, "as good stewards of God's dappled grace" (1 Pet 4:10). And Jesus tells us—using the same language—that he himself did not come on earth to be served; he came to serve (Mt 20:28; Mk 10:45).[2]

II

My second point: What does this mean for Christian living? I don't mean, what comes out of Cana—how do you make sure there's enough wine at a wedding reception? I mean rather what comes out of Paul and Peter and Jesus.

There is, to begin with, the principle that leaps out of Paul's statements. Not only Paul but each Christian is servant: servant of God, of the gospel, of the covenant, of the Church. We live to serve God. Recall the old catechism: "God made me to praise, reverence, and serve Him in this world." We live to serve the gospel. I mean the "good news" proclaimed by Jesus, that the kingdom of God has come, that God loves us and gave His Son to death for us. We live to serve the new covenant. I mean the solemn compact Christ made with us in his own blood. We live to serve the Church. Not a building; not a privileged hierarchy; but the Body of Christ, the communion of all who believe.

All that is true but awfully abstract. The Epistle of Peter puts living flesh on it. The way we serve God and gospel, covenant and Church, is by using the charisms God has given us. A charism is indeed a gift to me. But it is not given primarily *for* me. A charism is a gift God gives to me for the good of others, for the good of the community. Paul mentions a number of charisms, from wisdom and knowledge to healing and tongues (cf. 1 Cor 12:7–10). But hidden among those charisms is a gift we all have: faith. It's a startling, sobering statement, isn't it? The power to believe, the power to commit ourselves totally to Christ, is given us for the common good. In short, I am a Christian for others.

Not that my personal salvation is insignificant. If I save others but am myself shipwrecked, it's not like being captain of the *Titanic:* I'm not a hero. And still my own holiness, my status in God's sight, my salvation depends in large measure on whether I am a living member of a body, whether I contribute to the health of the whole. No one, spiritual writers like Thomas Merton insist, no one enters eternity alone.[3] To reach God, I need you, and you need me. We reach God through a community, through one another. Oh yes, we are called individually, we are loved as persons. "Nevertheless," a remarkable German theologian put it startlingly, "unique individuals as we are, we are loved by God only because we belong to all others and because they belong to us."[4] The astonishing thing about this body of Christ, the agony and the ecstasy, is that what I do or fail to do, my selflessness and my selfishness, affect the health of the body. Like it or not, aware of it or not, for good or ill we serve one another.

But what is it that a faithful servant does? Here one truth is of high importance. I am not simply or primarily a dispensing machine: Insert the exact change and you get the proper product. Christian service is a movement from a person to a person through a person. Through our Lord Jesus Christ, by his grace, I make it possible or easier for a man or woman to live a more human, a more Christian existence. It might be a word: a gracious greeting, a word of counsel, an expression of sympathy, a declaration of love, even a homily! It might be an action: food for the hungry, cold water for the thirsty, clothing for the naked, room for the stranger. Whatever the service, the Christian enables another in need to live more humanly, more Christianly. And the Christian does that in the power of Christ—for Christ's sake, literally.

To this theology of Christian service Jesus added a sobering provision. If he came to serve, it was not with the dignity of a British butler—John Gielgud serving a delightfully eccentric Arthur.[5] No, "He emptied himself," Paul tells us, "taking the form of a slave. . . .

He humbled himself, becoming obedient unto death, death on a cross" (Phil 2:7–8). In the image of Christ, the Christian is a suffering servant. It costs you to be a disciple.

III

All well and good. The Christian is a servant: We live to serve others, and service will cost us dearly. My third point: What does this say to you now, here, at this moment in your movement to God?

In one sense, I do not know; I cannot say; I dare not say. Not mine to command: "Center aisles, to the soup kitchens! Side aisles, off to Appalachia! Gallery gods, tickets to Thailand!" I don't know precisely the sort of service God is calling any of you to. This you discover, believe it or not, not by listening to me but by listening to the Lord. What Jesus said to the Jews holds true for Christians as well: "No one can come to me unless the Father . . . draws him/her. . . . It is written in the prophets, 'And they shall all be taught by God' " (Jn 6:44–45; cf. Isa 54:13).

But this I do know: God is talking to you—or soon will be. I know this simply because the need for you is so enormous, so prodigious. Not only in Lebanon or Latin America, not solely in Warsaw or Afghanistan, not primarily in Northern Ireland or South Africa. The need for you is all around you: the acre of God's world you till, the turf you trod each day, the people you pass, the work you do, the hidden hundreds behind some wall or window, the uncounted thousands who see little reason for living.

I see in your congregation what I see across the country: a generous people, hearts and wallets open to the underprivileged here and across the world. And yet, somehow we Christians do not come across to our less fortunate brothers and sisters as their servants. Rather than talk from an ivory tower, let me recall to you a Christian who was indeed a servant to all, a servant some of you knew, a servant who died last May at eighty-three.

Few of the powerful knew Father Horace McKenna, for he was one with the powerless. He simply lived Christ's criteria for inheriting his kingdom (Mt 25:31–46). Were people hungry? He founded SOME ("So Others Might Eat"), walked there day after day to break bread with the "street people" SOME served. Were people strangers? For half a century he labored to link black and white in love, gave blacks and poor whites a sense of their dignity. Were people homeless? He inspired Sursum Corda ("Lift Up Your Hearts"), low-income housing, placed families there, called each child by name; he started the House of Ruth for homeless and abused women, gave it its name and the first dollar for its property. Were people naked? He offered them showers and fresh clothing. Were people sick? He visited them recklessly, however dangerous the area. The first time I saw him in civies and tie (he was 75), I expressed surprise: "Horace, what gives?" His response, with that impish smile and delightful stammer: "Some of the fathers at St. Al's kidded me that I didn't have to worry about being mugged around there, because I always wore the Roman collar; so I thought I'd see what it would be like without the collar."

Horace McKenna described himself as a man with a stole and an apron—the twin symbols of his service. Like his Lord, he could grow black with anger, but only if *others* were hurting. At countless speeches his head slumped to his chest early; but at the end it invariably popped up with the same old question: "And what of the poor?" And yet he was never narrow. He encouraged us crusty eggheads who are poor only in spirit, and he always had time for the fledglings at Gonzaga High, even for their *West Side Story* when he could no longer see the players. No man, woman, or child ever bored him; for, as he said on his deathbed in the Georgetown University Hospital, one lesson above all others he had learned in living: "the presence of Jesus Christ in every human being." No wonder that when Horace McKenna died, Southern Maryland and the District of Columbia wept.

Few of us will do what Father McKenna did, as few of us will do what Mother Teresa does. That's not the point. We imitate them not in doing what they did, but in responding the way they did. We will be profitable servants only if we listen to what the Lord is saying to *us* and answer with the total self-giving of Mary: "Let it happen to me according to your word" (Lk 1:38).

Mother Teresa was so right: "All we can do" for our sisters and brothers in their need "is to give them tender, loving care. They are in God's hands." Our pride and our peril is, they are in *our* hands too.

Holy Trinity Church
Washington, D.C.
September 19, 1982

18

AT HIS GATE A POOR MAN
Twenty-sixth Sunday of the Year (C)

- Amos 6:1, 4–7
- 1 Timothy 6:11–16
- Luke 16:19–31

On the face of today's first and third readings, this is not a good day for the bourgeois, the capitalist, the man or woman of property. Neither Jew nor Christian. If you credit Amos, Jews who "lie upon beds of ivory . . . eat lambs and calves . . . drink wine in bowls" (Amos 6:4, 6) and get regular massages at Zion's health club will be the first to be exiled. If you listen to Luke's Jesus, the Christian in Brooks Brothers linen gorging at a gourmet table will end up in the hot seat, thirstily watching Lazarus and the lower classes making merry on the rolling lawns of paradise.

Now before you despair and give all your surplus to the Jesuits, it is important to grasp what this "word of God" meant then and what it means now. To save time, I focus on Luke. Three stages to my approach. First, a word on the rich man and Lazarus. Second, a word on Jesus. Third, a word on you and me.

I

First, the rich man and Lazarus.[1] Note one thing well: This story does not attack the rich man's riches. Oh yes, Luke's rich man does have a problem. But the problem is not that he is rich; the problem is, he doesn't care. Here he is, regularly arrayed in royal purple, feasting each day as if there will be no tomorrow. And here is a beggar lying before his door, a beggar oozing ulcers, too weak to keep dogs from licking his sores, so hungry that he wants only what falls from the rich man's table, only the scraps and leavings, only what the dogs might get. His situation was summed up in two segments of a rabbinical saying: "There are three whose life is no life: he who depends on the table of another, he who is ruled by his wife, and he whose body is burdened with sufferings."[2]

The point is, the rich man simply does not care about Lazarus. And Lazarus is lying not somewhere in Lebanon but at the gate of his mansion. He doesn't have to go looking for Lazarus; Lazarus is here. And yet the rich man's life goes on the same as ever. Not like the Samaritan who found the half-dead victim of robbers on the Jericho road, "bound up his wounds . . . set him on his own beast, brought him to an inn, and *took care of him*" (Lk 10:34). No, here business as usual, pleasure as usual.

The story illustrates for Luke what Jesus has said earlier in the same chapter: "No servant can serve two masters. . . . You cannot serve God and mammon" (Lk 16:13). You cannot make both God and riches your master, your lord; you cannot be slave to both. The rich man was enslaved to his wealth, and so he could not have God for his Lord.

Note a second facet of the story: its stern ending. The rich man moves out from his own tortured thirst, moves out to concern for his five brothers. Seemingly, they are living the way their brother used to live, and so they are in peril of the same fate. The rich man begs Abraham to "warn them." How? With a real shocker: Send Lazarus! Why Lazarus? Abraham asks. After all, they have God's word in their very midst, God's revelation in their sacred books. Let them listen to "Moses and the prophets" and they have it made. Oh no, wails the rich man, that may not be enough; "but if someone should come back to them from the dead, they will reform their lives." Uh-uh, Abraham responds. "If they do not listen to Moses and the prophets, they will not be convinced even if someone rises from the dead" (vv. 27–31).

A hard saying. If the carefree, uncaring brothers are not persuaded by God's word, they will not be moved by an apparition from beyond the grave. Not a logical argument; simply a flat statement from Jesus on the lips of Abraham. There is an uncommon irony to this prediction. When Luke wrote his Gospel—about the year 80— someone *had* come back from the dead, and apparently there were rich believers unmoved by the risen Christ. Abraham was so right: Those who can resist the word of the Lord in Scripture will not find it difficult to explain away some dude who says he's been in hell.

II

Second, a word on Jesus. If you ponder the Gospels, especially Luke, you may well be puzzled by Jesus' approach to riches.[3] At times he condemned wealth in harsh language. "Woe to you who are rich, for you have received your consolation" (Lk 6:24). It is to the poor that the kingdom of God belongs (v. 20). "Anyone of you who does not bid farewell to all he has cannot be a disciple of mine" (Lk 14:33). On the other hand, there is the Jesus who has well-to-do friends good enough to inherit the kingdom, the Jesus who counsels you to use your possessions prudently, to share what you have with the less fortunate.

A radical Jesus and a moderate Jesus—this is not the place to reconcile the paradox. For that, you might need a semester of Scripture. For our purposes today, simply take note of this: What was more important to Jesus than sheer wealth or poverty was whether people cared. Rich or poor, did their hearts go out to others?

That theme runs through the Gospels. Look at Luke alone. Jesus reverenced the Sabbath; but those who preferred the Sabbath rest to doing good or saving life were not good Jews in his book (cf. Lk 6:6–11). He ordered us to care for our enemies, those who hate us, curse us, abuse us (cf. 6:27). He chided his host Simon for not caring as much for him as did the sinner who washed his feet with her tears (cf. 7:44–47). When James and John asked if he wanted fire from heaven to burn a village of unfriendly Samaritans, "he turned and rebuked them" (9:54–55). When a lawyer asked how to inherit eternal life, he commanded him not only to love God with all his heart but to love his neighbor as much as he loved himself (cf. 10:25–28). He commended the Samaritan who cared for a half-dead Jew when a priest and Levite had passed him by (cf. 10:29–37). He told a high-placed Pharisee to invite to lavish dinners "the poor, the maimed, the lame, the blind" (14:13). He applauded the father who welcomed his sinning son home with a ring and the best of robes, with music and the fattest of calves (cf. 15:22–24). He advised his disciples: If your brother "sins against you seven times in the day, and turns to you seven times and says 'I repent,' you must forgive him" (17:3–4). He was put off by the Pharisee who thanked God that he was "not like the rest of humankind" (18:11). He rebuked the disciples when they tried to shelter him from little children (cf. 18:16). He wept over Jerusalem because the city "did not know the time of [its] visitation" (19:44). Even the cross could not keep him from caring for the thief who begged only to be remembered (cf. 23:42).

With this as background, you can understand why Jesus has the rich man "in Hades, in torment" (Lk 16:23). Not because he is rich, not because possessions are incompatible with love of God, with love of man or woman, but because Luke's rich man is indifferent to the unfortunate, simply does not care, is not concerned. His only concern is himself. Perhaps this is why Jesus tells us, through Abraham, that even a visitor from the dead would not help the five brothers. Not because they are rich, but because they are unfeeling, uncaring—so much so that even the word of God so dear to the Jewish community cannot touch them. Not caring affects not only the underprivileged at the gates; it affects those who do not care: They end up not caring even for God. They are "sad sacks" indeed. And they do not know it.

III

Finally, a word on you and me. There is something comfortable in today's parable, and there is something uncomfortable. Something comfortable: You are not damned because you have more than you need to survive. The haves are not automatically "in Hades," the have-nots automatically "in Abraham's bosom" (Lk 16:23). Jesus is not preaching communism; private property is not a no-no; a fat bankbook is not blasphemy; Crab Imperial is not unchristian; Calvin Klein on your skin is not a detestable sin.

Where, then, is the blasphemy, the unchristian, the sin? In not caring: unconcern for the unfortunate at my gates. Now there are very few of us who "feast sumptuously every day" (Lk 16:19). Georgetown students have never grown fat on Potomac perch and the only hamburger without a third dimension, and the Jesuit dining room, despite all calumnies to the contrary, does not really rival the Jockey Club. Our sumptuous feasting is far more subtle. So subtle it does not leave us as uncomfortable as it should. I dare not detail *your* richness of life; what that is you know far better than I. But I look at myself. I have a high-priced education, for which I did not personally pay, save in sweat. I have reasonably good health—some wonder at the year-round tan. I work hard, yes, but at a theology I love. I have time to research and write, to lecture and preach, to meet fascinating people. I have friends, find joy in loving and being loved. At times I can even feel the God who lives within me. You know, I am a very rich man!

At my doorstep lie many beggars. They may not look like Lazarus, but like him they are in need; in some way they are hurting. I mean every man, woman, or child who begs, loud or mute, for crumbs from my table. Not my Visa card; they ask a gift less expensive and yet more costly—what only a person can give, not a bank. They ask for my so precious time, for compassion even more than my competence, for understanding born of love At times they look for lips with a solution; more often they need an ear to listen, eyes to meet, hands to touch, a smile, even a tear.

And when I look at my response, I am appalled. Oh, not always, but much too often. It's all too easy to spread the table of my wealth for the beautiful people, for the educated and sophisticated, for the smooth and the smart, for the alligator shirt, for "our kind of guy." But what of the others, the disadvantaged, the unattractive, those who bore me, those I simply cannot stand?

That is why I thrill to Georgetown's response to Lazarus. Doctors and medical students bring healing to refugee camps in Thailand, touch their gifted hands to diseased children in the Bahamas, join dental and nursing colleagues in the Dominican Republic and Bogotá. College graduates give a year of their lives to the needy in Nicaragua; students move from class on the Hilltop to the disadvantaged in downtown D.C.; the choir sings Christ to the imprisoned. To all this, and more, I thrill not only because it is so strikingly Christlike. I thrill to it because it challenges me, challenges my selective charity, challenges me to risk more than I do, to touch my love to people who are nameless and faceless, men and women who may resent my touch, will rarely repay my caring.

Like the rich man in today's Gospel, I have at my disposal two basic ways in which God speaks to me: I have His word and I have His people. I have God's word that comes down to me from "Moses and the prophets," comes to me through God's Son and His Son's body, the Church. And I have God's living people, from the South Bronx to South Africa, from the loveless across the city to someone who hurts next door, all mutely begging for some scraps from my rich table. If neither God's word nor God's people speaks to me, gets through to me, I cannot expect a thunderclap from heaven or a visitor from hell. I would not listen to them anyway. If God's own word runs off my back like water, if the bloated bodies of starving children are no more than a TV picture, then hell itself would leave me cold.

My friends, each of you is wonderfully and fearfully rich. For your comfort, few if any of you will be asked by the Lord to "sell what you possess" (Mt 19:21), give it all away, follow the naked Christ naked. For your discomfort, every single one of you is asked by the Lord: How much do you care? And for whom?

Dahlgren Chapel
Georgetown University
September 25, 1983

EASIER FOR A CAMEL
Twenty-eighth Sunday of the Year (B)

♦ Wisdom 7:7–11
♦ Hebrews 4:12–13
♦ Mark 10:17–30

Prudent preachers tend to avoid today's Gospel. The wise will preach on wisdom: "I called upon God, and the spirit of wisdom came to me. . . . I accounted wealth as nothing in comparison with her" (Wis 7:7–8). Or they will leave the last half of the Gospel passage alone, and focus on the rich fellow whom our Lord looked on *and loved*. But a homily on "It is easier for a camel to go through the eye of a needle than for a rich man to enter the kingdom of God" (Mk 10:25)? How brash can a visiting homilist get?

And still, the issue has to be faced. But to face it intelligently, I suggest we do three things: (1) recapture some biblical background, to put the passage in context; (2) uncover what Jesus himself had in mind when he spoke this way about riches; (3) ask what all this might say to us today.

I

First, some biblical background.[1] Little wonder that "the disciples were amazed" at Jesus' words, were "exceedingly astonished" (vv. 24, 26). Not only because it seemed from his words that *no one* could enter the kingdom. What complicated their effort to understand was a powerful Jewish tradition, part of the air they breathed: Wealth was a mark, a sign, of God's favor. Not indeed the only Jewish tradition, but a strong one.[2] Remember how "the Lord blessed the latter days of Job more than his beginning"? God gave him "fourteen thousand sheep, six thousand camels, a thousand yoke of

134

oxen, and a thousand she-asses" (Job 42:12). The Lord blessed this God-fearing man by giving him "twice as much as he had before" (v. 10). Abraham, Isaac, Jacob, all were rich men; for God enriched those He loved. Wealth was part of life's peace, life's fulness. "In the days of famine," the Psalmist sings, the blameless "have abundance" (Ps 37:19). If the people obeyed God, Moses promised, they would prosper mightily in a land where they would "lack nothing" (Deut 8:9; see 28:1–12).

Not that everyone who was rich was therefore blessed by God. After all, Isaiah warns, "cursed are those who add house to house and join field to field, till [they] snatch up the whole area and become the sole inhabitants of the land" (Isa 5:8). Woe to those who forgot that the source of their wealth was God. But if you did fear God, if you really loved Him, you would surely be blessed with the good things of the earth.

> O fear the Lord, you His holy ones,
>   for those who fear Him have no want!
> The young lions suffer want and hunger;
>   but those who seek the Lord lack no good thing.
>   (Ps 34:9–10)

II

Now what did Jesus say to that revered tradition? He reversed it rudely, brutally. Not only did he have "nowhere to lay his head" (Mt 8:20; Lk 9:58). Not only did he live off the hospitality of others—the women of Galilee, the sisters of Bethany, the magistrates Nicodemus and Joseph of Arimathea, the tax superintendent Zacchaeus. He condemned wealth in harsh terms. "Woe to you who are rich, for you have received your consolation" (Lk 6:24).[3] It is to the poor that the kingdom of God belongs (v. 20). Ponder the parables: the rich fool who "lays up treasure for himself, and is not rich towards God" (Lk 12:16–21); the rich man who died and went to hell, the poor Lazarus who was carried off by angels (Lk 16:19–31). At one point Jesus called riches "unjust mammon" (Lk 16:9, 11), in contrast to "true" riches (v. 11). "You cannot serve both God and mammon" (v. 13). In harmony with all that, "Anyone of you who does not bid farewell to all he has cannot be a disciple of mine" (Lk 14:33).

This is raw language indeed. But there is another side to it—a side to Jesus that makes us hesitate about his harsher words. As far as we know, he never told Lazarus and his sisters, Martha and Mary, to give up all they had. He did not announce to Nicodemus and Joseph of Arimathea that they were excluded from the kingdom. Rich Zacchaeus proclaimed: "Behold, Lord, I give to the poor half of my goods" (Lk 19:8); not all, just half. And still Jesus told him: "Today salvation has come to this house . . ." (v. 9). Zacchaeus' response is good enough to inherit God's kingdom. This Jesus mirrors John the Baptist replying to the crowds: What should you do? If you have two coats, give away . . . one (Lk 3:11).

Well now, will the real Jesus please stand up? Which is it to be, no riches or some? I'm afraid the real Jesus, especially in Luke, is more complex than the TV preachers suspect. On riches, there is the radical Jesus and there is the moderate Jesus. There is the Jesus for whom wealth is "totally linked with evil,"[4] and there is the Jesus who counsels a prudent use of possessions to help the less fortunate. There is the Jesus who tells some people to give it all away, and there is the Jesus who advises others to share what they have. There is the Jesus who stresses how selfish and godless the rich become, and there is the Jesus who experiences how generous and God-fearing his well-to-do friends can be. There is the Jesus who forces you to choose between money and God, and there is the Jesus who loves a rich man who keeps both his wealth and God's commandments.

III

What might all this say to you today? One thing is clear: This is not the time or place to harmonize brilliantly the Gospel paradoxes on riches, to synthesize Jesus' theology of wealth. This is not a classroom. It is liturgy, where we recall God's wonderful works in the midst of His people, make the mystery of Christ present and active in our lives. Not that we may disregard the problems Scripture raises; only that the homily is not primarily a problem-solver. And still, the very paradox that baffles the Scripture scholar—the radical Jesus versus the moderate Jesus—can speak eloquently to us little folk.

On the one hand, the radical Jesus must never cease to challenge us. You see, nothing, absolutely nothing, should take precedence over Christ in my life, his right to rule over my heart. But history, my history, tells me that there is a peril in any possession— whether it's an adult's preferred stock or a child's "raggedy Ann," whether it's the presidency or a pastorate, whether it's profound knowledge or a touch of power, my health or my wealth, my child or my home—whatever I "own." The peril? Simply that it's mine, and it can become the center of my existence. It can organize my life, manipulate me, strangle me. When that happens, Christ takes second place. I don't listen, I don't hear his invitation or his command: to give it all up or only half, to care and to share, to let go. The radical Jesus poses a perennial question: What rules my life— the camel or the kingdom?

On the other hand, the moderate Jesus fixes my eye on something splendidly positive. I mean the gift I have in anything I possess, anything I "own." Ultimately, whatever is mine (save for sin) is God's gift. Even if it stems from my own fantastic talent, that talent itself owes its origin to God. But a gift of God is not given to be clutched; it is given to be given. Therein lies its glory, therein its Christian possibilities. The theology I have amassed through forty-five years is not merely my theology, packed away in my personal gray matter for my private delight. It is meant to be shared—at times even refuted! Each of you is a gifted man or woman—gifted in more ways perhaps than your modesty will admit. It matters not what your specific possessions are: millions or the widow's mite, intelligence or power, beauty or wisdom, faith and hope and love, gentleness and compassion. What the moderate Jesus tells you is to use your gifts as he invites or commands you to use them. To some he may say: Give all you have to the poor and come, follow me naked. To others: Share what you possess; use it for your brothers and sisters. Employ your power for peace, your wisdom to reconcile, your knowledge to open horizons, your compassion to heal, your hope to destroy despair, your very weakness to give strength. Remember, your most precious possession is yourself. Give it away . . . lavishly.

To do that, you dare not stare at the eye of the needle; you must look at our Lord. If you look too long at the needle's eye, trying to get your personal camel through it, you may despair. How can I ever reconcile my riches with God's kingdom, my possessions with Christ's command to let go? "With men and women," Jesus noted, "it is impossible, but not with God; for all things are possible with God" (Mk 10:27).

It was this kind of intense looking on the Lord that made possible one of the most remarkable renunciations recorded in recent history. This very day, in St. Peter's Basilica, a Polish Franciscan priest is being canonized, declared a saint. In 1941 Maximilian

Kolbe was a prisoner in the infamous concentration camp at Auschwitz. One day, in retaliation for an inmate's escape, ten prisoners were sentenced to die by starvation. Father Kolbe offered himself in place of one of the ten, a man with a wife and children. His offer was accepted. The man's number was erased, Kolbe's was inserted: 16670. That day he entered his starvation bunker, an underground pit filled with screaming, starving, despairing men—no light, no air, no food, no clothing whatsoever. On the eve of the Assumption he died, 47 years young, and his wasted body was burned in a furnace.

To such renunciation, the sacrifice of literally everything, the radical Christ invites only a relatively few. More likely is the summons of the moderate Jesus. I see it symbolized in a story told me last week by a Jesuit in our Georgetown community. Last year he left the slums of Santo Domingo for a needed change and to do graduate study here. But before he left he was worried: What would his impoverished people think of this—this movement from Santo Domingo to Washington, D.C., to a life style far higher than their own? Their reply, with almost one voice: "By all means go; relax; enjoy yourself; but . . . don't forget us, don't forget the poor!"

My brothers and sisters, the poor surround us; they walk our every street. Poor in so many ways. They need not only food but faith, not simply cash but caring, not merely Social Security but the touch of love. For the sake of the kingdom, for your salvation and theirs, don't forget the poor!

Holy Trinity Church
Washington, D.C.
October 10, 1982

20

O GOD, I THANK YOU—FOR WHAT?
Thirtieth Sunday of the Year (C)

◆ Sirach 35:12–14, 16–18
◆ 2 Timothy 4:6–8, 16–18
◆ Luke 18:9–14

Today's Gospel is a jewel, a gem. Here is another of Jesus' peerless parables. Pithy: depth without a wasted word. Pungent: a message that stings, pricks, bites. Luke appends the obvious lesson: Exalt yourself and you will be humbled; humble yourself and you will be exalted. But if you would plumb the parable at a level still more profound, I commend three movements of thought. First, get the background of the two actors in the parable. Second, uncover what it is in the prayer of each that turns Jesus on or off. Third, move the parable from Palestine to your own turf, your own temple: Who are you? And what is your stance towards God?

I

First, a look at the two actors on stage. One is a Pharisee, the other a toll collector. Now it's important to understand just who these two characters were, what kind of people they represented. Otherwise you may miss much of the story's significance.

When you and I hear "Pharisee," we get bad vibrations. Call me "pharisaical" and I resent it, I get angry. You are calling me a hypocrite: I am pretending to be what I am not; outwardly I seem religious, but deep down inside I am not. Or I am hung up on externals: I parade my virtues. It's something like the word "jesuitical." The dictionaries define it as "designing, crafty, intriguing, equivocating." Some of us sons of Ignatius may well be such, but remember, these disparaging definitions hark back to what our *ene-*

139

mies thought of us. And so, intelligent creatures all, you exercise great caution in using the word (at least before you graduate). In any event, you refuse to universalize, to tar all Jesuits with the same brush.

So for the Pharisees. Much of their history evokes respect.[1] Their lifeblood was the law of Moses. A Jew would be saved, the nation made holy, only by knowing the law thoroughly and following it exactly: Sabbath and feast days, ritual purity, tithing, dietary rules—all 613 imperatives. The code may repel you, but in fairness never forget that what the Pharisees were trying to codify was love, loyalty, compassion, make them inescapable religious duties, in this way to fashion an intimate relation between a Father who cared and the child He cared about.

Oh yes, some early Christians savaged the Pharisees. Matthew has Jesus himself assail them pitilessly: They were legalistic, overemphasized externals, laid impossible burdens on others, did what they did to be seen, were "outwardly beautiful, but within . . . full of dead men's bones" (Mt 23:27); a convert they made "twice as much a child of hell" as themselves (v. 15). And yet some Pharisees warned Jesus that Herod sought his blood (cf. Lk 13:31). The Pharisee Gamaliel told a council of Jews who wanted to kill the apostles: " . . . let them alone; for if . . . this undertaking is of men, it will fail; but if it is of God, you will not be able to overthrow them. You might even be found opposing God!" (Acts 5:38–39). And St. Paul, Paul the Christian, cried out to a council of Jews: "I am a Pharisee, a son of Pharisees" (Acts 23:6).

Now what of the other actor, the toll collector? Here too was a Jew, but a Jew whose job was to collect indirect taxes from his fellow Jews—for the Romans. He was not a quisling, a traitor to his country, but he was in the employ of the hated occupier. Even more of a a scandal to law-abiding Jews, his job lent itself to abuse, dishonesty, extortion. Remember the toll collectors who came to John the Baptist to be baptized? "Teacher, what shall we do?" John's answer: "Collect no more than you are authorized to collect" (Lk 3:12–13). Remember little Zacchaeus climbing out of his tree at Jesus' command? A chief of toll collectors, he promised: "Behold, Lord . . . if I have defrauded anyone of anything, I restore it fourfold" (Lk 19:8). That is why in the Gospels you find toll collectors bracketed in one breath with sinners. The Pharisees and their scribes grumbled to Jesus' disciples: "Why do you eat and drink with toll collectors and sinners?" (Lk 5:30). "Look at him!" Jesus' own people snarled. "A glutton and a sot, a friend of toll collectors and of sinners" (Lk 7:34). Simply not a respectable profession, though you might be as rich as Levi-Matthew (cf. Lk 5:29).

II

So much for the actors and their background. Second, each of them says something, each produces a prayer. The Pharisee's prayer is a prayer of thanksgiving: "O God, I thank you that I am not like the rest of humankind—robbers, evildoers, adulterers—or even like this toll collector. I fast two days a week, I pay [to the temple] a tithe (ten percent) on everything I acquire" (Lk 18:11–12). The toll collector's prayer is simply a cry for forgiveness, for mercy: "O God, be merciful to me the sinner!" (v. 13). And Jesus' reaction? The toll collector went home "upright in the sight of God"; the Pharisee did not. The self-confessed sinner was pleasing to God; the self-professed saint was not.

But why? Not because the Pharisee was lying, the toll collector telling the truth. Jesus does not challenge the Pharisee's facts. Jesus does not say: "Man, you're a liar. You know as well as I do that you rob your neighbor's pigeon house and sleep with his wife; on fast days you sneak Lady Godiva chocolates, and you actually give five percent to the temple, not ten." No, the parable has bite to it precisely because the Pharisee does every single thing his religion demands of him, and perhaps more. He observes the law of Moses and the pious practices of the Pharisees. Look at what he *does* and you cannot fault him.

Then where was the Pharisee's fault? Where did he fail? Listen to the opening sentence of today's Gospel: Jesus "told this parable to some who trusted in themselves that they were upright and despised everybody else" (v. 9). The parable had for target a number of Jews (not all of them Pharisees, and not all the Pharisees) with two damnable postures. They thought that what made them pleasing in God's sight was their own virtuous activity, a laundry list of good works, *and* they looked disdainfully down their arrogant noses at the rest of the human race, at "sinners and toll collectors" and everyone else who did not duplicate their good deeds.

No, says Jesus; not of such is the kingdom of heaven. If you want to see what saves, what makes for delight in heaven, look at the toll collector you condemn and contemn. He is upright before God, he has the stance the Lord applauds, because he trusts not in himself but in God, not in any good work that calls for reward but in God's gracious goodness, God's unmerited mercy. And in begging for mercy, in pleading for forgiveness, he does not contrast himself with anyone else—with the proud Pharisee or the hated Samaritan, with bigger and better thieves or a hot Middle East Casanova. He does not dare "lift up his eyes to heaven" (v. 13) and he does not care to comment on any member of the congregation save himself: "O God, be merciful to me the sinner!"

III

Third stage: Move the parable from Palestine to your own turf, your own temple. What does it say to you? After all, Luke did not write his Gospel for the Jews of Jesus' time (most of them were dead), did not write it simply for the Christians of his generation (around the year 80). The parables of Jesus are not sheer history; they are our parables. The parable of the Pharisee and the toll collector is terribly contemporary, for it raises the specter of two constant temptations. The first is a bit abstract, the second hounds our fragile humanity.

The first temptation is thinking that *I* save my soul. Jesus' parable is addressed to all who ascribe it to themselves that they are pleasing to God, all who lift themselves to heaven by their bootstraps. Oh indeed, I shall not be saved, I cannot be one with God, unless I want to be; but even that wanting, that very desire, is God's gift to me. I shall not be saved, I cannot be one with God, unless I do what God's law prescribes; but my ability to do that, and to do it freely, comes from God. An Arizona rabbi with an uncommon sense of humor once gave me a button that read "Jesus saves, Moses invests." I don't know about Moses, but the first phrase is, shall we say, right on the button: It is Jesus who saves. As Peter proclaimed to the powers in Jerusalem, "There is salvation in no one else, for there is no other name under heaven given among men and women by which we must be saved" (Acts 4:12).

Now don't misunderstand me or the parable. God will not mind if your prayer of thanksgiving sounds in part like the Pharisee's: "O God, I thank you for all I am. In brains I'm a 4.0, in looks a 10. I never miss Mass on Sunday (despite your boring preachers), haven't fractured a commandment this semester. I work with the poor and the lonely, with the cancerous and the cantankerous. I even support my pastor in the style to which he would like to become accustomed." Not a bad prayer, but useless unless you add, day in and day out, "O God, be merciful to me, sinner that I am." In your prayer of thanksgiving thank God for His mercy, from the birth of His Son in a stable, through his death on a cross, to his birth in your heart. Without that mercy, without God's ceaseless forgiveness, all your works would be worthless.

The second temptation is less subtle, a peril to everyday living: I compare myself with others. Perhaps not "I thank you, God, that I am not like the rest of humankind"; that is too much for even the most arrogant. But throughout history men and women have fallen prey in some measure to the Pharisee's fault. Early Christians looked down on Jews "rejected by God," Crusaders on infidels they would massacre. Protestants and Catholics despise one another in the north of Ireland, Shiites and Sunnites in the lands of the Moslems. The "upper" classes look down on the "lower," whites on blacks, GU on CU, "preppies" on punk rockers. And so on across the spectrum of human living.

I suggest that we raise our prayer of thanksgiving to a high Christian level: "O God, I thank you that I *am* like the rest of humankind. I thank you that, like everyone else, I too have been shaped in your image, with a mind to know and a heart to love. I thank you that, like everyone else, I too was embraced by the crucified arms of your Son, I too have him for a brother. I thank you that you judge me, like everyone else, not by my brains or beauty, my skin tone or muscle power, my clothes or my color, the size of my pad or the roar of my Datsun, but by the love that is your gift to me, by the way I share in the passion of your Christ. I thank you that, for all our thousand differences, I am so remarkably like the people all around me.

"I thank you for letting me see that there is a little of the Pharisee in me, that I too have this very human yearning for something that sets me apart from the rest—if only because I am the only Jesuit theologian-in-residence! If I am to thank you for making me different, let it be because, through your mercy, I am different from what I would have been without you. Thank you, Lord, for making me so splendidly the same as everyone else, because it means I am that much closer to your Son, who became what all of us are: wonderfully and fearfully human. Keep me that way, Lord, and . . . always "be merciful to me, sinner that I am."

Dahlgren Chapel
Georgetown University
October 23, 1983

21

OUT OF HER POVERTY
Thirty-second Sunday of the Year (B)

◆ 1 Kings 17:10–16
◆ Hebrews 9:24–28
◆ Mark 12:38–44

Today's first and third readings are deceptively simple. We are confronted with two nice ladies, two pious Jewish widows. Each is dreadfully poor, yet each gives all she has to a godly cause. One gives from her last handful of meal, her last drops of oil, to a prophet; the other puts her last two copper coins in the temple collection. One profits from a miracle; the other is praised by the Lord. Isn't that ever so touching? The moral? Why, give generously to your priest or rabbi, keep him in the style to which he would like to become accustomed, load the collection basket with all your greenery, and you can expect a miraculous hundredfold—or at least a pat on the back from the Master.

That is the surface story. Beneath the surface all sorts of kettles are boiling. As so often in the readings, so here, a basic Christian reality is at stake. Let me develop this in three stages: (1) the widows, (2) Jesus, (3) you and me.

I

First, the widows. You cannot simply read the seven verses from Mark in isolation. They are part and parcel of a larger drama. Around this snippet in Mark you find some startling contrasts: on the one hand, impressive appearances with little substance; on the other, stark simplicity with hidden depths. There is a fig tree in leaf, attractive to look upon from a distance; but when Jesus "went to see if he could find anything on it . . . he found nothing but leaves"; and he cursed it (Mk 12:13, 21). There is the temple, striking the disciples with wonder: "Look, Teacher, what wonderful stones and what wonderful buildings!" And Jesus' reply: "Do you see these great buildings? There will not be left here one stone upon another, that will not be thrown down" (Mk 13:1–2). And in our passage, note the contrast. On the one hand, the scribes in their trendy outfits, with their reserved seats in church, on the dais at big dinners, praying endlessly. It's all a fake, Jesus says, a pretense. These are the same people who "eat up widows' houses," that is, gobble them up illegally (Mk 12:38–40). How different from the poor widow: no pomp or parade, no show or display; just a small gift to the Lord. No big deal.

Surface show versus inner substance. But there is more: the gift itself. "Many rich people put in large sums"; the "poor widow . . . put in two copper coins" (vv. 41–42). She put in the smallest Greek coin in circulation; you would need 128 of these to make up the daily wage of which Jesus speaks in the parable of the laborers in the vineyard (cf. Mt 20:2). And still Jesus can tell his disciples: "Truly, I say to you, this poor widow has put in more than all" the rest. Why? Because they were tossing into the treasury "out of their abundance; but she out of her poverty has put in everything she had, her whole living" (vv. 43–44).

Be careful here. Jesus is not castigating the wealthy parishioners; he is not even accusing them of outward show. He is praising the widow. And his praise tells us something rich about human living, about the risk in giving. The widow's gift was greater than all because in giving the coins she gave up her security; she "put in her whole living." The others gave, and it was good; but they could leave the temple without anxiety, without indigestion. They had given a good deal, but there was more where that came from. For the widow, nothing left but to cast all her cares on God. Nothing left but to pray with the Psalmist:

> I lift up my eyes to the hills.
> Whence does my help come?
> My help comes from the Lord,
>   who made heaven and earth.
>   (Ps 121:1–2)

Similarly for the widow in 1 Kings. A handful of meal and a spot of oil—enough to bake a cake for herself and her son before they lie down to die. And a stranger says: "First make *me* a little cake . . ." (1 Kgs 17:13)! Not that she was giving up her security; she had none, even if Elijah had not dropped in on her. But to give the last cake of your life to a stranger because he says "Don't be afraid"? What would you have answered? "Man, get lost"?

II

Second, Jesus. You see, Jesus enters into Mark's story of the widow not only as a commentator like Walter Cronkite, not only as a supreme judge like Warren Burger. This section of Mark is leading up to Jesus' passion and death. Here the reading from Hebrews is highly pertinent: Christ came "once for all . . . to put away sin by the sacrifice of himself" (Heb 9:26). What made the widow's gift superbly human was that she gave everything she had: her last two coins. What made it splendidly religious was that it resembled what Jesus himself would offer on the cross: himself.

In Jesus' offering there was a terrible risk. We tend to think of him as going through an act. After all, wasn't he God as well as man? Didn't he know he would rise again? You can make a very good case for all of that. But even so you are faced with an undeniable fact: Jesus was afraid to die. So afraid that he sweated blood; so fearful that he begged his Father to let him live; so terrified that his Father sent an angel from heaven to strengthen him. All human security was gone: his mother, his disciples, his wealthy friends; none of them could help. He was alone, face to face with the awful blackness, the awesome blankness, of death.

It's a bloody moment on the cross when this Jesus gives up literally everything to the Father for us; when a naked Jesus, with no security against death, prays to the Father in the words of Psalm 22: "My God, my God, why have you forsaken me?" (Mt 27:46; Ps 22:1). But recall what Psalm 22 is all about. It is ultimately a prayer of trust, not in man or woman but in God:

> In you our fathers trusted;
>   they trusted, and you delivered them.
> To you they cried, and were saved;
>   in you they trusted, and were not disappointed.
>   (Ps 22:4–5)

Like the widow, Jesus gave all he had. More obviously than the widow, Jesus gave all he was. Nothing left to give, he gave himself: "This is my body, which is given for you" (Lk 22:19). Out of his poverty, he put in the treasury of the Father everything he had, his whole living, his whole dying. No security . . . total risk . . . trust in God alone. The result? Simply, redemption. You and I, the whole of humanity from Adam to the last of human flesh, all of us have our sins put away, all of us can bend the knee before God and say with confidence "Our Father."

III

But how do you and I fit into this liturgy of two widows? At bottom, the widows symbolize the Christlife, where the key words are "gift" and "risk." If Jesus is the perfect human, the prototype of what a Christian should be, then our lives are Christian in the measure that they are shaped to his risk-laden self-giving.

Let me make an uncommonly frank confession. When I look at myself, I find that in my giving I am very much part of an American syndrome. We have a long tradition of giving—giving out of our surplus. Surplus cheese for the hungry, surplus clothes for Goodwill, surplus books for the missions, surplus money for United Way, surplus time for friends, a surplus cup of cold water. A good thing, mind you; I am not talking it down. Without it, life would be a jungle, survival of the fittest, "dog eat dog."

Good indeed, this giving out of our surplus; but it raises a problem for Christians. Could not our Lord at once applaud this and still ask: Do not the pagans do as much (cf. Mt 5:46–47)? Not for love of Christ, but surely no less than *what* we give. Where, then, is our Christianness? Only in a different motivation, only because we give in the name of Christ?

The story of the widow, and even more the deed of Christ, suggest strongly that the new thing he brought into the world is summed up in his phrase "out of her poverty" (Mk 12:44). I mean, we are most Christian, because most Christlike, when our giving affects our existence, when it threatens our security, when it is ultimately ourselves we are giving away. How could it be otherwise? Like it or not, it is the *crucified* Christ who is the supreme pattern, the paradigm, the model for Christian living, for Christian giving. And the crucified Christ gives . . . himself.

I dare not suggest how or where or when this touches any given one of you. Christ speaks to you not in a xeroxed letter, impersonal, addressed to "all Christians everywhere." He speaks to you where you're at. You—and he—know who you are, where your gifts lie, what restrains you from risking, why you keep giving out of your surplus. Christ alone can tell you at what point, and in what way, you have to surrender what lends you security, go out to your brothers and sisters with trust only in the power of a loving God.

Christ alone. . . . Aye, there's the rub. Has Jesus Christ really gotten under my skin? How dearly do I love him? Isn't it appalling how little he moves most of us, how rarely he excites us? We watch *E.T.* and we go bonkers. A lovably strange character comes to earth from somewhere out there, shares awhile our human joys and griefs, dies and is resurrected, returns to wherever he came from— and we cannot forget him (or her, or it). E.T. dominates our Halloween, reshapes our pumpkins, may well displace old Santa. But the God-man who really came to our earth, really died and rose again, really returned to his Father "now to appear in the presence of God on our behalf" (Heb 9:24), why doesn't he turn more of us on? Perhaps he will . . . if we take that little fellow from outer space seriously.

American University
Washington, D.C.
November 7, 1982

22

WITH GREAT POWER AND GLORY
Thirty-third Sunday of the Year (B)

◆ Daniel 12:1–3
◆ Hebrews 10:11–14, 18
◆ Mark 13:24–32

When I spoke to you one month ago on camels and needles,[1] I did not suspect that a still more difficult Gospel would waylay us in November. The end of the world, the second coming of Christ, the gathering of all the elect—perhaps what you need is not a fifteen-minute homily but a six-credit course in the New Testament. It's true, the Church wants not exegesis but proclamation, not the solution to puzzles but a retelling of God's wonderful works among His people, not study but praise. The problem is, my proclamation and your praise should leap out of God's word—and today's word is mysterious, provocative, overpowering.

What to do? I suggest that, as so often, three elements enter into your assembly here today: the liturgy of the Church, the word of God, and the needs of the people. So, why don't we have a go at each in order: (1) what the Church is ritualizing in today's liturgy; (2) what the Gospel is describing; (3) how liturgy and Gospel might touch our human and Christian concerns.

I

First then, the Church's liturgy. What are we doing here each time we gather? What are we doing this morning? The difficulty is, we are such different people that we see different things even in the liturgy. Someone compared it to the story of four blind men experiencing an elephant. One said it was a very large tree; he had put his arms around the elephant's leg. No, said the second, it's a snake

149

with a very coarse skin and a strange, soft mouth; he had grasped the trunk. The third swore it was a sail on a ship; he had felt the elephant's ear. The fourth insisted it was a piece of old rope; he had grabbed the elephant's tail.[2]

For most of us, the Mass is what we see or would like to see, what we experience or would like to experience. An ageless Latin or an ephemeral English, Bach or the St. Louis Jesuits, a mystery-laden quiet or hyperthyroid activity, personal communion with Jesus or a community reach-out—and so on and so forth. For all their importance, these can be blind spots; they can keep us from seeing more deeply into the mystery we all cherish. In the liturgy we celebrate the ceaseless work of redemption; we proclaim God's wonderful works in the history of salvation. We don't just read about them, we don't just remember them; we re-present them, make them effectively present in us and in our lives.

In all this a major element is God's word. Year after year, repeatedly and endlessly, the readings recapture the movement of our salvation. Last Advent we re-presented the world's waiting for its Savior, a waiting readied through Isaiah and the Baptist and Mary of Nazareth. We welcomed the Lord Jesus as he came to us surprisingly in the flesh of an infant. We grew to manhood with him in a tiny Jewish town, walked in his steps through Galilee and Judea, recaptured his dying-rising through Lent and Easter. His ascension lifted all of us with him to the Father; his Spirit descended not only on the disciples but on each believer. And since Pentecost we have heard and lived the mission of the Church, its ups and downs, its pride and its passion, its agony and its ecstasy, its ceaseless struggle to grow into the fulness of its Lord, its living in hope for the final coming of its Savior.

And now, now we reach the end of the liturgical year. Next week the peak: We will crown Christ king. There the liturgy ritualizes what will be the high point of creation, when humankind and all it possesses, "the whole creation" that "has been groaning in travail together until now" (Rom 8:22), even death itself, will be subjected to Christ, "when he delivers the kingdom to God the Father after destroying every rule and every authority and power" (1 Cor 15:24). Today we celebrate the beginning of that end; today we live in anticipation the end of the world as we know it. If Advent was prologue to the Christian mystery, these two weeks are epilogue. We round out the history of salvation; we peer nearsightedly into its ending.

II

Second, the word of God. What is the Gospel describing? In brief, three interrelated realities: the end of this world as we know it; the coming of Christ, this time not in infant helplessness but "with great power and glory" (Mk 13:26); and the assembling into one place of all who are saved.

There is a danger here. In each of these three powerful prophecies you can be seduced by the images, distracted by the description. The language to which you have listened is the language of "apocalyptic." A big word, I know. Simply, apocalyptic was a special style of writing. The writers, seeing in vision the final struggle to establish God's kingdom, used incredibly vivid images, all sorts of symbols, to convey realities beyond their experience. If you have read the Apocalypse, the Book of Revelation, you know what I am saying: seven angels with trumpets, a woman sitting on a scarlet beast, the King of kings in blood-red robe on a white horse, Satan sealed in a pit for a thousand years, the new Jerusalem built of every glorious jewel—and so much more. The images are important, for they suggest the reality; but they are not to be taken with wooden literalism, extreme realism.

So here, in today's Gospel. There is some science-fiction—more fiction than science: sun and moon refusing to shine, stars falling from heaven's vault. This is first-century cosmology. There are fascinating images; but do not expect to see the Lord riding a gigantic pink cloud. And be not disappointed if you do not spy real angels flying like supermen from the rock-ribbed coasts of Maine to the sunny shores of L.A., gathering countless Christians beneath their wings and winging them to some giant superdome in the sky.

On the other hand, the Gospel *reality* is not fiction, is not an image. The fact is, this world, the sort of existence we know, this world of war and human wisdom, of sin and self-giving, of laughter mingled with tears, of skyscrapers and computers, of hunger and plenty—this world will come to an end. And with it will close the story of salvation here below, God's magnificent plan, from Adam through Christ to Antichrist, to bring all men and women to Him in endless joy.

All this, the Gospel insists, will end. It will end because it will be time, God's good time, for Jesus to come in "power and glory." Here Mark paints only one side of the picture: The elect are gathered into Christ's kingdom. It is a consoling prophecy, perhaps because Mark is writing for a community under persecution.[3] He does not include what Matthew has: The angels "will gather out of his kingdom all causes of sin and all evildoers, and throw them into the furnace of fire" (Mt 13:41–42). For Mark, Jesus does not come as judge; he comes as savior. He does not deny that the sheep and the goats will have different pens; for pastoral reasons, he is simply not interested in the lost, only in the elect.

<h1 style="text-align:center">III</h1>

Third, the needs of the people. How might today's liturgy and Gospel touch our human and Christian concerns? To begin with, there are two concerns we can only be curious about: When will the world end, and how? Is the last day tomorrow or thousands of years away? Will it all end in ice or in fire, from God's doing or our own madness? Despite the prophets of doom and the TV preachers, we simply do not know. Remember what Jesus himself said: "But of that day or that hour no one knows, not even the angels in heaven, and not even the Son, but only the Father" (Mk 13:32). Today the Son knows; but we—we would do well to confess our ignorance. In that sense at least, we can be like angels!

But such ignorance should not immobilize us, leave us impotent. Whenever and however the world will end, the second coming of Jesus is our ceaseless hope. Does that sound strange? It ought not. Without his second coming his first makes little sense. That original Christmas still takes our breath away—every year. We never tire of celebrating it: our Savior in straw. But it is only an apéritif, a stimulant, Dubonnet; it should make us hungry, make us yearn for more. For Christ on a cloud? It may not grab us, but the only unreal thing there is the cloud. *This* is why he came powerless, why he cried aloud ingloriously in a garden and on a cross, why he rose from the rock and returned to his Father: so that at last he might come "with great power and glory" and lift all his elect into the Father's presence forever.

Since that is so, let us affirm Christ's final coming with the intensity of the early Christians who expected him to return in their lifetime. After the Consecration let us proclaim with uncommon conviction what we confess to be the mystery of our faith: "Christ has died! Christ is risen! Christ will come again!"

But if Christ's coming "with great power and glory" is mostly a matter of Christian hope, if it may well be a millennium or more away, if I can do nothing to hasten or delay it, isn't it quite irrelevant to my day-to-day existence? On this I like what a fine Episcopalian New Testament scholar has written: "Christian faith always lives 'as if' the second coming were just around the corner. . . . "4 As if. . . . Not pure fantasy, not imagination run wild. If you are convinced that "Christ will come again," that the final moment is the moment to which all of history, including your own, is marching, that this is the climax of Christian yearning, then you will live in its light. You will become now what you want to be then.

How do you assure that? The significant single word here is the command of Jesus at the end of this chapter in Mark: "Watch!" (Mk 13:35, 37). Be on the alert! Keep your eyes open!

Watch for what? On the alert for what? Eyes open for what? For the constant coming of Christ into your life. Rabbi Abraham Joshua Heschel used to say that the question of religion is not what we do with our solitude; the question of religion is what we do with the presence of God. A Christian might rephrase it: What do I do with the presence of Christ? He comes to you ceaselessly: each time you come together; each time his word is proclaimed to you; each time his body rests in your hand or on your tongue. Christ comes to you in each man, woman, and child whose eyes meet yours—especially those who hunger for food or justice or love. We should never grow weary of the words of Jesus in Matthew's Gospel:

> When the Son of man comes in his glory . . . [he] will say to those at his right hand: "Come, O blessed of my Father, inherit the kingdom prepared for you from the foundation of the world; for I was hungry and you gave me food, I was thirsty and you gave me drink, I was a stranger and you welcomed me, I was naked and you clothed me, I was sick and you visited me, I was in prison and you came to me." Then the righteous will answer him: "Lord, when did we see you hungry and feed you, or thirsty and give you drink? And when did we see you a stranger and welcome you, or naked and clothe you? And when did we see you sick or in prison and visit you?" And the King will answer them: "Truly, I say to you, in so far as you did it to one of the least of these my brothers and sisters, you did it to me."
>
> (Mt 25:31–40)

My brothers and sisters: It is good indeed to fix our eyes on Christ's final coming "with great power and glory." Here, after all, is our Christian hope. But it would be tragic if the far horizon blinded us to Christ's daily coming in rags and tatters, lonely, frightened, joyless, sick in so many ways, lost in a strange world that does not seem to care. Here, after all, is our Christian love.

Holy Trinity Church
Washington, D.C.
November 14, 1982

23

COME, LORD JESUS?
Thirty-third Sunday of the Year (C)

> ◆ Malachi 3:19–20
> ◆ 2 Thessalonians 3:7–12
> ◆ Luke 21:5–19

Today's first and third readings, I noticed, did not send smiles to your faces. And no wonder. The prophet Malachi promises you that when the Day of Judgment comes, sinners will burn up like stumps left in the field after reaping. Luke predicts a desolation that is frightening: wars and quakes, famine and plague, persecution and betrayal, days of distress and grapes of wrath. A prudent preacher might be persuaded to bypass such futurology, focus on a simpler sentence of St. Paul in the second reading: "If anyone will not work, let him not eat" (2 Thess 3:10).

But the liturgy forbids escapism. It forces us to face our future, compels us to ask three questions. First, why do we have these specific readings at this time in the Church's year? Second, what do Luke and Malachi mean? What sense can we make of this "word of the Lord," this "gospel of the Lord"? Third, what might God be saying to you and me through these distressing passages? In other words, we ought to talk about (1) the liturgy, (2) Scripture, (3) ourselves.[1]

I

First, the liturgy. Why these readings now? Why not something pleasant, encouraging, hopeful? Why read from Luke what we can read in the *Post:* war in the Middle East, starvation in the sub-Sahara, religious persecution in Russia and her satellites, and "the year of the earthquake"?

Why these readings now? To grasp this, you must grasp what the Eucharistic liturgy is about. The liturgy is not primarily an obligation under penalty of hell-fire, not a sure-fire scheme for collecting money. The liturgy is the whole Church celebrating the story of salvation, reliving it, making it a reality in our lives. Each twelve months the cycle of salvation is repeated. We not only reread it; we re-present it, make God's wonderful works effectively present in us.

We began with Advent, when we relived a whole world's expectation of its Savior, made ready to receive God's salvation into our hearts. We embraced him when he came, God enfolded in straw, "omnipotence in bonds." We grew up with him in his three silent decades, expanded with him in Nazareth our experience of human living. We walked the ways of Palestine in his company, as he preached ceaselessly that the kingdom of God is in our midst. We shared his last supper, sweated his blood in Gethsemane, ached with Mary beneath the cross, looked on helplessly as he died for us. We rose with him at Easter, breakfasted with him by the Sea of Tiberias. In him we too ascended to the Father; his Spirit descended on each of us who believes. In the months since Pentecost we have captured with our ears and experienced in our lives the mission of the Church, shared its endless effort to grow into Christ, while we waited in hope for the coming of the Lord, this time not in imprisoning infancy but trailing clouds of glory.

And now the final act of the liturgical drama is upon us. Next week the curtain will fall: We will crown Christ king. But not quite yet. Today we celebrate in anticipation what will precede the second coming of the Lord: the end of this world as we know it. We are rounding out in ritual the story that began on the first page of Scripture: "In the beginning God created the heavens and the earth" (Gen 1:1), the story that ends on the last page of Scripture: "Come, Lord Jesus!" (Rev 22:20).

II

Our second question: What do Luke and Malachi mean? Malachi is simple enough: He simply foretells that on Judgment Day the wicked will be punished, the righteous spared "as a man spares his son who serves him" (Mal 3:17). If you read on a bit, you find some triumphalism: "You [the righteous, the saved] shall tread down the wicked, for they will be ashes under the soles of your feet

. . ." (Mal 3:21). But that is biblical imagery; it does not raise real problems.

Not so for the Gospel. If you are puzzled, join the crowd. A first-rate New Testament scholar has written of Luke 21: "There are almost as many interpretations of it as there are heads that think about it."[2] A homily is not an exercise in exegesis; still, it is important for today's liturgy and for intelligent Christian existence that you get some sense of what the Gospel is saying.

Note first that Luke 21 contains not one prediction but two: the destruction of Jerusalem and the end of the world. Our problem at this moment is, today's Gospel foretells only the fate of Jerusalem; there it stops.[3] Now this was indeed a disaster, a catastrophe comparable to Hitler's Holocaust. In the year 70 the Romans crushed a Jewish rebellion, burned the temple, destroyed Jerusalem, left the city desolate save for a garrison camp. The Jewish historian Josephus, who witnessed the siege of Jerusalem, tells of 6000 refugees perishing in the flames of the temple. He tells how Titus' army surrounded Jerusalem, put 1,100,000 Jews to the sword, took 97,000 captives to Rome.[4]

Disastrous indeed, this end of Jerusalem, a cause for Christian tears; but Jerusalem would be rebuilt. More pertinent for our liturgy is the second prediction, the end of the world (Lk 21:25–36). As for Jerusalem, Luke was writing about a prophecy fulfilled ten years before he wrote. Here now is a prophecy still to be fulfilled. For Luke, the end of Jerusalem is springboard for an end more astonishing still. Cosmic signs will attend it, signs in sun and moon and stars, signs in the raging of the sea. With these signs you will "know that the kingdom of God is near" (v. 30). After these signs you will "see the Son of Man coming in a cloud with power and great glory" (v. 27). Here is the end of this world as we know it.

Now Luke's Jesus does not tell us what will happen to the sun that heats and lights our earth, to the moon on which we have so recently walked, to 200 billion billion stars, to the seas that cover more than 70 percent of the earth's surface. His discourse on "the end" is not a lesson in astronomy or oceanography; he is not Carl Sagan on TV. What he does tell us is that this absurd little earth where a billion humans fall asleep hungry, this glorious globe that was freed from slavery by the crucifixion of its God, this paradoxical planet that nurtures love and hate, despair and hope, skepticism and faith, this creation of divine love where men and women die for one another and kill one another—this kind of existence we experience will not last forever. And he tells us this not to add to our worldly knowledge. He tells us this only because "the end" will be a beginning. The end is prelude, an overture. The end of human history as we know it is important because it will usher in the kingdom of Christ in its glorious fulness. It is the consummation of "the mystery of faith" we proclaim in each liturgy: "Christ has died! Christ is risen! Christ will come again!"

III

My third question ran as follows: What might God be saying to you and me through these distressing passages? Let me correct one word in that question. At bottom, these are not "distressing" passages; they are harbingers of hope. At least for those who are trying to serve God. Malachi promises that on Judgment Day you who fear the Lord "shall go forth leaping like calves from the stall" (Mal 3:20b). The comparison with a young cow or bull may not "grab" you, but the idea behind it should: When the Lord comes, your joy will know no bounds; for you will be the Lord's "special possession" (3:17). And Jesus tells you: When the signs of the end "begin to take place, look up and raise your heads, because your redemption is drawing near" (Lk 21:28).

All well and good; these are messages of hope. But, dear preacher, let's get down to the nitty-gritty, to the hard core of Christian living. What do we do *now?* While waiting for Christ to come again, how should we act, how should we live?

Very simply: Live as if the Lord were coming tomorrow! Perhaps he is. There are Christians who claim he will be here tomorrow . . . or the next day . . . or the next. They find every sign of the end in our generation—from Luke's wars and quakes and famines to Revelation's "scarlet beast" (Rev 17:3). They expect this world to end not in ice but in nuclear fire. Perhaps. But that is not the point. We don't begin to live like Christians when "the end" is in sight. Jesus does indeed warn us not to let "that day come upon [us] suddenly like a snare," when we are "weighed down with dissipation and drunkenness" (Lk 21:34), heavy with lust and Löwenbräu. But this is not the Christian ideal: Don't be caught with your pants down. That's like being good because you're afraid of hell—and only *when* you're afraid.

No, my friends. Whether the Lord is coming this Thanksgiving or a thousand years from now, our task is to live as if he were arriving tomorrow. Better still, as if he were already here. Because he is. Some day he will come in power and glory to place all creation at the feet of his Father. But today he comes quietly, subtly, invisibly wherever you are. Look for him not on a pink cloud or with a jeweled crown. Look for him in your gathering together. Look for him in the preached word, in the Host you cradle in your hand and on your tongue. Look for him inside you. Look for him at home, on the faces of your dear ones. But look for him especially where he told you to look: in the hungry and thirsty, the stranger and the naked, the sick and the imprisoned (cf. Mt 25:35–36).

You know, the "signs" we see around us—endless war on earth and the race for outer space, political and religious persecution, nations bleeding in captivity and children starving to death—need not tell us that Christ the King is on the next cumulus of clouds. But this much they do tell us: We are hardly ready to receive him. And not just the Arafats and the Andropovs. Would *I* open my arms in rapture, pirouette gracefully, and cry out: "Here I am, Lord. Do you like what you see?"

Christ will like what he sees only if I am preparing the kind of kingdom he proclaimed: a world where justice reigns, and peace, and love. That kingdom is conceived not in the Kremlin or on Pennsylvania Avenue, but where each of us lives and operates; not in the United Nations, but in each human heart. In your heart. Do *you* like what you see?[5]

> Dahlgren Chapel
> Georgetown University
> and
> Holy Trinity Church
> Washington, D.C
> November 13, 1983

FEASTS

24

WHAT SHALL I DO, LORD?
Conversion of St. Paul the Apostle

◆ Acts 22:3–16
◆ Mark 16:15–18

Preaching St. Paul to Paulists—it's carrying coals to Newcastle, grapefruit to Florida, pizza to Pisa. You can stomach just so much, even from a friendly son of Ignatius. I shall pass over the stale analogies that link you to your favorite apostle: the missionary journeys from Columbus Circle to San Diego; becoming "all things to all" Americans; disputing with academics from Boston to Berkeley; a step ahead of the other apostles, even Peter; hustled out of a Texas town by religious authorities; at times even inducing a modern young Eutychus "into a deep sleep" by talking too long (Acts 20:9).

And yet there is one analogy that today's liturgy will not let you forget. Your special feast, the celebration of your predilection, is not, as with other saints, Paul's passage to glory; it is not Paul the apostle to the Gentiles. Your feast is Paul's conversion. A singular liturgical celebration. With this in mind, suppose we look successively at (1) St. Paul, (2) the Paulists of the past, (3) today's Paulist.

I

First, St. Paul. The accounts of his conversion in Acts (9:1–18; 22:3–16; 26:4–23) make four pointed observations about conversion. First, it is God who takes the initiative. It was Jesus who knocked Paul from his horse: "I am Jesus" (Acts 9:5; 22:8; 26:15). As Augustine insisted, if we but turn to God, that itself is a gift of God. We do not choose Him; He chooses us.

Second, Paul's response when he discovers it is Jesus who is speaking: "What shall I do, Lord?" (Acts 22:10). The Lord does not tell him immediately; he tells him to go into the city, into Damascus: "There you will be told what you are to do" (Acts 22:10; 9:6). Like Mary before the angel, Paul does not know all that the Lord's call will ask of him; he knows only that it is the Lord who is calling.

Third, the basic call, as Ananias told it to him: "The God of our fathers appointed you to know His will, to see the Just One and to hear a voice from his mouth; for you will be a witness for him to all men and women of what you have seen and heard" (Acts 22:14–15; cf. 26:16). An apostle is a witness, and the essential task of a witness—John, Magdalene, Paul—is to testify to what he or she has seen or heard.

Fourth, a fact of Christian life inseparable from the apostolate. The Lord said to Ananias: "He is a chosen instrument of mine to carry my name before the Gentiles and kings and the sons of Israel; for I will show him how much he will suffer for the sake of my name" (Acts 9:15–16). To turn to Jesus is to turn to a crucified Master who insisted that to follow him is to carry his cross, to save your life you must lose it.

The conversion of Paul? God calling: "I am Jesus." A total yes: "What shall I do, Lord?" A mission: "You will be a witness." Inevitable crucifixion: "I will show him how much he must suffer."

II

When I turn from St. Paul to the Paulists, I find conversion part and parcel of your historic story.[1] It seems foreshadowed in the fact that your four charter Paulists—Baker, Deshon, Hecker, and Hewit—were converts. It is even more obvious in your primeval purpose: a missionary society with a "mission impossible," to convert America.

But the conversion that fascinates me in your history is a broader conversion, the four elements I culled from St. Paul. There is, to begin with, a fresh call from God, the experience of being knocked off a comfortable old horse. Your oldest symbol is Hecker. Happily Redemptorist, he heard a small call. It did not seem all that revolutionary, except to German brethren: to found a house in Newark for English-speaking Redemptorists. But of that small voice to Isaac was born, through bloody parturition, a new society, to make Catholic truth pervasive and persuasive in Protestant America.

Second, there is the response of that fervent foursome. Once withdrawn from their earlier allegiance, they knew only that they would continue to live in community and spread the Catholic faith over America. They were not utterly sure how they would operate, knew not what would happen to them in the process. Conversion was indeed primary, but what strikes me even more forcibly is a phrase from Hecker in 1858: "other apostolic labors as the wants of the Church may demand or develop."[2] It is Mary's "Whatever you wish, Lord"; it is Paul's "What shall I do, Lord?"

Third, your history is largely a story of witness, extraordinary and ordinary. In your apostolates of press and pulpit, of radio and TV, on America's campuses and in her hinterlands, even when opening, in Archbishop Ireland's words, "death-dealing batteries upon the saloon,"[3] wherever your people have been, it is consistently a question of being witnesses. Witnesses not to yourselves, but for Jesus. Witnesses to "all men and women." Witnesses "of what you have seen and heard." To many of us Jesuits with our thousands in the U.S., it is amazing how a few hundred apostles have borne such Pauline witness to this nation—with intelligence, with courage, with humor, with friendship and love for all. I sometimes suspect Hecker had a secret cloning process.

Fourth, Paulist witness has made for suffering servants. Your congregation was conceived in pain, the pain of four sensitive and courageous men. Your devotion to the American way of life made you suspect (even to French Jesuits) of an Americanism you never dreamed of. Your missions to areas where the word "Catholic" was a curse, your efforts in academe's groves to graft the sacred onto the secular, every pioneering movement to the far reaches of America—all these lodged the death pangs of Jesus in the flesh of your forefathers.

III

So much for the Paulists of the past. What of the Paulist today? Where is your conversion experience? Here is where the visiting homilist must walk warily and talk charily. I can only suggest that your conversion must be a continuing process on the lines of St. Paul and the Paulists of your past. Not slavish imitation; only fidelity to the four facets of their experience.

First, openness to God's voice today. Your own tradition commands it; for since 1858 you have stressed individuality and initiative. You turn ceaselessly to God speaking in new ways: "other apostolic labors as the wants of the Church may demand." Symbolically, your *Catholic World* becomes the *New Catholic World.* It does not mean that 245 Paulists run around like headless chickens cackling "Here I am, Lord." You are a community, a band of apostles, a missionary society. And not every good idea calls for a Paulist. But the death knell of a community is the stubborn nonargument "We've always done it this way." You serve a God who speaks in unexpected ways—speaks even in the least and youngest of His servants. Hecker was under 38 when he made his bold journey to Rome.

Second, your response. Is it Paul's "What shall I do, Lord?" Is it God's will that turns you on, or your own? At times it's not simple to say. Superiors can be wrong, and community discernment can be dreadfully undiscerning. And I—why, I can be self-centered; I too can have glaucoma—defined by Webster as "a diseased condition . . . marked by hardness and inelasticity . . . due to excessive internal pressure, causing impairment of vision or blindness." The $64 question is, how sincerely do I say "What do *you* want me to do, Lord?"

Third, what sort of witness do you bear to Jesus? Only what *Paul* saw and heard? What the world outside these walls asks is that you attest what *you* have seen and heard. Have you experienced what you are proclaiming? You will move hearts only if you are yourself a sort of sacrament, an outward sign of inward grace, only if it comes through to questing men and women that you have seen Jesus, have been fired by his presence, have experienced that presence in yourself and in the assembly, in the preached word and in the blessed bread. As in Gospel days, so now, there is one thing the Gentiles want before all else—what they asked of Philip: "Sir, we would like to see Jesus" (Jn 12:21). They will see him more easily if *you* have seen him.

Fourth, suffering. No disciple of Christ can avoid the cross of Christ. Perhaps the fresh cross religious congregations must carry today is confusion and anxiety: confusion about our primary mission, anxiety about our continued existence. Who are we, and how long will we last? If Jesuits are hung up on the central mission spelled out by our last General Congregation, "faith and justice," I shall be surprised if within your own communities the hermeneutical question—how to interpret your original vision, "making America Catholic"—does not make for gas pains. And why do so many leave us, so few join us? Is "society" to blame for this too, or is it we who make religious life unattractive—paradoxically because we refuse to live the crucified Jesus? Do we deserve to die?

My brothers in Christ: Despite the gloom of the last several sentences, you have good reason to rejoice. In Paul, in your past, in yourselves. Over four decades I have counted many of your company as dear friends, beginning with a youthful Gene Burke. I have lectured to your faithful from Toronto to L.A., found your young men as a group my best-balanced students at Catholic University, even impoverish the Paulist Press with my publications. Through all of this, one reaction abides, refuses to retreat: grateful admiration. I thank God for a small group of men with a large vision, for missionary men open to every significant stirring of grace in this land they love, for apostolic men who convert to Christ not only others but themselves first and always. I only pray that each Yankee Paul may never cease asking of Christ what the Hebrew Paul asked: "What do *you* want me to do, Lord?"

St. Paul's College
Washington, D.C.
January 23, 1982

25

I ASKED FOR WONDER
Corpus Christi (B)

- ◆ Exodus 24:3–8
- ◆ Hebrews 9:11–15
- ◆ Mark 14:12–16, 22–26

Several years before his death in '72, a remarkable rabbi, Abraham Joshua Heschel, suffered a near-fatal heart attack from which he never fully recovered. A dear friend visiting him then found him woefully weak. Just about able to whisper, Heschel said to him: "Sam, when I regained consciousness, my first feeling was not of despair or anger. I felt only gratitude to God for my life, for every moment I had lived. I was ready to depart. 'Take me, O Lord,' I thought, 'I have seen so many miracles in my lifetime.'" Exhausted by the effort, Heschel paused, then added: "That is what I meant when I wrote [in the preface to his book of Yiddish poems]: 'I did not ask for success; I asked for wonder. And You gave it to me.'"[1]

Today's feast, Corpus Christi, the Body and Blood of Christ, is a splendid moment to reflect on one of God's most striking gifts to us: the gift of wonder. Three stages to our reflection. First, a word on the feast itself. Second, our Christian response to the feast. Third, more broadly, our response to human and Christian living.

I

First then, today's feast. In a sense, it is an unexpected feast. Unexpected for several reasons. Unexpected because Corpus Christi duplicates Holy Thursday. We are repeating that lovely Last Supper celebration, but without the sadness of Holy Week. Unexpected because *every* Eucharist is a feast of the body and blood of Christ: "Take this, all of you, and eat it; for this is my body. Drink from this, all of you; for this is the cup of my blood." Unexpected if you know how the feast came to be. About 1209, an Augustinian nun, Juliana of Liège, reported a vision. She had seen the full moon in splendor, save for a dark area on one side. As she understood it, the moon was the Church, and one area was dark because there was no feast of the Blessed Sacrament. Juliana must have been one persuasive woman: Fifty-five years later, this "feast of the Eucharist" was a feast of the universal Church.

Unexpected, it is still a welcome feast. We can too easily take the Eucharist for granted, especially if we are regular guests at the Supper. What dulls excitement is repetition; what creates a rut is routine. College cuisines are unexciting, in part because the menu is predictable; you know what's coming. And there is a sameness that surrounds our Eucharist: the same Consecration, the same Communion, the same Real Presence. With few exceptions, much the same words, much the same gestures. Stand, sit, answer "Amen," shake hands. . . .

Oh yes, changes are possible. Rome can give you several penitential formulas, four canons instead of one, three dismissals, a Mass for children. We ask our celebrants to "celebrate." We even dare liturgical dance. And still, at bottom, there is a sameness to our Supper.

The one significant change comes with the word of God. Here imagination interrupts routine. Here Christ himself speaks to you. Today he reminds you through Exodus how God made a covenant with Israel—in blood: "Moses took the blood and threw it upon the people, and said: 'Behold the blood of the covenant which the Lord has made with you . . .' " (Exod 24:8). Today he reminds you through Hebrews that your own covenant was consummated not "with the blood of goats and bulls and with the ashes of a heifer" but with his own blood (Heb 9:12, 14). Today he brings you back to the Supper room to hear him say once again: "This is my blood of the covenant . . ." (Mk 14:24), to remind you that what you eat here is not bread but his body, what you drink is not wine but his blood.

II

All well and good—you are reminded. But what should your reaction be? Not theology. I am not downgrading theology; I make a modest living off it. And still, the liturgy is not a classroom. This is not the place for your theology of transubstantiation: *how* the substance of bread and wine is transformed into Christ's body and blood. Your proper reaction is not even simply an act of faith. Oh yes, you should exclaim with Thomas Aquinas:

> On the cross thy godhead made no sign to men;
> Here thy very manhood steals from human ken:
> Both are my confession, both are my belief,
> And I pray the prayer of the dying thief.[2]

But you need more than an act of faith; you need the very first stanza of that same hymn:

> Godhead here in hiding, whom I do adore
> Masked by these bare shadows, shape and nothing more,
> See, Lord, at thy service low lies here a heart
> Lost, all lost in wonder at the God thou art.[3]

"All lost in wonder. . . ." I don't mean curiosity—the Hatter in Alice's Wonderland singing:

> Twinkle, twinkle, little bat!
> How I wonder what you're at![4]

I don't mean doubt or despair: I wonder if life is really worth living. I don't mean uncertainty: I wonder whether Britain should yield the Falklands to Argentina. No, in the grasp of wonder I'm surprised, I'm amazed, I marvel, I'm delighted, I'm enraptured, I'm in awe. It's Moses before the burning bush "afraid to look at God" (Exod 3:6), and Mary newly God's mother: "My spirit rejoices in God my Savior" (Lk 1:47). It's Stephen about to be stoned: "I see . . . the Son of Man standing at the right hand of God" (Acts 7:46), and Michelangelo striking his sculptured Moses and commanding him: "Speak!" It's Ignatius Loyola in ecstasy as he eyes the sky at night, Teresa of Avila ravished by a rose. It's doubting Thomas discovering his God in the wounds of Jesus, Mother Teresa spying the face of Christ in the tortured poor. It's America thrilling to footsteps on the moon, a child casting his kite to the winds. It's a mother looking with love on her newborn infant. It's the wonder of a first kiss.

Such should be our reaction to Eucharist, to the body and blood of Christ. I'm surprised, I'm amazed, I marvel, I'm delighted, I'm enraptured, I'm in awe. Why? Because something surprising, amazing, marvelous, delightful, enrapturing, awesome has broken into my commonplace world. The God-man . . . out of sheer love . . .

gives to this "strange, piteous, futile thing"[5] . . . his flesh to eat and his blood to drink. I don't pretend to understand it, any more than I understand how God is three and one, any more than I understand how God could wed Himself to flesh in the womb of a virgin. I don't understand it. I simply welcome this hidden God in awe and delight: "Lost, all lost in wonder at the God thou art."

III

But how on earth do you get that way? My own conviction is that we are born that way. But as we grow older, most of us lose it. We get blasé and worldly-wise and sophisticated. We no longer run our fingers through water, no longer shout at the stars, no longer make faces at the moon. Water is H_2O, the stars have been classified, and the moon is not made of green cheese. We've grown up. Heschel saw it as modern man's trap: "believing that everything can be explained, that reality is a simple affair which has only to be organized in order to be mastered. All enigmas can be solved, and all wonder is nothing but 'the effect of novelty upon ignorance.' "[6] The new can indeed amaze us: a space shuttle, the latest computer game, the softest diaper in history. Till tomorrow; till the new becomes old; till yesterday's wonder is discarded or taken for granted. Little wonder Heschel concluded: "As civilization advances, the sense of wonder declines."[7]

Now this is not a tirade against technology. I am simply resonating to Heschel's alarm: "Mankind will not perish for want of information . . . only for want of appreciation."[8] To appreciate not only the new but the old, not only the miracle that shatters nature but the wonder that is every day. When did I last marvel not at *what* I saw—the Rodin exhibit, *Star Wars,* Hoyas in the NCAA finals, Mother Teresa—but *that* I see, that with a flicker of eyelids I can span a small world? Must I grow deaf with Beethoven before I touch my ears with reverence? Does it amaze me that I can shape an idea, tell you how I feel, touch my fingers to another's face, to a flower? The religious Jew thanks God three times a day for the wonder of being, for God's amazing blessings: "We thank thee . . . for thy miracles which are daily with us, for thy continued marvels." About to drink a glass of water, the Jew recalls the eternal mystery of creation: "Blessed be thou . . . by whose word all things come into being."

This is not to blind ourselves to sin and war, to disease and death. These are terribly real. And still we have to see, with Gerard Manley Hopkins, that "the world is charged with the grandeur of God," that even if all "wears man's smudge and shares man's smell,"

> ... for all this, nature is never spent;
>   There lives the dearest freshness deep down things ...
> Because the Holy Ghost over the bent
>   World broods with warm breast and with ah! bright wings.[9]

The enemy of wonder is to take things for granted. If I am to be lost in wonder within this chapel, I have to be lost in wonder outside of it. Put another way, I have to live my ordinary day in the presence of the living God. Such, very simply, was Rabbi Heschel's secret. For him, the question of religion was not what we do with our solitude; the question of religion was what we do with the presence of God. Here He is, Paul told the Athenians, "not far from each one of us" (Acts 17:27). Here He is, in our gathering together and in our war-torn world, on our altar and on the face of humanity. How do we live in the presence of the living God?

In wonder indeed, ceaselessly surprised by the trace of God all around us. But wonder need not paralyze us; wonder need not mean wide-eyed inactivity. Heschel proved that. Theologian and historian, poet and mystic, he moved from his study to social issues: Vietnam and poverty, civil rights and racism, Russian Jewry and Israel. In his words, as with Jeremiah, Amos, and Joel, God raged and roared (cf. Jer 26:30, Joel 3:16, Amos 1:2). He had experienced Hitler's Germany, but because he was spared the flames that devoured his family and his community, he felt a special burden: to remind us that, despite the absurdity and apathy that surround us, "the world is filled with mystery, meaning and mercy, with wonder, joy and fulfillment; that men have the power to do God's will and that the divine image in which we are made, though distorted, cannot be obliterated. In the end, the likeness of God will triumph over the mark of Cain."[10] When Heschel died, at his bedside were two books: a Hasidic classic and a work on the Vietnam war. They symbolized the movement of his life: from wonder to deeds, and back again to wonder.

Have I wandered from Corpus Christi? Not at all. This feast of the Eucharist is not an isolated event in your Christian existence. Unique, perhaps; isolated, no. The Eucharist fits into the endless series of God's wonderful works in the story of salvation, the story of a God who, the Book of Job tells us, "does great things and unsearchable,/marvelous things without number" (Job 5:9). I do not escape to Dahlgren Chapel from a dull, unexciting, secularized, godless world to celebrate a solitary miracle of grace. I come *to* miracle *from* miracle. The entire world is charged with God's grandeur. The divine milieu, as Teilhard de Chardin saw, is not only the mystical body of Christ; it is the cosmic body of Christ. The world is different because Christ is there. Not only here—there!

To this divine milieu, to this God-filled atmosphere in which we are bathed, to all of this my whole being must thrill. And so, as we cradle the body of Christ in our hands and on our tongues, I suggest that we ask for the gift God gave to an unforgettable rabbi: "Dear Lord, grant me the grace of wonder. Surprise me, amaze me, awe me in every crevice of your universe. Delight me to see how your

> . . . Christ plays in ten thousand places,
> Lovely in limbs, and lovely in eyes not his
> To the Father through the features of men's faces.[11]

Each day enrapture me with your 'marvelous things without number.' I do not ask to see the reason for it all; I ask only to share the wonder of it all."

Dahlgren Chapel
Georgetown University
June 13, 1982

26
OF CABBAGES AND KINGS?
Christ the King

♦ Daniel 7:13–14
♦ Revelation 1:5–8
♦ John 18:33–37

When I say "king," what comes to your mind? A romantic legend like Arthur and his Knights of the Round Table? Shakespeare's Henry V, roaming the camp at night, musing on the burdens of kings: "What infinite heart's ease/ Must kings neglect, that private men enjoy"?[1] David, the man after God's own heart, type of the Messiah—adulterer and murderer? Wise Solomon the magnificent with his "seven hundred wives and three hundred concubines" (1 Kgs 11:3)? A ceremonial figure like Sweden's Carl XVI Gustav? A butcher of innocents like Herod the Great? France's Louis IX, crusader and saint? Bavaria's mad King Ludwig with his crazy castles? Is it Old King Cole, that "merry old soul" who "called for his pipe, and . . . called for his bowl, and . . . called for his fiddlers three"? Perhaps the Burger King? Or are kings of no consequence to you, out of style, spoken in the same breath with other small items? Remember *Through the Looking-Glass?*

> "The time has come," the Walrus said,
> "To talk of many things:
> Of shoes—and ships—and sealing wax—
> Of cabbages—and kings—
> And why the sea is boiling hot—
> And whether pigs have wings."[2]

What comes to your mind is important, for it influences your reaction to today's feast. What does "Christ the King" say to you? Frankly, I don't know. So, let me complicate your instinctive reactions with three questions: (1) Why does the Church insist on a liturgy like this? (2) What does God's word add to our understanding? (3) How might the kingship of Christ help to make us more Christian, more human?

I

First, why does the Church insist on a liturgy of Christ the King? Why now, at this point in the liturgical year? Not too many years ago, the feast of Christ the King was celebrated on the last Sunday of October. But there it made little sense; it was an intrusion in the movement of our salvation story. It was like having Pavarotti high-C an "Ave Maria" into the second act of *Samson and Delilah,* or before Mimi's death rattle in *La Bohème.*

But today is different; Christ the King fits beautifully here. In the course of this past year, our liturgical cycle has moved from a whole world's waiting for its Savior, through his coming in infant impotence, his dying-rising, his return to the Father, the Church's own pilgrimage in the image of Christ, to his final coming trailing clouds of glory. Today we reach in ritual the end of the story. Today the liturgy ritualizes the high point of creation, when humankind and all that is, even death itself, will be subjected to Christ, "when he delivers the kingdom to God the Father after destroying every rule and every authority and power" (1 Cor 15:24). This is the way the Church uses the prophecy of Daniel, the seer's vision of a messianic king to whom God gives a universal, endless reign: "And to him was given dominion and glory and kingdom, that all peoples, nations, and languages should serve him; his dominion is an everlasting dominion, which shall not pass away, and his kingdom one that shall not be destroyed" (Dan 7:14).

At the close of the church year, celebration of Christ the King is like the coda in a Beethoven symphony. It not only brings the movement to a decisive end, forms a climax to what has gone before; it is at once a summing up and something splendidly new.

II

So much for liturgical positioning; now for biblical understanding. It is one thing to agree that today is a more convenient date to celebrate Christ our King than the last Sunday in October. It is quite another thing to make sense out of Christ's kingship, especially in an America which hasn't had much use for kings ever since we thumbed our colonial noses at George III. Does God's word add to our understanding? Here the Gospels raise problems and offer insight.

One problem is a seeming contradiction. On the one hand, "king" was not a title Jesus particularly liked. And you may remember that when the people "were about to come and take him by force to make him king," Jesus took "to the hills" (Jn 6:15). On the other hand, at a critical moment of his life, he did not deny he was a king. He did not give Pilate an unequivocal "No, I am not a king." He did not plead "not guilty."

The point is, Jesus did come to establish a kingdom. He made it clear the moment he began to preach: "The time is fulfilled, and the kingdom of God is at hand" (Mk 1:15). When Jesus sent the Twelve out "to the lost sheep of the house of Israel," he charged them to preach "The kingdom of heaven is at hand" (Mt 10:7). What Jesus' parables unfold progressively is the kingdom and its mysteries: "The kingdom of heaven is like mustard seed . . . leaven . . . treasure hidden in a field . . . a merchant in search of fine pearls . . . a net thrown into the sea" (Mt 13:31, 33, 44, 45, 47). And what did the early Church preach? Read the last verses of the Acts of the Apostles: Paul "welcomed all who came to him, preaching the kingdom of God and teaching about the Lord Jesus Christ . . ." (Acts 28:30–31). The kingdom of God and the Lord Jesus.

But what does kingship mean here? Not political power: "My kingship is not of this world" (Jn 18:36). Christ is not about to stride regally down Pennsylvania Avenue and take his seat in the Oval Office. And yet we *are* dealing with dominion, with rule, with authority, with that dirty word "power." The question is not *whether* there is dominion, kingship, in our lives. The question is: Who or what exercises dominion over human existence? Who or what rules our lives? Who or what is lord of us flies?[3]

When the Son of God invaded this world in our skin, a powerful triumvirate, a trinity of tyrants, terrorized man, woman, and child. I mean Satan, sin, and death. Jesus himself called Satan "the ruler of this world" (Jn 14:30). For St. Paul, sin was an evil force, almost personal, a malevolent power, that tyrannized every human born into time, a power hostile to God, a power that alienated from God. Death was not simply an inescapable experience; death seemed to destroy. Listen to Job addressing God: "Now I shall lie in the earth; you will seek me, but I shall not be" (Job 7:21).

What did Jesus do? He crushed the three kings. Not that they have vanished from the face of the earth. The forces of evil are diabolically active across the globe; even in grace we remain paradoxically sinful; we die as surely as did Eve and Adam, and like them we experience death as a contradiction, an insult, an absurdity, a "night" into which (with Dylan Thomas) we do "not go gentle." But their despotic power has been broken. We need no longer be slaves to Satan and sin; we die only to live more gloriously still.

Yes, Jesus has conquered the three kings. Remarkably, not by force of arms, not by pomp and power; he defeated them by dying . . . and rising. A unique coronation, for Christ's only crown is braided with thorns. Ever since that first Holy Week "None of us lives to himself, and none of us dies to herself. If we live, we live to the Lord, and if we die, we die to the Lord; so then, whether we live or whether we die, we are the Lord's. For to this end Christ died and lived again, that he might be Lord both of the dead and of the living" (Rom 14:7–9).

But though the Lord owns me flesh and spirit—for he has purchased me with his blood—he will not compel my obedience. I am really and truly the Lord's to the extent that I acknowledge him as Lord. Empty words will not do. "Not everyone who says to me 'Lord, Lord' shall enter the kingdom of heaven but he/she who does the will of my Father who is in heaven" (Mt 7:21). Only if God's will shapes my will in graced freedom do I allow Christ to rule over me. If the ruling principle in my life is my independent will, that rebel will is the Satan and the sin in me. And such a will shall be my death, shall exclude me from Christ's kingdom; for with such a will I am protesting with the citizens of the parable "We do not want this man to rule over us" (Lk 19:14).

In the final analysis, Jesus Christ is a King of hearts. Which means he will never force himself on us; he will only draw us, as Augustine saw, with the cords of love.

III

Now all this is quite broad—a swift theology of Christ's kingship. It calls for a third question: How might the kingship of Christ help to make us more Christian, more human? Here two texts are splendidly suggestive.

The first text announces, in breathless accents, your role and mine, your function and mine, in the kingdom. Recall the reading from Revelation: "To him who loves us and has freed us from our sins by his blood and made us a kingdom, priests to his God and Father, to him be glory and dominion for ever and ever" (Rev 1:5–6). The kingdom is not a place, a Ludwiglike castle in the sky; we are the kingdom. If the kingship of Christ is his rule over our hearts, then the kingdom of God at its root is within us. The kingdom is a people—a people responding passionately to the passion of their King.

More wondrous still, in this kingdom we are priests. Not only the ordained; all of us. The first Epistle of Peter proclaims it not only to persecuted Christians in Asia Minor but to you and me: "Like living stones, be yourselves built into a spiritual house, to be a holy priesthood, to offer spiritual sacrifices acceptable to God through Jesus Christ" (1 Pet 2:5). And again: "You are a chosen race, a royal priesthood, a holy nation, God's own people, that you may declare the wonderful deeds of Him who called you out of darkness into His marvelous light" (v. 9). Like the royal priesthood of Israel (cf. Exod 19:6; Isa 61:6), it is your task to carry the word of God to an unbelieving world. You have the power to do it, thanks to the King of kings, who lets you share his own kingship, his own priesthood.

The second text strongly suggests what your priesthood involves. Not only "spiritual sacrifices" like praise and thanksgiving in your temple of red brick. In a few moments you will resonate to the rousing Preface of Christ the King. His kingdom, the Preface affirms, is "a kingdom of truth and life, a kingdom of holiness and grace, a kingdom of justice, love, and peace." Here is the kingdom you and I must extend into our acre of God's world. A "mission impossible"? Only if that kind of kingdom is not within us, is not part and parcel of this priestly people.

The pungent question, therefore: Do those seven qualities of Christ's kingdom describe us, distinguish our Dahlgren community? Are we "men [and women] of truth" (Exod 18:21; Neh 7:2) in the biblical sense: men and women faithful to God's covenant, to His law, to one another (cf. Gen 47:29; Josh 2:14; Zech 7:9)? Is the life we live the life of "Christ who lives in [us]" (Gal 2:20)? Does our holiness, our oneness with a living Lord, exceed the holiness of men and women who do not eat his flesh and drink his blood? How radically does the Spirit of grace transmute our minds and hearts, make us St. Paul's "new creation" (2 Cor 5:17)? Is our justice only rational ethics—give to others what each has a strict right to demand—or do we father the fatherless and house the stranger, lift up the downtrodden and free the oppressed, because this is how God has acted with us (cf. Deut 10:18–19)? Is our love as outstretched as the arms of Christ on the cross, or is it locked off from 14th Street and Iran, from the Kremlin and the Klan? Are we a people consumingly engaged in the struggle for peace, or do we merely mouth "Peace" in the safety of a sanctuary?

These are not, God knows, accusations. I simply cannot read the Preface of Christ the King without shivering. I, a priest of the kingdom, how frightfully far I am from the kingdom! And one further thought. If Christ the King were to deliver the kingdom to his Father today, would it be "a kingdom of truth and life, a kingdom of holiness and grace, a kingdom of justice, love, and peace"? Till the kingdom comes, my friends, you and I have a fair piece of priestly work to do. For your consolation, it can be done; for we do it with the King, in the power of his dying and rising.

Dahlgren Chapel
Georgetown University
November 21, 1982

MEDLEY

27

CHARIOTS OF FIRE
University Mass of the Holy Spirit 1

♦ Acts 2:1–8, 11b
♦ John 14:15–17, 26

Today's liturgy, I hope, will challenge you. Challenge you not so much to change, to convert, to be other than you are. Challenge you rather to live consciously and merrily what you already are. Let me make my point in three stages. First, I shall take you to the movies . . . free. Second, I shall move from life on the screen to life in the Spirit. Third, a blunt word on how all this touches the Hilltop—some Saxa sundries.

I

First, a quick trip to the movies. Most of you have seen *Chariots of Fire*. The title stems from a poem by William Blake. Blake took an age-old legend, that Jesus came to England with the man who had buried his bruised body, Joseph of Arimathea. From this legend he fashioned a fresh vision: a spiritual Israel, a new Jerusalem, on his native soil. His vow to fight without ceasing "Till we have built Jerusalem/ In England's green and pleasant land" is prefaced by his passionate cry:

> Bring me my bow of burning gold!
> Bring me my Arrows of desire!
> Bring me my Spear! O clouds, unfold!
> Bring me my Chariot of fire![1]

The film is the story of two British runners, upset winners in the 1924 Olympics. It tells how Harold Abrahams and Eric Liddell won against the odds through character, discipline, courage. Visually, it is a stunning film. But I am not now interested in its sensuous beauty. I was more mightily moved by three suggestive phrases—suggestive because they provoked me to think of the Spirit, to muse on you and me.

First, the uncompromising Scottish Congregationalist Liddell remarks to his sister, who is depicted as opposed to Eric's running: "God made me fast." Yes, God has called him to ministry, to preach the gospel, to return to China. And still it is true: "God made me fast." He can glorify God with his legs and his lungs. Whereas Abrahams runs as a kind of defense against upper-class anti-Semitism, Liddell runs for love of God.

Second, Eric explains where his extraordinary power comes from. Indeed he is healthy and strong; he has powerful limbs, singular stamina. But these would be insufficient, were they not driven by a deeper force: "The power," he declares, "the power is within."

Third, Eric has an even more startling phrase to link what he is doing with the God he serves. "When I run," he says, "I feel His pleasure." I think he meant: When I run, I feel that God is pleased with me. It might also mean: When I run, I share in God's own pleasure, I experience God's own delight.

Intrinsic to all this is the film's title, *Chariots of Fire*. Blake borrowed the phrase from the Old Testament: from the Lord coming "in fire" to destroy His enemies, "His chariots like the stormwind" (Isa 66:15), or Elijah carried to heaven in "a chariot of fire" (2 Kgs 2:11; cf. Sir 48:9). In the film the phrase is not easy to decipher. Like other good symbols, it says different things to different people. To me, as I followed the runners, "chariots of fire" suggested frightening force and burning heat, flaming speed and fluid grace. These two bodies, these two spirits, were themselves chariots of fire, overpowering and irresistible.

II

Three striking statements: "God made me fast." "The power is within." "When I run, I feel His pleasure." Let's move out from the movie; for these expressions are remarkably expressive of life in the Spirit, of Christian chariots of fire.

First, God made each of you "fast." I don't mean "foot-loose and fancy-free"; I don't mean that you play fast and loose. If you're that "fast," it's your own doing! I am thinking rather of the gifts God has given you. St. Paul insists that the Spirit distributes among us all sorts of gifts, from wisdom and faith to healing and tongues (cf. 1 Cor 12:7–10). These are indeed charisms, gifts from the Spirit to individuals for the good of the community. But we dare not limit God's gifts to the dramatic, high-powered, obviously spiritual gifts. God's gift to others is *you*, this living bundle of paradoxes and contradictions. You will discover all sorts of talents if you will only stop contrasting yourself with the beautiful and the brilliant, with the powerful and the personable, with the exotic and the eccentric, with the "tens" of this world.

Eric had a special gift he used for God: He was fast. It sounds so fantastic when he says it: "God made me fast." And it is fantastic, till you remember that you (and he) have even greater gifts—on the level of sheer humanness. Gifts to be given. God made you to look with love into others' eyes and listen to the music of their voices, made you to touch a face or a flower, to taste and smell the human condition. God made you to think and feel, to laugh and weep, to dance and play, to sing and strum, to walk and talk, to sweat in fear and tremble for joy. Whatever you are, whoever you are, you are God's gift, a gift that in its turn can be given.

But if you are to be given, the power has to come from within. It is a glorious thing to be human, to be yourself, to be "natural." But if God's gifts to you are to shape you and others to Christ, you cannot rely on the naked you, on the talents that are your sheer humanness. These, like Eric's legs and lungs and heart, must be driven by a deeper force. I mean the Spirit of God who lives so silently, so secretly, deep inside you. "The power is within." It is St. Paul's challenging cry to the Christians of Corinth: "Do you not know that you are God's temple and that God's Spirit dwells in you?" (1 Cor 3:16). That is why Paul has a special name for Christians who "have the mind of Christ" (1 Cor 2:16). He calls them "spiritual," because they possess the Spirit (1 Cor 2:13, 15), are possessed by the Spirit. They are incredibly alive to all that goes on; they never stifle the Spirit, never disregard the Spirit's whisperings (1 Thess 5:22).

And so must you be. Not just a "nice guy" or a "cool chick." Not living two lives, natural and supernatural, secular and sacred, material and spiritual. You are one man, one woman, a single you; and everything you do—work and play, Mass and Michelob—should find its force and its meaning in the Spirit who has made you a new creature in Christ. "The power is within."

Once that grabs hold of you, once you start running your life in the power of the Spirit, then you experience what Eric expressed

so eloquently: "When I run, I feel His pleasure." Not only an intellectual conviction that God is pleased with you. More happily still,
you taste God's delight in you, feel it in your bones, tingle with it.
This is the insight a perceptive Sister has shared with us in verse under the title "Discovery":

> It's this that makes
>   My spirit spin,
> My bones to quake,
>   My blood run thin,
> My flesh to melt
>   Inside my skin,
> My very pulse
>   Create a din—
> It's this that makes
>   My spirit spin:
> That Heaven is
>   Not *up*, but *in!*[2]

This is not merely for mystics and martyrs, for Teresa of Avila
and John the Apostle. To a felt experience of God we are all called.
For our God is not some far-off, inaccessible abstraction. Our God,
for all that He is beyond us, lives within us. And He lives within us
to be known and loved—yes, felt. Not that we escape the dark night
of the soul. Rather that, despite our experience of God's absence, we
increasingly sense His presence. Not only His presence. . . . His
pleasure.

Gifted by God, powered by the Spirit, feeling divine pleasure—
how can you fail to be chariots of fire? The symbolism is splendidly
suggestive of the Holy Spirit: force and heat, speed and grace,
something overpowering and irresistible. But suggestive not only of
the Spirit. This is what our Lord had in mind for all of us on the first
Pentecost, when "a sound came from heaven like the rush of a
mighty wind," when "there appeared to [the apostles] tongues as of
fire . . . resting on each one of them. And they were all filled with
the Holy Spirit . . ." (Acts 2:2–4).

The question is, does the Holy Spirit turn you on? Does the
Spirit rock you and roll you? Do you ever dance for joy in the Spirit,
or wince with others' pain? If not, why not? Some of us speak slight-
ingly of Spirit baptism, of "born again" Christians, of charismatics
and pentecostals. Kooks we call them, "off the wall." That sort of excitement might do for first-century Palestinian fishermen; it's em-

barrassing for sophisticated folk like us. We get our kicks from sex and stereo, from foaming mugs and bouncing basketballs. Turned on by the Spirit? What are you, some sort of weirdo? Chariots of fire? Man, you've seen too many movies!

III

Which brings me to my third point: a blunt word on how all this touches your Hilltop existence. You see, it is a fascinating and risky adventure on which you've embarked. This is not the pious eructation of an impious Jesuit; it is a fact. On the one hand, Hoya life can be fascinating: the ecstasy of discovery, the exhilaration of freedom, the joys of friendship, 325 faculty focused on you, a paradoxical city that exhibits at once the grandeur of democratic government and the machinations of Machiavelli, the glories of El Greco and the ceaseless rape of the poor, the glitter of black-tie parties and the cynical sex of 14th Street. On the other hand, the adventure is laden with risk. College life can dehumanize you. You can emerge as the rugged individualist the sociologist Robert Bellah finds newly rampant in our nation: responsible to no one save yourself. And you dare not disregard a disturbing survey in *Psychology Today*. From the responses of your peers, a central passion between 18 and 25 is money—at times second only to food! In consequence, many in your age bracket confess themselves sexually unsatisfied, in worsening health, worried and anxious, discontented with their jobs, and . . . lonely as hell.[3]

The question is, how do you become fully human these four years? Jesus suggested the answer the night before he died for you: "[The Father] will give you another Counselor, to be with you for ever, even the Spirit of truth, whom the world cannot receive, because it neither sees Him nor knows Him. You will know Him, for He dwells with you and will be in you" (Jn 14:16–17). Can you get a 4.0 average without the Spirit? Probably. Can you "get high" apart from the Spirit? Undoubtedly. Can you be *fully* human without the assistance of the Spirit? I'm afraid not.

You see, ever since God took flesh in Jesus, to be fully human is to be in the image of Christ. But only the God who made you "fast" can take that sharp intellect of yours and shape it into "the mind of Christ," winnow sheer knowledge into a wisdom not of this world. Only the Power within you can make your every day a new creation, because only the Spirit can make you what St. Paul called "a new creature" (2 Cor 5:17), alive with the life of the risen Christ, alive not only for yourself but for the lonely and despairing, the furious and frustrated, a few miles east of your Eden. Only the Spirit who lives in you can bring you to *feel* God's own pleasure, guarantee you a delight in living far deeper than even Pepsi can promise. It will be tragic if you profit from professor and Pub but neglect the Power inside you, the Counselor who alone can lead you into all truth, the Spirit who alone can make you chariots of fire.

Little wonder we pray: "Come, Holy Spirit, fill the hearts of your faithful ones and enkindle in them the fire of your love. Send forth your Spirit, O Lord, and they will be created; and you will renew the face of the earth."

Gaston Hall
Georgetown University
September 12, 1982

28

ZAPPING THE ZELIG
University Mass of the Holy Spirit 2

♦ 1 Corinthians 2:9–13
♦ John 14:15–17, 26

Woody Allen is loose again! This time he is *Zelig*. Leonard Zelig is a Jewish nobody, a 1920's nothing. He has no personality of his own, so he assumes whatever strong personalities he meets up with. With Chinese, he is straight out of China. With rabbis, he miraculously grows a beard and side curls. With psychiatrists, he apes their jargon, strokes his chin with solemn wisdom. At the Vatican, he is part of Pius XI's clerical retinue. In spring training, he wears a Yankee uniform and stands in the on-deck circle to bat after Babe Ruth. He takes on the black skin of a jazz trumpeter, the blubber of a fatty, the profile of a Mohawk Indian. He is a chameleon: He changes color, accent, shape as the world about him changes. He has no ideas or opinions of his own; he simply conforms. He wants only to be safe, to fit in, to be accepted, to be liked.

For a while Zelig's freakish transformations make him the rage; New York welcomes him with confetti and ticker tape. He is famous for being nobody, a nonperson. His psychiatrist, Mia Farrow, is of no help to him: In her presence he cannot help playing psychiatrist. Only when she pretends to be, like him, a patient with no personality, only then does he begin to see himself for what he is: a disturbed person looking for identity, looking for himself. He identifies with her. And ultimately, after he's been a guinea pig and a side-show freak, through all manner of bitter anguish, love liberates Leonard Zelig's true self. Through comedy and tragedy, nobody becomes somebody.[1]

This morning, my friends, the Mass of the Holy Spirit inaugurates or continues your search for yourself. What this liturgy tells

you is that the search is not merely academic, not simply psycho-
logic. What makes Georgetown different is that the quest is under-
taken under the wings of a divine Person. On the Hilltop you can
easily end up a nobody: no personality of your own, a chameleon
changing color with each new contact. To become somebody, you
need three gifts: light, life, and love. And the Holy Spirit is the Spirit
of all three: of light, of life, of love. A word on each.

I

To become somebody, you need light. Such is the function of
intelligence, of understanding, on a college campus. Some cynic defined college as "the notes of the teacher passing into the notes of
the student without passing through the mind of either." It happens—but $40,000 is a steep price to pay for shared ignorance. To
be educated is to be enlightened—light for the mind.

With this mind you look into a microscope and are filled with
the wonder of life the naked eye cannot see.[2] With this mind you
speed over oceans more swiftly than the jet and touch human persons from Afghanistan to Zaire, from Belfast to Beirut. With this
mind you flee back into the past and rediscover a universe 15 to 20
billion years old, rediscover an America five centuries young. With
this mind you pluck meaning from the strings of a harp and the
whisper of the wind, from a sonnet or a sonata, from Michelangelo's
Pietà and the Mona Lisa, from Beethoven's *Pastoral Symphony* and
Tchaikovsky's *Sleeping Beauty* and Verdi's *Aïda*—yes, from Linda
Ronstadt and from David Bowie's brave new world. With this mind
you look into the minds of philosophers from ancient Greece to
modern Britain, from Plato's world of ideas to Whitehead's world of
experience, to share their tortured search for what is real, for what
is true. With this mind you look into the mind of God as He reveals
Himself in creation, on a cross, and in the lines of His own book.

If your mind is open to light, you can begin to become your own
person; for you begin to see, not just a small light at the end of a
single narrow tunnel, but infinite possibilities, the endless ways a
personality can be shaped. For you will be experiencing mystery. I
mean the realization that reality, the real, is incredibly complex and
perplexing, profound and open-ended. Whether it's the inner you
or outer space, whether it's the story of man and woman or the life
of God, whether it's the whiz kid inside that computer or the people

who surround you, the real is a fascinating and frustrating, entranc-
ing and enrapturing wedding of what you can grasp and what is still
beyond your grasp. It's the beginning of understanding.

But that razor edge of knowledge is not enough, that facile
memory, that bright light of human brilliance, that 4.0. You can
have all that and end up a Zelig, famous for being everybody and
nobody: the anonymous white coat or Green Beret, the three-piece
suit or beaded cocktail dress, faceless in Calvin Klein. The light you
need to make you unique, somebody, is the Spirit.

I don't mean a divine crib sheet, all the answers to a four-year
inquisition. I mean the same Holy Spirit who moved Mary to say yes
to an angel, who guided the steps of Jesus from a crib to a cross, who
loosed the tongues of fearful apostles on the first Pentecost, who
leads the disciple of Jesus "into all the truth" (Jn 16:13). This is the
Spirit who plays on your mind as on harp strings, plucks gently here
and strongly there, never compelling, always inspiring. This is the
Spirit who lets you see beneath the surface of things, beneath the
veneer of your fear, lets you see what you can become if, like Jesus,
you allow his Spirit to take hold of you. This is the Spirit who zaps
the Zelig in you, makes you uncomfortable with "fitting in," following the crowd, imbibing morality with a Michelob. This is the Spirit
who really liberates your mind, not from Adam's apple and grade-
school dogma, but from the blackness of sin and selfishness, of prejudice and smallness, of narrowness and blindness, from all that
makes for darkness above your eyeballs.

Little wonder we pray today, "Father of light, send your Spirit
into our lives with the power of a mighty wind, and by the flame of
your wisdom open the horizons of our minds."

II

To become somebody, you have to be alive. The problem is,
you are not genuinely alive simply because you are not medically
dead. Simply because you go to class in the morning, a carrel in the
afternoon, Clyde's at night. Simply because your standard of living
is high, your cholesterol low. Simply because you eat and drink, talk
and sleep, rock and roll. Simply because you are going through the
motions of living—all the routines that enable a man or woman to
get through life without living it.

A function of college is to bring out the life in you. From the

ICC to the Yates to the GUTS,[3] Georgetown lives to touch you to human living. Your mind, of course; for when you really know, your mind comes alive. To know is to image God's life; an idea mimics God's own creative magic; discovery is a share in divinity. But life is more than mind, more than thought. Not only must your intellect come alive; *you* must. Living is your whole person reacting to the real. And so Georgetown offers not only a campus but a city, not only blackboards but footlights, not only a podium but a pub and a pool. Georgetown is jubilant when you *delight* in what you experience, from a chemical formula to the vibrant flesh of a Rubens, from *Swan Lake* to the Tidal Basin, from a simple amoeba to a three-point homily. Georgetown is proud when you thrill to Hoya poetry-in-motion, sports that shape grace and fluidity, strength and heart: a hoop or the Henley, cinders or clay, a diamond or a diving board. Georgetown is glad when D.C. poverty is not a statistic but twists your gut, when injustice in Johannesburg makes you black with anger and the assassination of Aquino makes you weep, when refugee camps in Thailand stab you to the heart. Georgetown is sad when living is artificial, stimulated by a tube in the winter of life or a syringe at its spring.

But this, glorious as it is, is not the be-all and the end-all of Georgetown life. The uniqueness of life here, what makes you not only somebody but somebody special, is something the naked eye cannot see, the ear hear, the human heart conceive. Within you lives the Spirit of life, a divine Person. The Spirit you "have received," St. Paul proclaims, is "the Spirit which is from God, that [you] might understand the gifts bestowed on [you] by God" (1 Cor 2:12). Within you is God's life coursing through you like another bloodstream, making you brothers and sisters of Jesus, able to live as Jesus lived, to believe where others doubt, to hope where others despair, to love where others hate.

No Zelig here. You do indeed take on the character of Christ: "It is no longer I who live, but Christ who lives in me" (Gal 2:20). But the paradox is, the new life is a new you. Alive with the life of the risen Christ, yes, but you never cease to be yourself, not quite the same as any other, shaped uniquely into a unique Christ. A new creation that does not destroy or swallow up what is native to you—your wit and wisdom, your freedom and spontaneity, your laughter and your tears—but raises all this to a new pitch, a fresh intensity. If the Spirit of life lays hold of you, you cannot but shout with Eugene O'Neill's Lazarus newly lifted from the grave:

Laugh with me!
Death is dead!
Fear is no more!
There is only life!
There is only laughter![4]

III

To become somebody, you have to love. The real person is not the rugged individualist who can make it on a desert isle or in a penthouse for one—not Robinson Crusoe or Howard Hughes. To be a person is to be in relation, oriented to an "other." And this is to love; for to love is, as Aquinas saw, to go out of yourself, to be one with the other: with God's mute creation, with God's free images, with God Himself.

And so Georgetown insists that you know most perfectly when your knowledge is love. Not a cold grasp on an object from outside, but oneness with it from within. Water is indeed H_2O, but you know water best when you run your fingers through the Chesapeake, joy in a Jacuzzi, feel it bathing your brow in baptism. I can know your ancestry and IQ, your life style and vital measurements, but none of this compares with my knowledge when eyes meet, words pass, hands touch. It is one thing—and a good thing—to study "the problem of God." But such knowledge will never save. It is not enough to know *about* God; you must know God, encounter and experience the living God—not simply a theology of God but the God of theology.

Here the Spirit of love enters in. Not that true love has to be Christian. But I much fear that, unless this divine Person within you inspires your quest for truth, little of your knowledge will be love. Sociologist Robert Bellah is distressed by "a new middle class," largely the young, that "believes in the gospel of success 1980 style. It is an ethic of how to get ahead in the corporate bureaucratic world while maximizing one's private goodies. In the world of the zero-sum society it is important to get to the well first before it dries up, to look out for number one. . . ." It is summed up by a young woman therapist in Atlanta: "In the end you're really alone, and you really have to answer to yourself. You're responsible for yourself and no one else."[5]

In contradiction to this ethic, 500 "Spirited" students fanned out from here last year to D.C.'s ignorant and indigent, to the homeless and the hopeless, to the imprisoned in body and the captive in spirit. Once again nine graduates have flown to Nicaragua for a year, to serve the poor, the downtrodden, the degraded. In the power of the same Spirit, please God, you will experience, within these gates and without, what it means and how it feels to fall in love with an idea, with all manner of people, with the triune God. If you do not, you will leave Hoyaland with a gigantic "incomplete." For unless you love, you are at best half a woman, half a man.

My friends, Zelig is not sheer fantasy. He/she lives all around you, even among the brilliant. You remember Peter Sellers. This "prime minister of mirth," as *Time* dubbed him at his death, was alive only when he was impersonating, playing to perfection the role of another: a German scientist or an R.A.F. officer, president of the U.S. or Cockney Marxist, an Indian doctor or a bumbling French detective, a dowager and her friends. Rootless, he changed residences like clothes; 70 cars in six years; four marriages; few relationships that were lasting or intimate. And "when the world closed in, he sought refuge variously in women, yoga, vegetarianism and overwork."[6]

Ironically, *zelig* in Yiddish means "blessed." But not on the Hilltop. Blessed are you only if the Spirit of light puts His torch to your intelligence. Blessed are you only if the Spirit of life thrills you each day to your bone and marrow. Blessed are you only if the Spirit of love links you to "the other" all around you, links you to the Other within you. Blessed are you when, in the power of the Spirit, you zap the Zelig in you—when nobody becomes somebody, somebody special, somebody unique. It's worth 40,000.

Gaston Hall
Georgetown University
September 11, 1983

29

ON LEAVING THE ASYLUM
Baccalaureate Homily

♦ Wisdom 6:12–20; 7:7–12
♦ John 16:12–15

I suspect that, as you listened to the Gospel, some among the graduates were hoping I would take to heart the opening words of Jesus: "I have yet many things to say to you, but you cannot bear them now" (Jn 16:12). Indeed, the liturgy of the Trinity, closing out your years on the Hilltop, calls not for much speaking but for prayerful musing; for Father, Son, and Spirit have made their home within you.[1] Still, let me move your musings in a distinct direction. Three stages: first, a parable from the present; second, the Wisdom reading from the past; third, a quick fix on your future.

I

First, a parable from the present. Several weeks ago, a 1967 French film returned briefly to D.C.: *The King of Hearts.* We are in the last days of World War II. An amiable Scot, Alan Bates, is sent to a small French village to find and dismantle a giant booby trap left by departing Germans. The citizens have fled in fear, leaving the village to the inmates who have escaped from the local asylum. Charming lunatics: dukes and duchesses, generals, "a marvelously compliant madam and a virginal whore."[2] All find Bates's efforts to save them utterly incomprehensible. Instead, they dub him the King of Hearts, celebrate a mad coronation. Finally he succumbs to their logic.

After defusing the booby trap, Bates does gymnastic exercises on the cathedral clock. Now the citizens return. Seeing them, the inmates stream back to the asylum with one accord. In the last scene, Bates, ornithologist by profession, is standing at the gate of the madhouse, stark naked, a bird cage in his hand. He is seeking asylum from the "real" world.

The thesis of the parable? The certified insane of this world are a lot less lunatic than the madmen who persist in making lunatic wars.

II

Since *The King of Hearts* is not an allegory, it would be a mistake (happy perhaps, but still a mistake) to apply the details rigorously to your situation: the asylum inside the gates, the carousing inmates out on the town, hidden booby traps from the MX to the final exam, the hands on the tower clock, the supposedly sane citizens of Pennsylvania Avenue. But the parable does raise a disturbing question: Who are the really sane? What does it mean to be "in your right mind"?

I am not playing the pessimist when I say you are moving out into a world where madness is global. In my short span of living, I have seen eight million Ukrainians and Cossacks systematically starved by a Stalin; half the world's Jews gassed by an Aryan anthropology; new hells fashioned by the atom in Hiroshima and Nagasaki; Eastern Europe chained to the Russian Bear; Vietnam converted by napalm into family incinerators; half of Cambodia done to savage death; nine million refugees clogging the roads of East Pakistan; terrorist bombs maiming women and children in Christian Ireland; black slavery in Watts and Harlem, in D.C. and South Chicago; Arab and Israeli, Iranian and Iraqi at each other's throat; pope and president bloodied by bullets; a billion humans bedding down hungry each night; 50 million innocents aborted each year; and right now the threat of "mutual assured destruction": MAD.

How do you enter such a world sane, bring some sanity to it, stay sane yourself? Now a sermon is not a seminar, not a class in psychology. It tries to touch God's living word to a live issue. Since the best of Burghardt is not necessarily the cream of Catholicism, I commend to you today's Wisdom reading from the past. Regrettably, it is a liturgical snippet, out of context. Let me replace it in the rich wisdom literature of the Old Testament; for here are inspired insights that put a picture together: the wise man, the wise woman. In our terms this morning, the sane woman, the sane man. Who are they? What do they do that is so wise, so sane? And where do they get their wisdom, their sanity?[3]

Who are the wise woman, the sane man, of Scripture? They are experts in an art: how to live well. Passion does not sear them nor wrath wreck them; they are "cool." Knowledge fills their heads without puffing them up; it rests lightly yet securely upon them. Technical competence they complement with artistic feel. They muse and mull over existence, but not in abstruse abstraction; rather, they have a sixth sense of where they sit in this world. Pious they are, but never saccharine—only faithful, dutiful, impressively reverent. Aware that God rules the world, they have a salutary fear of the Lord.

But what is it they do that is so wise, so sane? They indeed do something; for they are not Olympian observers of the human scene, "scopers,"[4] tenured to a "seat of wisdom," a funded chair of sanity. Old Testament wisdom is practical wisdom; it is a technique whereby the wise can work their way through the perils and pitfalls of human living to the goal they have in view. They are intimately interested in others—not only in "the people" but primarily in persons. They know the human heart, its joys and sorrows. They sense our grandeur and our wretchedness, our loneliness, our anguish in face of suffering and death, our unease and disquiet before God. With all and each they yearn to share their wisdom, their sanity. Marvel of marvels, they know how to enjoy life. Oh, they realize how imperfect and passing is the world that surrounds them, how sinful and selfish the human heart, how hostile the earth they trod, the air they breathe; but none of this shatters them. Through all of this they walk with sympathy and serenity; they enjoy being alive.

Where do the wise of Scripture get their wisdom? From three sources. (1) There is the accumulated wisdom of the past, the tradition of the fathers. (2) There is their own experience: From openness to all that is real, they have grown in wisdom, in sanity, never cease to grow. (3) It is, at bottom, a gift of God. Ultimately, the master of wisdom is Jesus. He is the Wisdom of God, in whom the sapiential texts find their definitive meaning. He it is who, as Wisdom in flesh, communicates wisdom not to the wise of the world but to his little ones. In a world ceaselessly seesawing towards insanity, he is the Sane Man par excellence. *He* is the King of Hearts.

III

From the parable of the present and the Scripture of the past, a quick fix on your future. Not a computerized program; not directly "a word from your Creator." Rather, a challenge forged from that word, a challenge addressed not to unbelievers but to young men and women who avow Christ as their Wisdom, who will in a few moments feed on his flesh and drink of his blood.

For sweet sanity's sake, I single out one quality from the wisdom of the fathers and the Wisdom that is Jesus. I mean their openness. Here I challenge you on three levels. (1) Because you are creatures of intelligence, you should be open to ideas. (2) Because you are creatures of flesh and blood, you should be open to people. (3) Because you are creatures of Christ, you should be open to the Spirit. A word on each.

Because you are creatures of intelligence, you should be open to ideas. If you respect the roots of the word, there is a certain "insanity" in the closed mind: it is "not whole," "not healthy." That is all too obvious where the madness is bloody, where dialectical materialism or religious fanaticism, racial purity or white supremacy, sheer lust for power kills the body. But the "insanity" I have in mind need not be gory; it can be terribly subtle. I fear much for the lawyer whose only life is corporate tax, the doctor whose whole existence is someone else's prostate, the business executive whose single responsibility is to his stockholders, the athlete who puts all his eggs in an 18-inch basket, the theologian who thinks the world can be saved by theology. I am afraid of, afraid for, men and women who claim there is only one way to God, one morality of the majority, one way to interpret the Bible or the First Amendment, even one way to say Mass—in Latin, because that's the way Jesus said it! It kills marriages and human relations; it deadens feelings and sensitivities; it makes for a society that lives in a thousand and one tunnels, with no communication and no exit.

I don't know how much you've learned on the Hilltop; I like to think that you exit with an open mind. Not a mind without fixed points; not a mind that accepts everything—Marxism and capitalism, Christianity and atheism, love and lust—as equally good or bad, absorbs all ideas like a sponge and is just as soft. I mean rather a realization that the life of the mind is incredibly open-ended, if only because reality is a participation in God, a reflection of the Beauty, Truth, and Goodness that cannot be imprisoned in a definition.

If you are open-minded, you challenge—challenge fixed ideas, established structures, including your own. You listen—to people in other disciplines, other ways of thinking. You don't impute evil to those with whom you disagree: They must be living in sin! You don't turn cocktail parties into small warrens of the same profession, those who mouth the same jargon. You are touchingly humble, because your knowledge, however vast, is a drop in a measureless ocean. You rarely live on either-or: either creation or evolution, body or soul, church or world, liberty or law, sacred or secular, God or man, home or career, Jesus human or divine, Beethoven or Bruce Springsteen. Like the Church in its highest tradition, you focus on both-and; for any decent heresy tells us something important to which we have been deaf.

But you are not naked intellect, disembodied spirit. Because you are creatures of flesh and blood, you should be open to people. The distinguished sociologist Philip Rieff sees a fresh character ideal coming to dominate Western civilization. Over against the old pagan commitment to the polis, to public life, over against the Judeo-Christian commitment to a transcendent God, over against the Enlightenment commitment to the irresistible progress of reason, today's ideal type is "anti-heroic, shrewd, carefully counting his satisfactions and dissatisfactions, studying unprofitable commitments as the sins most to be avoided." The "highest science"? Self-concern. Devotion and self-sacrifice? "Constraining ideals" that must be rejected. We have to "emancipate man's 'I' from the communal 'we.' "[5]

This ideal of human living I call "insane"; it is unhealthy, for you and for your world whelmed by injustice and pain. If Georgetown's normal product is a man or woman simply of enlightened self-interest, Georgetown's bicentennial should be its swan song.

I like to think that you exit these gates with sensitivity and compassion. For if you do, then the competence and skill that are yours—in nursing or economics, in linguistics or liberal arts, in physical science or foreign service—will touch not only bodies and budgets, semantics and ideas, technology and diplomacy. The gifts you have honed here will reach out to that before which all knowledge and wisdom pales, that which alone is of everlasting value: the human person.

The paradox is, only in this way can you get your own act together: not in isolation, only in relation. You will become yourself to the extent that you go out of yourself. You will find wisdom in the measure that you are ready to share it. When you can say, to a single person or to an acre of God's world, "Your life is my life," then will your wisdom catch fire. Only when knowledge is wed to love will wisdom come alive in you.

But you are not just flesh and blood. Because you are creatures of Christ, you should be open to the Spirit. This is not pious twaddle. If you are "in Christ," St. Paul trumpeted, you are "a new creation" (2 Cor 5:17). And this new creation, Jesus promised, the Holy Spirit "will guide into all the truth" (Jn 16:13). Not economic theory or historical facts; these stem from sweat, blood, tears, midnight oil. But everything God took flesh to reveal, everything you need to be sane, to be a whole person, to be wise with the wisdom of Jesus.

I do not claim that unless you are open to the Spirit within you, you will be unhappy or unsuccessful. You may well be the life of a party, the power behind a throne, make money like mad. I do predict that if you listen to this Spirit of life and love who whispers and thunders within you, you will love wisdom "more than health and beauty" (Wis 7:10), more than wealth and power. Then, I promise, you will rarely find existence unexciting; you may thrill to human living the way you thrill to the *Return of the Jedi*.[6] X-number of the dead and despairing will be quickened to life by you. Above all, you will touch—yes, touch—a living God whose presence in you challenges not your logic but your love. For, as metaphysician Jacques Maritain insisted, the culmination of knowledge is not conceptual but experiential: You "feel" God.

Open to strange ideas, open in love to strangers, open to a strange Spirit—the world outside these gates will find you a bit mad. But remember, they said the same thing about the King of Hearts: "He's out of his mind" (Mk 3:21). Bring something of Jesus' strange sanity to the manic earth on which you will walk, and when you return to this happy asylum you may, with our glad blessing, dance on the hands of the Healy clock. Till then, my friends, God love you . . . as we do.

Georgetown University
May 29, 1983

30

IF I HAVE NOT LOVE. . . .
Wedding Homily 1

♦ Genesis 2:18–24
♦ 1 Corinthians 12:31—13:13
♦ Mark 10:6–9

Dear Jane and Remy: In an action characteristic of two first-rate lawyers, you have chosen three pertinent texts as precedents for the legal step you are about to take. The texts are pertinent because they speak powerfully of three basic needs you have: a human person, a divine Person, and a love that links them to you. As a "friend of the court," I suggest that these texts may be even more pertinent than you realize. A brief word on each.

I

First, the text from Genesis (2:18–24).[1] After the Lord has fashioned the first man, He declares: "It is not good for the man to be alone; I will make him a helper fit for him." Now be careful not to read too much into that sentence. Do not conclude that it would be good for a *woman* to be alone. God's statement has for springboard a fact: Adam is there. If Eve had been created first, I doubt not that God would have said: "It is not good for the woman to be alone."

The point is, both man and woman need a counterpart, someone who "corresponds to" him or her. Genesis 2 develops that idea with incomparable imagery. After declaring that the man should not be alone, God brings to Adam the beasts and birds He has just created. Why? To have Adam "name" them, "to see what he would call them." Oh, not a bare description like road runner or robin redbreast. In the Hebrew mentality, for Adam to "name" something was for Adam to recognize its nature, see it for what it is, give it the meaning it had for Adam in his world. And what the first man saw was this: Not one of these creatures of field or sky—however swift or lovely, however gentle and affectionate—was "fit for him," suitable for him, could complement him, complete his being. For all their likeness to him, they were not like enough to him.

So the man remains alone; but the Lord God is not yet done. He shapes a creature at once different from him and strikingly similar. So similar, so kin to him, that Scripture imagines God fashioning this other out of the man's very body. But don't be distracted by poetic detail: Adam is not really losing a rib, he is gaining a woman.

Now note Adam's reaction. When God brings the first woman to the first man, as before he had brought bird and beast, the effect is electric. When first he sets eyes on her, he exclaims in ecstasy: "This one, at last, is bone of my bone and flesh of my flesh!" "This one" (three times he shouts it)—here is man's joyful surprise as he welcomes his one equal on earth, his peer and companion. Now, and for ever, we have two; neither man nor woman is alone. Here, the author adds, is a kinship, an attraction, so strong that it will loosen the strongest bonds in early life, the bonds that bind to parents and home: "That is why a man leaves his father and his mother and cleaves to his wife, and they become one flesh."

The first need? A human person. From the opening act of creation, to be a person is to be with and for another. And personhood is more perfect as communion is more complete, a gradual growth in mutual giving that removes aloneness from flesh and spirit. It is a sharing that will make each of you, Remy and Jane, far more of a person than you were in your first quarter century, more of a person each today than you were yesterday, more of a person than your wildest dreams can this day fantasize.

II

Second, the text from Mark (Mk 10:6–9). In this confrontation with the Pharisees, Jesus repeats some of the Genesis story: "For this reason a man shall leave his father and mother. . . ." But he adds something as breath-taking as it is brief: "What therefore God has joined together, let not man put asunder." What we have here is not simply the likeness in spirit and flesh that makes man and woman "fit" for each other; not only the powerful attraction that compels them to leave father and mother and become one person in two. This is indeed from God. But Jesus suggests that God enters marriage even more intimately: When the two join together, He joins them together. Not to leave them as they leave the church, but to stay with them as long as they will have Him.

Here the Roman Catholic tradition on marriage is remarkably rich. It insists that in this sacred ritual the priest does not play the part he plays in baptism; here I am only the Church's official witness. I do not marry these two; *they* are the celebrants of the ceremony. I do not make them man and wife; *they* are the ministers of this mystery. This means that they are channels of grace each to the other. When they say yes, Jane will give to Remy, Remy to Jane, not only themselves; each will channel to the other . . . God.

More than that: God will be faithful to them days without end; He will always be there. This awesome rite is a solemn pledge thereof. The God who revealed to us that the marriage of two Christians is a profound symbol of the love that links Christ and his Church will never be far from them. This day He promises them His pervasive presence in good times and in bad, in sickness and in health, in poverty and in wealth.

The second need? A divine Person. Remy and Jane, for all your shining, sterling qualities, marriage is still too perilous to entrust solely to a man and a woman. Our 50% casualty rate is a terrifying testimony to that. You need God: the Father who fashioned you, the Son who died for you, the Spirit who lives in you. But remember, presence can never be one-sided. You have to be present to God; His faithfulness calls for your fidelity; He must be as real to you as you are to each other. If He is, the odds are in your favor; if He is not, I tremble for you.

III

Third, the text from St. Paul (1 Cor 12:31—13:13). Ponder once again this paean to love sung by the Apostle to the Christians of Corinth:

I will show you a still more excellent way [more excellent than tongues or prophecy or healing, more remarkable than being an administrator, a teacher, or even an apostle].

I may speak with every tongue that men and angels use; but if I have not love, I am a noisy gong or a clanging cymbal. I may have powers of prophecy, no secret hidden from me, no knowledge too deep for me; I may have utter faith, so as to move mountains; but if I have not love, I am nothing. I may give away all I

have, deliver my body to be burned [as a martyr], but if I have not
love, it does me no good.

Love is patient, love is kind. Love feels no envy, will not boast,
is not arrogant, is not rude. Love has no selfish aims, cannot be
provoked, is not resentful. Love refuses to rejoice at wrong, rejoices only in the right. Love bears all things, believes all things,
hopes all things, endures to the last.

Love never ends. Prophecies will pass, tongues cease, knowledge be swept away; [we shall never have finished with love.] . . .
In this moment three things abide: faith, hope, love; all three
abide. But the greatest of these is love.

Yes, Jane and Remy, you need a human person and you need
a divine Person. But the need that links both persons to you is love.
Now the love whose praises Paul sings so lyrically is not love in its
usual understanding, not love in some shadowy sense. It is not simply the love you enjoy because you are human. This is the love Paul
calls "God's love poured into our hearts through the Holy Spirit
who has been given to us" (Rom 5:5). This is the Spirit's most precious gift. It can include, indeed, all the closeness and tenderness,
all the intimacy and passion, you associate with human loving. But
it is more. The love Paul describes is genuinely divine, because the
power to love like this comes not from your native gifts, your powerful personality, your emotional stability, your exceptional talents.
You have it because a loving God has sent His Spirit, the Holy Spirit
of love, into your hearts.

The third need? A love at once human and divine. Human because it is you who love this way; divine because it is God who enables you to love this way. Because it is divine, it is not something you
deserve; it is a gift. Because it is a gift, you may never take it for
granted; you ceaselessly thank God for it.

Dear friends, in these Scripture texts a peril lurks. Because it is
Remy and Jane who have chosen them as precedents, we could be
tempted to conclude, in legalistic fashion, that only they are bound
by the texts. A judge might so rule; a theologian would not. These
passages speak compellingly to all of us who believe, Christian and
Jew alike. They express in deathless phrases what Jane and Remy
are proclaiming by their presence. First, it is not good for any of us
to be alone. Nation or person, tribe or family, we need one another
. . . desperately. Otherwise we perish, in bitter loneliness or nuclear
holocaust. Second, for all our priceless freedom and technological
magic, we humans are not self-sufficient. We need a Lord at once
above us and within us, a Lord who alone can save us from our-

selves, a Lord who alone can join us together till death do us part. Third, to link others and the Other to us, each of us needs a love that is patient and kind, free of envy and arrogance, unselfish and unresentful, a love that "bears all things, believes all things, hopes all things, endures to the last." Without love, you and I are "nothing."

And so we thank you, Jane and Remy, good lawyers and better lovers. Thank you for revealing to us—through God's word just uttered and your own word now to be spoken—who we can be if only we live "God's love poured into our hearts." In return, we promise you not just Waterford crystal or another set of Blackstone's *Commentaries*. We promise a love that will never end—for you, for one another, and in a special way for the loveless who surround us, who beg mutely that our love of law be transformed into a law of love.

The Congregational Church
New Canaan, Connecticut
October 29, 1983

31

AS I HAVE LOVED YOU
Wedding Homily 2

◆ Genesis 1:26–28, 31a
◆ Romans 8:31b–35, 37–39
◆ John 15:9–12

Good friends: Three powerful passages have just been proclaimed in your hearing. These passages are important to us today not only because they are plucked from God's own Book. They are especially important because they were chosen with care by Bernadette and Jim out of a host of possibilities. They express, therefore, certain values that these two hold particularly precious. And so it makes sense for us to ponder these passages. What is it that God might be saying—to one man and one woman, to each man and each woman here this morning? Ultimately, only you can answer for yourself; let me simply stimulate you with my own musing.

I

First, the reading from Genesis (3:26–28, 31a). It offers three insights into God and the human person, into God and those who marry in God. (1) The God who had fashioned heaven and earth, the birds of the air and the beasts of the field and the fish of the sea, crowned His creation by shaping two creatures in such a way that they, and they alone, were images of His very self. (2) God commanded them to be creative themselves: to fashion other selves from their own flesh and spirit. (3) God looked back upon all He had done . . . and it was "very good" (v. 31).

It is another marvel of God's creation, of God's caring, that the first chapter of Genesis is not imprisoned on a page. It moves today from a garden to a church, from Eden to Haddonfield. Two products of God's creating hand stand before us today, stand before God today. This new Adam, this new Eve, are special; for each is like God. I mean, each entered this world possessing two of God's prerogatives: Each can know and each can love.[1] Each mirrors the Christ who is *the* Image of the Father; for each carries Christ deep within. Each has been molded through two decades by a loving God in such wise that each can cry with St. Paul: "It is no longer I who live, but Christ who lives in me; and the life I now live in the flesh I live by faith in the Son of God, who loved me and gave himself for me" (Gal 2:20).

More than that. This morning God asks of them, as He asked of the primal pair, that they carry on His own creating. Not like bird or beast, by a God-given instinct to outlive themselves, to survive their own mortality. Rather like God Himself: to shape, consciously and lovingly, images not only of themselves ("chips off the old block") but of God.

We can get lost in God's command "Be fruitful and multiply, and fill the earth" (v. 28), confused by an earth already filled, where little ones die like September flies. We can get lost in numbers and miss the miracle that is each child. Each child fashioned not solely by God, as were Adam and Eve, but from the flesh and spirit of a man and woman. Each child so wonder-full that God's own Son became a child. Each child imaging the Christmas child we shall reverence a week from tomorrow. Each child Christ-come-again.

And the same God who looked back on the world's first week surely looks with a smile on what His love has fashioned in Jim and Bernadette, on the love that has linked them in such singular oneness, on the gift they will express in a moment, the gift of each to the other. This God must surely smile on what this love promises: other images of His own Christ. Surely He must say this day: This too is "very good."

II

Second, the reading from Romans (8:31–35, 37–39). This is St. Paul's cry of utter confidence in God. In the Roman winter of 57–58, he declares that nothing, absolutely nothing, can make the true Christian forget God's love made manifest in the dying and rising of Christ. Not starvation or the sword, not political repression or religious persecution, not supernatural beings or astrological powers. For all their destructive force, they are no match for crucified love.

But why such bitter memories, why such unpleasant problems from ancient Rome, at a joy-filled wedding? Not because the dangers that confronted early Christians are likely to confront Jim and Bernadette. Dentists may live "from hand to mouth" but they rarely starve. Neither Democrats nor Republicans will oppress them because they are Catholic. Save for an occasional full moon, the zodiac should not seriously strain their marriage.

And still there are dangers—from without and from within. We inhabit a culture that is highly pragmatic: If something works, fine; if it doesn't, get rid of it! Splendid, as long as you're speaking of Apple or Radio Shack, of IBM or Texas Instruments. Devastating, when you apply the principle to human relations, to marriage. And we do. Not all of us, of course. But when 50% of the men and women who vow love unto death disavow that vow,[2] something new and frightening has invaded our culture. Broken contracts no longer raise our eyebrows. The sixth wedding of a brilliant actress only makes us chuckle. If TV is a king-size bed of infidelity, it merely reflects a culture that takes this for granted, is more amused than scandalized. And so Jimmy the Greek would not lay odds on any marriage enduring till death do you part.[3]

Possibly more perilous are dangers from within. However skeptical you may be of "original sin," our minds are indeed dreadfully dark, our wills woefully weak. We can so often resonate to St. Paul's agonizing confession: "I do not do the good I want, but the evil I do not want is what I do" (Rom 7:19). It must be difficult to live with one other person a whole life long. (Perhaps the only thing more difficult is *not* to live with another.) Our small selves get in the way. I take you for granted; I say things I do not mean—or do mean; I take out my frustrations on you; I don't care for your friends; I detest your ring of dirt inside our bathtub; I like Monday Night Football and you adore Merv Griffin. And there are problems not small at all. In the full flush of love it is easy enough to say "I take you for better or worse, in good times and bad, in sickness and health, in poverty and wealth." But illness can wear away not only her who is ill but him who is whole. It is not only the poor whose love can cool; the "good life"—too much too soon or too long—has its own high casualties.

Marriage would be too risky an adventure if Bernadette and Jim had only themselves to rest on, or only us to depend on. What St. Paul proclaims is that our Christian hope is not in man or woman but in God. And not in some far-off, gossamer God whose existence we can prove with philosophical arguments. Married or single, we can live unafraid of the future because our God has proven He cares: He gave His own Son to a bloody cross for us. Moreover, as Paul puts it, "hope does not disappoint us, because God's love has been poured into our hearts through the Holy Spirit who has been given to us" (Rom 5:5).

Bernadette and Jim, I am not a palmist; I cannot read the life lines or the liver lines in your hands. I can only promise you that God's love for you will never cease, that He will always be there, that if you respond to His love with your whole heart you have good reason to hope for deep happiness in your life together . . . for life.

III

The third text you have chosen takes my breath away: "This is my commandment, that you love one another as I have loved you" (Jn 15:12). Not simply "love one another." That much we expect of you; without love, marriage is hell. But "love one another as [Jesus has] loved you"? Do you know what you are promising?

How has Jesus loved us? We cannot count the ways. Out of love, he stripped himself of all that would make him look different, clothed himself in our flesh, became all we are save for our sin. Out of love, he had compassion on the sick and the hungry, the harassed and the helpless, the blind and the leprous, on a father and his epileptic boy, on a mother who had lost her only son. Out of love, he experienced how lonely we can be, how frightened of death. Out of love, he gave us his flesh for food, his blood as drink. Out of love, he died a criminal's death, in unspeakable agony. Out of love, he came back to life, shared his Spirit with us, promised us life without end in a joy we cannot conceive.

Knowing you, I think you know what you are promising. You know that love is more than a rub and a tickle. Genuine love, lifelong love, marital love is indeed your whole self given to one other. But in the Christian vision it is more: Together you give yourselves to a little acre of God's world. Unlike the Pharisee in the temple, you will not delight in what makes you different from others; you will thank God that, like Jesus, you *are* like the rest of humankind, that at root each person you touch is brother or sister. Your compassion will rarely be selective, never "Who is it?" but only "Do you hurt?" Your very oneness should make you more sensitive to the unloved, the lonely. The strength you draw from each other must draw you to so many who are afraid—afraid of death, afraid of life. You too must murmur to those who hunger: "This is my body, which is given for you" (Lk 22:19). You know that Christian love is a crucified love, a ceaseless dying and rising; that love makes demands, and demands can nail your hands and your feet. A remarkable Presbyterian preacher phrased it profoundly: ". . . when someone we love suffers, we suffer with him, and we would not have it otherwise because the suffering and the love are one, just as it is with God's love for us."[4]

From such love springs joy, abiding joy. Otherwise your life is lived in two pigeonholes—good times and bad times; the good you enjoy, the bad you endure. No, dear Bernadette and Jim, not for you. The joy no human being can take from you (cf. Jn 16:22) is the joy you discover in that most joyous of men, the Jesus who found his joy not only on the mount of his transfiguration but on the hill of his crucifixion. Not because he enjoyed suffering, but because love transformed sheer suffering into meaningful sacrifice, made joy the inmost core of his sorrow.

Bernadette and Jim: Your choice of biblical texts for today almost matches your choice of each other for life. I pray that the three passages you have selected for your wedding day will overshadow your every day. Creative images of your Creator, confident for the future because your confidence rests in God, alive with a love like that of Jesus—there is no better way to begin life together, no better way to live life together.

Christ the King Church
Haddonfield, New Jersey
December 17, 1983

32

TO MAKE OF IT A NEW CREATION
Twenty-fifth Anniversary of a Retreat House

◆ Ephesians 3:14–21
◆ John 1:35–39

More than a century ago, in 1867, Msgr. George Talbot, adviser to Pope Pius X on English affairs, wrote a letter to the Archbishop of Westminster, Henry Manning. That letter contained an important question and provided a provocative reply. "What," he asked, "is the province of the laity?" His answer: "To hunt, to shoot, to entertain. These matters they understand, but to meddle with ecclesiastical affairs they have no right at all."[1]

Almost a century later, in 1965, the bishops of the Catholic Church in solemn council proclaimed: "Let the laity not imagine that their pastors are always such experts that to every problem which arises, however complicated, they can readily give a concrete solution, or even that such is their mission. Rather, enlightened by Christian wisdom and paying close attention to the teaching of the magisterium, let them take on their own distinctive role."[2]

My friends, you gather here to celebrate Faulkner's 25 years[3] because you are keenly aware of three realities. (1) You have a "distinctive role" to play in the Church's apostolate. (2) To play this role effectively, you need a distinctive spirituality. (3) For you, this spirituality is absorbed in distinctive fashion through the Spiritual Exercises of St. Ignatius. A word on each.

I

First, you have a "distinctive role" to play in the Church's apostolate. Your basic charter is a pregnant paragraph in Vatican II's Decree on the Apostolate of the Laity:

> The redemptive work of Christ has for essential purpose the salvation of man and woman; and still it involves as well the renewal of the whole temporal order. Consequently, the Church's mission is not only to bring to men and women the message of Christ and his grace, but also to penetrate and perfect the temporal sphere with the spirit of the gospel. In carrying out this mission of the Church, the laity therefore exercise their apostolate in the world as well as in the Church, in the temporal order as well as in the spiritual. These areas, though distinct, are so intimately linked in the single plan of God that God Himself intends, in Christ, to take up the whole world again and make of it a new creation, initially here on earth, consummately on the last day. In both areas the lay person, at once believer and citizen, should be guided ceaselessly by one and the same Christian conscience.[4]

My fellow Christians, there are not two churches—clergy and laity. There is one Church of Christ with different functions, varied gifts of the Spirit. The mission of that single Church is a twin mission: to link every man, woman, and child to God, and to shape this earthly city into a city of justice, a city of peace, a city of love. Each of you shares in that mission; for the root mission that sends a Christian to sanctify the Church and reshape the world is not ordination, not a vow ceremony, not a special adult commissioning. You were sent on mission the moment you were baptized—you and I and every Christian without exception.

Let me stress your mission to the world. God indeed *made* you, as the old catechisms insisted, "to praise, reverence, and serve Him in this life and to be happy with Him for ever in the next." That is true of every human being. But Christ *baptized* you not simply for your own salvation, not solely to save souls, but to transform the world on which you walk, in which you work. Where you fulfil your distinctive function, where you play your irreplaceable role, is not the sanctuary but our sin-scarred earth. Few of you will fly to a refugee camp in Thailand, a leper colony in the Philippines. Your mission territory is where you live and move and have your being. Your apostolic turf is Merrill Lynch or the Department of Defense, CBS or the C.I.A., Sibley Hospital or the Washington *Post,* a contract or a computer, the people on your street or the youngsters in CCD, your own family which is the Church in miniature. Your mission land is surprisingly simple and discouragingly vast: Your mission land is wherever you are. For, with rare exceptions, only lay Christians can bring Christ to law office and legislature, to media and medicine, to public school and private industry, to executive suite and union hall, to the thousand and one areas of human living seldom open to the ordained.

Note well, my friends: In these areas you are not replacing a shrinking clergy; you are not substitutes waiting for the first team to come back on. These are your home grounds; here is your arena of action; here *you* are the Church, by right and duty.

But how do you bring Christ there or expand his presence? At times, by the power of the word: your word and God's. The ethics of nuclear war, human rights in the womb and in El Salvador, homosexuality and premarital sex, ERA and women in the Church, who Christ is and what it means to be a Christian—these are not priestly preserves, off limits to laity. They should challenge your competence, engage your conversation, as often as do the Redskins or the Orioles.

More effectively still, you transform your turf by the attraction of your life. It does no good to preach peace if your heart harbors hatred. "If," says our Scripture, "a brother or sister is ill-clad and in lack of daily food, and one of you says to them, 'Go in peace, be warmed and filled,' without giving them the things needed for the body, what does it profit?" (Jas 2:15–16). If your business practices are no more ethical than the unbeliever's—"after all, everybody does it"—why should anyone believe your gospel? If you are color-conscious, if on principle and in practice you pass by the black or the yellow or the brown, who will be moved if you parrot the parable of the Good Samaritan? If you differ from your fellows only for an hour on Sunday, why should they think it worth while to turn their lives around?

II

Which leads quite naturally into my second point. I take it you come to Faulkner, at least in part, because to play your apostolic role effectively, you need a spirituality, a distinctive spirituality. I don't mean a Christian existence different in essence from that of other Christians, different from mine. All Christian spirituality is the response of a man or woman to God revealing His love in Christ. In the concrete, it consists in knowing, loving, and serving God and His children in the context of a community of faith, hope, and love. All Christian spirituality is a new, intimate relationship with the Blessed Trinity, a sharing in God's own life, a conscious experience of God and His love that thrusts you out in loving service to the very least of Christ's brothers and sisters. Simply yet profoundly, all Christian spirituality is St. Paul's outburst to the churches of Galatia: "I have been crucified with Christ. It is no longer I who live: Christ lives in me" (Gal 2:20).[5]

Still, there is something distinctive about your spirituality.[6] Not all Christians develop their likeness to Christ in the same way. A Trappist monk sanctifies himself singing God's praises in choir and field and workshop, in long hours of silence and contemplation. Not so you. Oh yes, your holiness, like the monk's, is centered in the Eucharist. But it works itself out, it is shaped, in your encounter with the world: with wife or husband and children, with the tools of your trade and the ideas that inspire your business, with money and material possessions, with technology. It is indeed a secular world, divorced from the medieval marriage to Christ. But secular is not the same as evil. It means only that God's creation, from the amoeba to technology, has its own proper purposes, and God is not programed in much of it. Technology is not evil, as none of God's creation is evil—marriage, the body, politics, poetry. But it does demand to be sanctified; it must be directed to justice, to peace, to love.

And so, unlike the monks of old, you do not renounce the world, or simply suffer it as a necessary evil, fashion your life with God on weekends, at Sunday Mass or between halves of a football game. You embrace the world. Not the sin it contains, the evil uses to which it is put. You embrace it because it mirrors the God who made it. You embrace it because here is your task: to move your acre of God's world closer to His kingdom. You embrace it because here your likeness to Christ unfolds—or else you will hardly resemble him whose crucified arms were outstretched to embrace not only Jerusalem but the entire world.

III

So far, then, two basic truths. First, the laity have a distinctive mission in the Church: to penetrate the world with the spirit of the gospel. Second, to do that effectively, the laity need a distinctive spirituality: an interior life shaped by and in their encounter with that world. My third point: You Faulkner folk absorb this spirituality in distinctive fashion through the Spiritual Exercises of St. Ignatius.

I have not come to canonize Ignatius or his Exercises; that has already been done by higher authority than mine. Nor do I claim that the Exercises are the only way to shape a Christian spirituality; that would be not only brazen but untrue (there were saints before Ignatius). What I want to assert is that these Exercises, which you rightly esteem so highly, are not a mandate for a me-and-Jesus spirituality; the Exercises force you out of Faulkner; they drive you back to the city; they have to be lived, not here but where you work and play, where you suffer and joy, where you live and die.

Today's Gospel can be deceptive, can mislead you. Jesus sees two disciples of John the Baptist walking behind him. He questions them: "What are you looking for?" They reply: "Teacher, where do you live? Where do you stay?" His response: "Come and see." And so "the disciples went to see where he was staying and they stayed on with him that day" (Jn 1:38–39).[7]

It sounds like a one-day retreat, and in a sense it is: just the two disciples and Jesus. But the Gospel does not end there, and the Exercises do not end here. All the disciples found out where Jesus lived: only rarely in isolation, only briefly in "the hills by himself" (Jn 6:15). They had to "follow" him not only "to a lonely place, and rest a while" (Mk 6:31). They followed him to his townspeople in Nazareth and to his enemies in Jerusalem, to the temple and the city, to a garden called Gethsemane and a hill called Golgotha. And when he left them for good, they followed him not to his Father's heaven but to the ends of the earth.

And so for the Exercises. They are not private meditations that begin and end at the Potomac. Oh yes, you retire a while, and you ask ceaselessly (as *Godspell* puts it) to "know [him] more clearly, love [him] more dearly, follow [him] more nearly." That word "follow" is again the operative word. A few do follow Jesus into a more lonely place: the monastery at Gethsemani, a Carmelite convent in Baltimore. But for most of you, as for Ignatius, the Exercises mold a contemplative in action: knowledge and love that look to service. They help fashion men and women who live the four Weeks of the Exercises in the world, for whom the four Weeks are the framework of life in the city: the proper use of God's creatures, the movement from sin to reconciliation, the standard of Christ and the standard of Satan, a ceaseless dying and rising wherever you are.

A weekend at Faulkner is not primarily an escape from the world; it is a fresh introduction to your world. You should not return to the city ready to endure it; you return graced to transform it. You return with new vision and energy to walk through your city as Jesus walked through Palestine, healing with your touch, comforting the sorrowful and strengthening the feeble, driving out today's devils: injustice, hatred, and war.

Idealistic? Of course! But the Exercises were not intended as pap for tender children, or a narcotic for the neurotic. They fashion Christs . . . or they fashion nothing.

My brothers and sisters in Christ: Twenty years ago last month, Pope Paul VI opened the second session of the Second Vatican Council. In the last section of his discourse, he addressed himself to the fourth aim of the Council: "The Church will build a bridge to the contemporary world." He noted that the conciliar fathers, in response to John XXIII's open-door policy, had unexpectedly determined "to treat no longer of your own limited affairs but rather those of the world, no longer to conduct a dialogue among yourselves but rather to open one with the world." He confessed that he was tempted to be frightened, to be saddened, to defend and condemn; for he was a realist, and his eyes were not blind to the Iron Curtain, to the spread of atheism, to the emptiness, sadness, and despair in the human heart. He was tempted to dwell pessimistically on these aspects of contemporary society, but he refused to: "not now," he said—not while love was filling his heart and the heart of the Church assembled in council. Rather he went on to say:

> Let the world know this: The Church looks at the world with profound understanding, with sincere admiration, and with the sincere intention not of conquering it, but of serving it; not of despising it, but of appreciating it; not of condemning it, but of strengthening and saving it.

The conclusion of Pope Paul's address is a remarkable image of the Church you are called to be, the attitude Vatican II calls you to have:

> From the window of the Council, opened wide on the world, the Church looks toward some categories of persons with particular solicitude: She looks toward the poor, the needy, the afflicted, the hungry, the suffering and sorrowing. . . .
> She looks toward men of culture and learning, scientists, artists; and also for these she has great esteem and a great desire to receive the fruit of their experience, to strengthen their intellec-

tual life, to defend their liberty, to provide a space in which their troubled spirits can expand joyously within the luminous sphere of the divine word and divine grace.

She looks toward the workers, toward the dignity of their person and their labors, toward the legitimacy of their hopes, toward the need, which still afflicts them so greatly, of social improvement and of interior elevation, to the mission which may be recognized as theirs, if it is good, if it is Christian, to create a new world, of free men and brothers. . . .

She looks to the leaders of nations, and in the place of the grave words of warning which the Church must often address to them, she substitutes today a word of encouragement and confidence. Take courage, rulers of nations; today you can give to your peoples many good things necessary for their life: bread, education, work, order, the dignity of free and peaceful citizens, provided only you truly know who man is, and only Christian wisdom can show you this in its true light. Working together in justice and love, you can create peace, that greatest good which is so longed for and which the Church defends and promotes so greatly, and you can make of humanity a single city. . . .

Other vast fields of humanity fall under her gaze: the new generation of youth desirous of living and expressing themselves; the new peoples now coming to self-awareness, independence, and civil organization; the innumerable men and women who feel isolated in a troubled society that has no message for their spirit; and to all without exception she proclaims the good news of salvation and hope. . . ."[8]

On finishing, Paul "tried to read greetings in various languages. His voice was hoarse. He was emotionally drained. He read a few lines in Greek. Then he said with a tired gesture to his master of ceremonies, Archbishop Enrico Dante, *Basta!* 'Enough.' He waved aside the other pages and rose to leave. The ovation was thunderous. . . ."[9]

These exciting words, my friends, were spoken to the world's bishops, but they are meant for the world's Christians. They are meant most urgently for the laity, for you. The world Paul described is your world; you, above all, are the Church's presence therein. The approach Paul took to this world suggests your own spirituality, thoroughly Ignatian: realism in the face of facts, optimism in the light of Christ's irrepressible grace. Go forth, then, men and women of Faulkner, men and women of Christ; go forth, "rooted and grounded in love . . . the love of Christ which surpasses knowledge" (Eph 3:17–19); go forth in love to this world which is your arena, your playground, yes your house of prayer; go forth to change it, to restore it in the image of the God who created it and saw "it was very good" (Gen 1:31). If not you, then who?

St. Bernard's Church
Riverdale, Maryland
October 22, 1983

33

EVEN SO I SEND YOU
Mission Congress '83

♦ Jeremiah 1:4–10
♦ John 20:19–23

A sermon at a "sending" ceremony provokes a powerful challenge: What can the sermonizer say that might "send" you? On the one hand, you are quite a motley set of sendees. How does one "send" you to Malawi or Guatemala or Appalachia, to unemployed miners and illegal migrants, to the starving and the stuffed, to the suburbs and the slums, to those who laugh and those who weep, to black and white and brown? On the other hand, your heads are filled with four days of intellectual fare: pluralism and dialogue, inculturation and regionalization, sexism and racism. . . . Not mine to force-feed the goose for a still richer *pâté*.

What, then, to do? I suggest a slender meditation on a single syllable. I mean that simple, profound word "send." You see, it sums up the role of the Church from the first apostles to the Second Coming. Three scenes to my scenario. First, the word itself in its Christian context: Who is it that is sent? Second, the task of the sent: What is sending all about? Third, the psyche of the sent: What kind of Christian creature ought he or she to be? Not demonstrative argument; only a prayerful musing.

I

First then, the word in its Christian context: Who is it that is sent? "Send" has an exciting history, plays a striking role in the story of salvation. For centuries Yahweh sent servants to His people—patriarchs like Moses and prophets like Jeremiah—to convey His word and His will, to threaten and to cheer, to prepare His people for the Messiah to come. But at the midpoint of history, God "sent" His own Son to tent among us, "that the world might be saved through him" (Jn 3:17). This Savior "sent" a select Twelve "to the lost sheep of the house of Israel," to proclaim "The kingdom of heaven is at hand" (Mt 10:5–6). Their very name "apostles" meant "those who are sent." Risen to new life, Jesus sent his fearful disciples into the world with his own authority: "As the Father has sent me, even so I send you" (Jn 20:21). That missionary mandate took wing on the day of Pentecost, when, in the words of Vatican II, "The Holy Spirit was sent, that He might forever sanctify the Church."[1] Then it was that the apostles, "filled with the Holy Spirit" (Acts 2:4), went forth a fellowship of faith and hope and love, so that "every soul was struck with awe, [so] many were the wonders and signs" they performed (v. 43).

Here, dear friends, a footnote for remembrance. When searching Scripture for signs of sending, don't miss the Magdalene of John's Gospel. In John, Simon Peter and the Beloved Disciple go to the empty tomb and do *not* see Jesus. It is to a woman that Jesus first appears. It is Mary Magdalene who is instructed to tell the disciples that Jesus is ascending to his Father. She is sent by the risen Lord himself, and what she proclaims is the standard apostolic announcement of the Resurrection: "I have seen the Lord" (Jn 20:18). And so Magdalene comes awfully close to meeting the basic Pauline requisites for an apostle: She has seen the risen Lord and she has been sent to proclaim him. Little wonder that in the tradition of the Western Church she is the only woman, besides the mother of Jesus, on whose feast the Creed was recited. And this precisely because she was regarded as an apostle—in a striking expression, she was "the apostle to the apostles."[2]

But not only those who have seen the risen Lord are "sent." The whole Church is sent, is apostle, is mission. And the primary mission ceremony is not a commissioning that wings you to a special spot—Tanzania or Taiwan, Lima or Leyte. On this the Second Vatican Council rings loud and clear:

> Incorporated into Christ's Mystical Body through baptism and strengthened by the power of the Holy Spirit through confirmation, [the laity] are assigned to the apostolate by the Lord himself. They are consecrated into a royal priesthood and a holy people (cf. 1 Pet 2:4–10) in order that they may offer spiritual sacrifices through everything they do, and may witness to Christ

throughout the world. . . . On all Christians, therefore, is laid the special burden of working to make the divine message of salvation known and accepted by all men and women throughout the world.[3]

The sending ceremony, at its most radical, is baptism; and so it is that every man or woman baptized into Christ is sent, is an apostle, is on mission to proclaim the risen Lord. I thrill to the insight of Cardinal Suenens: The greatest day in the life of a pope is not his coronation but his baptism, the day of his mission "to live the Christian life in obedience to the gospel."[4]

II

This leads to the second scene in my scenario, the task of the sent: What is sending all about? I've already stated it in broad terms: We are sent to proclaim the risen Lord. "Christ has died; Christ is risen; Christ will come again." True enough, but awfully skimpy, dangerously individualistic. How do I preach the risen Lord in the context of community, the People of God, the Church of Christ? This is not a cram course in ecclesiology, and so I shall not torment you with mission theory, heap hypothesis upon hypothesis. Let me merely mold your musing in one direction—a pregnant expression from Vatican II: The risen Christ established his Church as "the universal sacrament of salvation."[5]

I am not concerned to prove that the Church of Christ is the only way to salvation. What the Council says succinctly is that the risen Christ wanted and wants his community everywhere—whether three or three million—to be a sign, a special kind of sign. Not simply a sign that points elsewhere: "180 miles to New York"; "Christ that-a-way." The Church as sacrament not only *tells* you where you can find God's saving love in Christ; the Church embodies that love, incorporates it, incarnates it, lets you sense it, touch it.

Not that the Church is ever completely Church. There will always be acres of God's planting untilled by a Christian community. And even where the Church has taken root, the sign is rarely all it should be. Much too weakly does it signal to those outside that God loves the world and Christ has died for it. After all, it is not only unbelievers who keep peasants in grinding poverty or blast babies to bits with their bombs.

Hence the never-ending need for mission, for sending. In

every age, at each moment, the Church must struggle to make the redemptive love of Christ a tangible reality, reveal that love in the flesh and bones of Christians. Wherever you are sent—only through the Harbor Tunnel or across the vast Pacific, over the Bay Bridge or over the Andes—you go to fashion or refashion a people whose faith, hope, and love will be a living sign, an effective sign, that God is there, that the bread you break is more than manna, is food for the life of the world.

The Church can be such a sign only if Christians are such signs. For the Church is not a Platonic idea suspended in space; the Church is living people. The Church, as early Christians loved to say, is "the 'we' of Christians." We are, in the first instance, not an institution but a communion, an interpersonal community united to the Father and to one another through Christ in the Spirit. But are we? Are we really united to one another? Four decades of priestly experience across this country have raised in me a frightening question: Are Catholic differences destroying our catholic love? From color to contraception to Communion in the hand, from ERA to the I.R.A., from nuclear weapons to food stamps, we cannot disagree without disliking, cannot argue without accusing, bring our gifts to the same altar without really being reconciled.

Ironic, isn't it? The task of this community is to reach out, through the Spirit of love that is its inner form, so as to draw all men and women into the communion of love, so that they too will respond in faith and love to the love whereby the Father loves His own People. The People are essentially a missionary people, with a catholic mission of love. And yet we find it so hard to hold out our hearts to our own household. Little wonder that the unbeliever seeking a sign turns away sadly: "Look how these Christians hate one another!"

III

This suggests quite naturally the third scene in my scenario, the psyche of the sent: What kind of Christian creature ought he or she to be? Since being sent is synonymous with being a Christian, the psyche of the sent should obviously be graced with at least 26 qualities: the three theological virtues, the four cardinal virtues, the seven gifts of the Holy Spirit, and the 12 fruits of the Spirit! To touch each of the 26 to your missionary existence would not only weary you; it might keep you from ever getting where you are sent. Let me rather pluck from the pack three graces *I* have found more and more compelling for Christian mission.

First, a faith-full trust. I commend to you the Scripture segment you have heard from Jeremiah (1:4–10), the prelude to his prophesying. It is the year 627 B.C. The word of the Lord comes to this young man, perhaps in his early twenties. The Lord who knew him so intimately before He shaped him in the womb has appointed him "a prophet to the nations." Keenly conscious of his inexperience, his youthful incompetence, Jeremiah protests: "Ah, Lord God! Look, I don't know how to speak; I am much too young for this sort of sending." The Lord stops him right there: "Don't tell me you're too young; for to all to whom I send you you shall go, and whatever I command you you shall speak. Don't be afraid of them, for I am with you to deliver you." And the Lord stretches forth His hand, touches the mouth of Jeremiah: "Behold, I have put my words in your mouth."

Jeremiah reminds us that, from our first sending to our very last, ultimately the one who sends is God; that, if I am open to the whispering of His Spirit, it is the word of God I speak; that, for all the risk in mission—Paul's danger from rivers and robbers, from the city and the wilderness, from false brethren and inner anxiety (cf. 2 Cor 11:26–28)—I need not be afraid, because He is with me.

Second, understanding. Not understanding in the sense of sheer knowledge or intelligence, the ability to comprehend and judge, the power of perception, the capacity to form opinions. With that sort of understanding most of us are jampacked from ear to ear. I am speaking of that understanding which involves a special kind of personal relationship, marked by an innerness that comes through to another as empathy. I mean what the *American Heritage Dictionary* defines as an "understanding so intimate that the feelings, thoughts and motives of one are readily comprehended by another."

Such is the understanding Jesus possessed pre-eminently. "Who touched me?" he calls to the crowd, to the amazement and amusement of his disciples (Mk 5:30–31). Such is the understanding we must recapture if the precious people to whom we are sent are to touch not an impersonal institution but a risen Christ. We do this in our day when we approach with reverence and sensitivity a culture alien to us, aware that in His own strange ways God is already there. That same sensitivity and reverence we must touch to each child of God from Appalachia to Zimbabwe, aware that each, from the starving child to the hostile chieftain, has been fashioned in the image of God's own Son.

That sort of understanding, my friends, can only *begin* with your native charm, your irresistible personality, even your sheerly human caring. In its depths, it is a gift of the Spirit. "The Spirit of the Lord shall rest upon him," Isaiah foretells of the messianic king, "the spirit of wisdom and understanding . . ." (Isa 11:2).

Third, joy. This "fruit of the Spirit" (Gal 5:22) is at the core of Mary's Magnificat: "My spirit rejoices in God my Savior" (Lk 1:47). Understandably so, for joy is at the heart of our Gospels.[6] There joy is linked with *life*, especially new life. The birth of Jesus is "good news of a great joy" (Lk 2:10). The father of the prodigal calls for joy because "this my son was dead, and is alive again" (Lk 15:24). There joy is linked with *discovery:* the man who discovers the word (Mt 13:20), the shepherd who discovers his stray sheep (Mt 18:13), the disciples who discover demons subject to them (Lk 10:17), little Zacchaeus when he discovers Jesus (Lk 19:6), Jesus himself rejoicing because the Father has "discovered" Himself not to the wise but to little ones (Lk 10:21). There joy is linked with *repentance:* "more joy in heaven over one sinner who repents than over 99 righteous who need no repentance" (Lk 15:7). There joy is linked with *suffering*. The disciples are to rejoice when slandered and persecuted (Mt 5:11–12). When reviled for Jesus' sake, they are to "leap for joy" (Lk 6:23)—as indeed they do when they leave the council "rejoicing that they [are] counted worthy to suffer dishonor for the name" (Acts 5:41). There joy is linked with *Jesus,* the fulness of joy. Only if the disciples abide in Jesus' love will their "joy be full" (Jn 15:11). It is his joy they are to have "fulfilled in themselves" (Jn 17:13). When they see him again, it will bring a joy no man or woman can take from them (Jn 16:22). And so it proves after his rising from the dead—for the disciples and for Magdalene (Jn 20:20; Mt 28:8). Why, in his risen presence the disciples even "disbelieve for joy" (Lk 24:41).

From a half century of people-watching, I am persuaded that the most effective sign we can raise to unbelievers is our joy in believing. The German philosopher Nietzsche was so correct in his caustic critique of Christians: We do not look redeemed. There is indeed a discouraging amount of death in our world; and, like God, we take no delight in death. But the message of our sending is life, the breath-taking promise of Christ the night before he died: "I live, and you shall live" (Jn 14:19). If *we*, the sent, show no joy in being alive with the life of the risen Christ, why should anyone believe us when we proclaim without passion "Christ is risen"?

My sisters and brothers on mission: A Jesuit for fifty-two years, I do not dare or care to disparage your patron, St. Francis Xavier. But may I recommend as supplementary model a friend of Jesus named Lazarus? Not the Lazarus of whom his sister Martha said: "Lord, by this time there will be an odor, for he has been dead four days" (Jn 11:39). Rather the Lazarus summoned by the Son of God from the grave. The Lazarus of Eugene O'Neill's play *Lazarus Laughed:* the lover of Christ who has tasted death and sees it for what it is; a man whose one invitation to the living is his constant refrain:

> Laugh with me!
> Death is dead!
> Fear is no more!
> There is only life!
> There is only laughter!

And O'Neill tells us: Lazarus "begins to laugh, softly at first," then full-throated—"a laugh so full of a complete acceptance of life, a profound assertion of joy in living, so devoid of all fear, that it is infectious with love," so infectious that, despite themselves, his listeners are caught by it and carried away.[7]

For your sake, my friends, and for the sake of those to whom you are sent, I make bold to issue one only mandate, the charge of St. Paul to the Christians of Philippi: "Rejoice in the Lord always! Again I will say, Rejoice!" (Phil 4:4).

Convention Center
Baltimore, Maryland
March 21, 1983

34

THAT THE WORLD MAY KNOW. . . .
Reformation Sunday 1983

◆ John 17:20–23

This morning, dear Christians, your Christianness may be put to the test. One sentence from the lips of Jesus is a striking symbol of Luther Place Memorial Church: "I was a stranger and you welcomed me" (Mt 25:35). You welcome the homeless and the hungry, the commuter and the wanderer, the sick who need healing and the lonely who seek communion. But at this moment you are asked to welcome a strange sort of stranger. On Reformation Sunday, when you celebrate 95 theses that changed the face of Christendom, you are asked to welcome a Roman Catholic, a priest, a Jesuit, a theologian—all in one! The images these words conjure up are not part of your "love boat"[1]: the Catholic saving himself by works; the priest preaching indulgences for a price; the Jesuit leading the Counter Reformation; the theologian arguing with Luther as if the Reform were an academic debate, not a matter of life or death.

We have been strangers far too long: 466 years tomorrow. Ever since good Pope John XXIII, the situation has indeed changed for the better. We are talking to one another like human beings; we are seeking ways to break down barriers. And still many of us are strangers. Our change and our estrangement are symbolized here this morning. Change: I am preaching to you in your place of worship. Estrangement: I am preaching *after* your service, not during it. So Rome wishes it, and many a Lutheran wishes it so. We have traveled a fair piece, but a long road lies ahead. We are not yet as perfectly one as our common Lord prayed his disciples would be. In the title of a fairly good film, we are, at best, "lovers and strangers."

In these circumstances, what message can I bring to you that might justify delaying your Sunday brunch? What can I say, after four centuries and a half, that might shorten the distance between us? Let me speak to you as one who was slow to see our separation as unchristian, one who has labored long with your Lutheran theologians to lessen our isolation, one who harbors high hopes for the way you have chosen to destroy distance. Let me speak, very personally, about oneness, about becoming one. Three stages: (1) the oneness of the Church; (2) the oneness of Christians; (3) the oneness of our world.

I

First, the oneness of the Church. I mean the struggle for the unity of the churches—Anglican and Roman Catholic, Protestant and Orthodox—the quest for a single Church of Christ. This search takes place principally on two levels: those who have authority in the churches and those who carry on dialogue for the churches. For example, in 1965 the Patriarch of Constantinople, Athenagoras I, and the Bishop of Rome, Paul VI, simultaneously canceled, removed, blotted out the anathemas their predecessors had pronounced back in 1054. Only one month ago, the U.S. Lutheran–Roman Catholic dialogue released a 24,000-word document stating that these theologians had reached a "fundamental consensus on the gospel."[1] These are but examples—two from among thousands of activities across the earth that are whittling away our ingrained estrangement.

Now there are untold Christians who have no use for that sort of thing. They come in two stripes. For some, such whittling is a waste of precious time. The world is aflame, and Rome and Geneva are fiddling! This abstract stuff just keeps us from where the action actually is. Away with this intellectual gamesmanship, this theological Atari! On with the real work of the world, the blood and guts of human hostility! You'll still be mouthing words, making fine distinctions, when the Bomb obliterates your hideout.

For others, Catholics and Protestants, this is betrayal of what Rome or the Reformation stood for. Between Protestant and Catholic there is no common ground. Nothing will do save unconditional surrender. Otherwise you end up with compromise: Roman Catholics will soon have no saint save Luther, and Protestants will have to kiss the toe of the Beast in Rome.

Now a sermon is not a debate. Let me simply respond that both reactions are off target. Here three realities seem undeniable. First, doctrine does divide us, has divided us close to five centuries. Second, even though doctrine will never save us (only a living faith saves), doctrine is not unimportant. It is simply our stumbling effort to understand what the Son of God took flesh to tell us. If the Bomb interrupts our probing, it's not a bad way to go: getting to know more intimately the Jesus we love so passionately, the Christ we confess as Lord and Savior. No compromise in our dialogues, I assure you; only a struggle to uproot our ancient prejudices, so that together we may see more clearly, together proclaim "This is the Word of the Lord." Third, to cease striving for one Church of Christ would be un-Christlike. I admit we do not yet know what sort of oneness the Lord is asking of us, the precise form our unity should take. But this much we do know: Our present disunity cannot be God's will for us; it is a scandal, to angels in heaven and to men and women on earth.

So, dear friends, be patient with us eggheads as we wrestle with words, with ideas, with history. We are not playing games; we too are searching the Scriptures, as scholars indeed but also as men and women of faith. May God give us eyes to see what "one Church" means . . . to Him.

II

Second, the oneness of Christians. I said above that our present disunity is a scandal. But not only because we cannot agree on where to locate the Church Christ founded. The greater scandal is the hostility and hatred, the indifference and prejudice, that have characterized Christian living since 1517. I look at our distant past, and I am appalled. Your ancestors and mine waged war, killed one another, in the name of Christ. The Thirty Years' War that afflicted the Holy Roman Empire and most western European states from 1618 to 1648 "left behind it a trail of destruction and death. Bohemia, Saxony, Thuringia, and Württemberg were devastated. Cities, towns, and villages were burned and plundered; some of them disappeared. The Empire was depopulated; the German states were fragmented and divided. Religious life was demoralized and political institutions badly weakened."[2] Our own "land of the free" has been pockmarked, from colonial times, by religious repression—legal and violent, economic and social, ice-cold and fanatical.

Nor is this ancient history. In the year of our Lord 1983, Christians are slaughtering Christians in the north of Ireland; Christians and Moslems are at one another's throats in Lebanon; the anti-Catholic comics that flood the market and rape the minds of little children make me weep; and all too many of us have been reared on a religious diet of suspicion and mistrust, of ignorance and misrepresentation, of horror stories literally "out of this world."

Now for the good news. We who have lived on tight little islands or behind barricades for 450 years have begun to talk. We who avoided one another like the Asian flu have looked into one another's eyes and discovered real people, ordinary men and women very much like ourselves. We who grew up reading only our own side of the Christian story now feast on books authored by "the enemy." Catholics have uncovered a new Luther, wonderfully warm, refreshingly fearful of his own frailty, convincingly Christian in his utter reliance on God's grace; Protestants have glimpsed in Pope John XXIII how the specter of papal authority can fade before a man of God who rules with love.

More remarkable still, ecumenically, is your own Luther Place experience. I wonder if you realize how powerful a force you are for the oneness of Christians. I mean, concretely, your close bonding with your Roman Catholic brothers and sisters from Holy Trinity Church in Georgetown. I mean your ministries together for justice' sake. I mean Bread for the City, ministering the essentials of life, mental, physical, and spiritual; Zacchaeus Medical Clinic, offering holistic health care without cost; Deborah's Place, for homeless women to call home; Sarah House, for fragmented hearts and minds; Abraham House, for refugees from across the ocean, and Wallenberg House, for refugees from the economic plight of our own city, this Capital in contradiction.

All this, and so much more, is a striking contribution to the oneness of Christians. Here Lutherans and Romans become one not because their minds meet but because their hands clasp; because, despite differences in doctrine, they love one another somewhat as the Lord Jesus loves them. Here is Christian unity on the grass-roots level, ecumenism in the streets. And believe me, my friends, unless you and I are one at this level, all the doctrinal consensus across the world will be meaningless for salvation.

III

So much for the oneness of the Church, so much for the oneness of Christians. Important as these are in themselves, however, both the oneness of the Church and the oneness of Christians serve me today as prelude—overture to a oneness even more desirable, a oneness more difficult still. I mean the oneness of the world.

You see, you have gathered here for worship at a critical moment for human unity. The deadly enemies are especially three: war, hatred, injustice. This year the governments of the world are spending close to 600 billion dollars on weapons to deter and to kill. Official estimates calmly conjecture that in a nuclear exchange between the superpowers, U.S. fatalities alone would range from a low of 20 million to a high of 165 million. Terrorists have shot president and pope, have massacred over 200 Marines in Beirut, blast even babies to bits with their bombs. While we rage at such barbarians, we civilized folk across the earth kill more little innocents in a single year than all who died in two world wars—because we are not quite sure they are human, have rights. Each night one out of every four persons on this planet goes to sleep hungry; each day 50,000 of the hungry die. Not to mention, in our own dear country, the frightening hostility between black and white, between man and woman, between the middle class and the poor—the panic in our streets.

But what has all this—war, hatred, injustice—what has the world's disunity to do with our Christian unity, our Christian disunity? Our Lord answered that question in his high-priestly prayer to the Father the night before he died: "I do not pray for these only [for the disciples at the Supper], but also for those who believe in me through their word, that they may all be one; even as you, Father, are in me and I in you, that they also may be [one] in us, *so that the world may believe that you have sent me*. The glory which you have given me I have given to them, that they may be one even as we are one, I in them and you in me, that they may become perfectly one, *so that the world may know that you have sent me and have loved them even as you have loved me*" (Jn 17:20–23).

From the prayer of Christ two ideas emerge. First, we who believe are to be one. Not loosely one, but "perfectly one"—so perfect a oneness that it images the oneness that obtains between God the Father and His only Son. Second, the reason why the churches, why Christians, can never cease seeking for unity is not something selfish: United we stand, divided we fall. It is not (what may well be true) that only a tightly-knit Christianity can withstand today's many-layered assaults on our faith. The reason lies deeper: Christian oneness is a witness. To the extent that those who confess Christ are united in understanding and linked in love, the world outside will recognize two crucial Christian mysteries: Christ was sent by God, and we are loved by God.

The tragedy is, we have not given the world that witness—not convincingly. The proof? Quite simple: Most of the world simply does not see Christ in us. And why should it? How dare we urge Lebanese Moslems to come to terms with Lebanese Christians, Shiites with Sunnites, when Protestants and Catholics are bloodying Belfast in deathless bitterness? How dare we demand that South African whites treat blacks as equals, when for decades we segregated blacks from whites in our very worshiping? How dare we ask Jews to take a second look at Jesus, when the Holocaust that gassed six million Jews took place in a Christian country? How dare we send missionaries to Latin America, when what the natives witness is a sectarian struggle for their souls? How dare we exhort the nations to be reconciled, to extend the hand of fellowship, when for centuries we have refused to call one another brothers and sisters? Were I part of that world, I am afraid I would look at Protestants and Catholics and cry "A plague on both your houses!"

My friends, time may very well be running out on us. I cannot remember ever feeling so frightened for our world as I do now. I am afraid that with each passing day the children of God are growing further and further apart. Words have lost their power to persuade; only naked force has any effect. Iran and Iraq, Israel and Lebanon, Libya and Chad, Northern Ireland, Afghanistan, and now Grenada—and over all this the ceaseless menace of the earth's last Bomb. It's as if the world were charged with hellish hate.

What alone can give us hope is that, ever since Bethlehem and Calvary, the world is charged with Christ. But not a Christ who magically pulls peace out of a top hat. Rather a Christ who works his miracles of love through other Christs who love as he did, as he does. Through you and me. But not you and I in splendid isolation, each of us doing our own "thing" as if the other did not exist. You and I working together in love, in a co-operation which, as the Second Vatican Council put it, "vividly expresses that bond which already unites [all Christians] and . . . sets in clearer relief the features of Christ the Servant."[3] Co-operation not for our self-satisfaction but in service of those outside this structure who experience only the crucifixion of Christ, little or nothing of his resurrection.

My sisters and brothers in Christ: Eleven days from now, you will celebrate the 500th anniversary of Martin Luther's birth. Have you wondered what sort of celebration Luther would enjoy most at this perilous moment for humankind? Oh, I'm sure he will be delighted as you extol his theology, as computers spew forth volume after volume on the letter and the spirit, on the law and the gospel, on the kingdom of Christ and the kingdom of the world, on the bondage of the will and the freedom of a Christian. But with a certain amount of Catholic chutzpa, I submit that the Luther of 1983 will find his deepest satisfaction if you shout from the housetops and live in the streets a thesis of his that commands the assent of every Christian: The freedom a Christian has through faith is freedom to render the service of love. "Lo, that is how love and joy in God flow out of faith, and how love gives rise to a free, eager, and glad life of serving one's neighbor without reward."[4]

Here, my friends, here is freedom for the Christian: the freedom to serve. And here, my friends, here is hope for humankind.

Luther Place Memorial Church
Washington, D.C.
October 30, 1983

NOTES

Prologue

1. Constitution on the Sacred Liturgy, no. 35 (tr. *The Documents of Vatican II*, ed. Walter M. Abbott [New York: America, c1966] 149–50).
2. Dogmatic Constitution on Divine Revelation, no. 25 (*Documents* 127).
3. Gerard Manley Hopkins, "God's Grandeur," in W. H. Gardner and N. H. MacKenzie, eds., *The Poems of Gerard Manley Hopkins* (4th ed.; New York: Oxford University, 1970) 66.
4. In this connection see Raymond E. Brown, S.S., " 'And the Lord Said'? Biblical Reflections on Scripture as the Word of God," *Theological Studies* 42 (1981) 3–19.
5. See my article "Fathers of the Church," *New Catholic Encyclopedia* 5 (1967) 853–55.
6. Hans von Campenhausen, *The Fathers of the Greek Church* (New York: Pantheon, c1959) 10.
7. *Acta apostolicae sedis* 35 (1943) 312.
8. Pierre Benoit, in A. Robert and A. Tricot, *Initiation biblique* (3rd ed.; Paris: Desclée, 1954) 43 (translation mine).
9. Here I am much indebted to F. van der Meer, *Augustine the Bishop* (New York: Sheed and Ward, c1961) 412–52 ("The Servant of the Word").
10. Ibid. 414.
11. Ibid. 419–20.
12. *Sermon 96*, no. 4.
13. *Treatises on the Gospel of John* 7, 6.
14. Van der Meer, *Augustine the Bishop* 440–41.
15. Jaroslav Pelikan, ed., *The Preaching of Augustine: "Our Lord's Sermon on the Mount"* (Philadelphia: Fortress, c1973) xxi.
16. Van der Meer, *Augustine the Bishop* 443.

17. See Johannes Quasten, *Patrology* 3: *The Golden Age of Greek Patristic Literature from the Council of Nicaea to the Council of Chalcedon* (Westminster, Md.: Newman, c1960) 433–51.
18. Philadelphia: Fortress, c1966.
19. Ibid. 12–13.
20. Cf. Jared Wicks, S.J., *Man Yearning for Grace: Luther's Early Spiritual Teaching* (Washington, D.C.: Corpus, c1968).
21. I have used the translation in Gerhard Ebeling, *Luther: An Introduction to His Thought,* tr. R. A. Wilson (Philadelphia: Fortress, c1970) 45–46.
22. Jared Wicks, S.J., "Justification and Faith in Luther's Theology," *Theological Studies* 44 (1983) 15–16.
23. For a development of some of these nourishments, see, e.g., Paul-Marie of the Cross, O.C.D., *Spirituality of the Old Testament* (3 vols.; St. Louis: Herder, c1961–63).
24. Cf. Carroll Stuhlmueller, C.P., *Thirsting for the Lord: Essays in Biblical Spirituality* (Garden City, N.Y.: Image Books, 1979) 62–70.
25. Ibid. 69.

Homily 1

1. See the homily "Prepare the Way of the Lord" in my *Sir, We Would Like To See Jesus: Homilies from a Hilltop* (New York: Paulist, c1982) 23–28.
2. See Homily 2 in this volume, "Advent with Mary." Note, however, the twofold waiting I develop there: Mary, as mother, waiting for Jesus' first coming and, as perfect disciple, waiting for his second coming.
3. For those unfamiliar with campus rhetoric, Hoyas are Georgetown University students, Terrapins swear fealty to the University of Maryland.
4. Sister Mary Ignatius, "Discovery," *Messenger of the Sacred Heart* 77, no. 2 (February 1942) 58.

Homily 2

1. I have developed this theme in a homily for the second Sunday of Advent (B), "Prepare the Way of the Lord," which can be found in my book of homilies *Sir, We Would Like To See Jesus* (New York: Paulist, c1982) 23–28. I realize that readings from Isaiah do not dominate the liturgy in the C cycle, but I think my point is still basically valid. Note, too, how Isaiah dominates the office of readings in the Advent breviary.
2. See the informative, inspiring article of Patrick J. Bearsley, S.M., "Mary

the Perfect Disciple: A Paradigm for Mariology," *Theological Studies* 41 (1980) 461–504, at 478.

3. See the useful article by Raymond E. Brown, "Mary in the New Testament and in Catholic Life," *America* 146, no. 19 (May 15, 1982) 374–79.

4. Ibid. 377.

Homily 3

1. See the article "Repentance" by John L. McKenzie, S.J., in his *Dictionary of the Bible* (New York: Macmillan, c1965) 728–30.

2. See the liturgies of repentance mentioned or quoted in Neh 9; Isa 63:7—64:12; Bar 1:15—3:8; Dan 9:3–19; Hos 6:1–3; 7:14; 14:2–3; Joel 2:15–17; Jon 3:7–9.

3. The reference is to the liturgical dance performed by Betsey Beckman and William Noonan interpreting the powerful section in John Shea's *Stories of Faith* (Chicago: Thomas More, 1980) 213–18, on Death, Sin, and Fate and the risen Christ's victory over each.

4. Shea, *Stories of Faith* 214.

5. Ibid. 217.

6. Ibid.

7. Ibid. 215.

8. The reference is to an immensely popular TV serial.

9. Another TV serial.

10. Shea, *Stories of Faith* 216.

Homily 4

1. For the basic information on which this first point is based, I am indebted to Raymond E. Brown, S.S., *The Gospel According to John (i-xii)* (Anchor Bible 29; Garden City, N.Y.: Doubleday, 1966) 465–80.

2. A reference to a well-publicized contemporary event: Pope John Paul II, provoked by certain trends he discerned in the Society of Jesus, appointed his own delegate, Paolo Dezza, S.J., to run the Order until the next general congregation would be convoked.

3. See Charles Augrain, P.S.S., and Jacques Guillet, S.J., "Obedience," in X. Léon-Dufour, *Dictionary of Biblical Theology* (2nd ed.; New York: Seabury, 1973) 397–98.

4. For this understanding of Jeremiah's covenant, see Guy P. Couturier, C.S.C., "Jeremiah," *Jerome Biblical Commentary* (Englewood Cliffs, N.J.: Prentice-Hall, c1968) 19:89.

Homily 5

1. Scripture scholars dispute whether the Letter to the Philippians stems from Paul's house arrest in Rome (61–63) or from his imprisonment in Ephesus ca. 56–57. I do not believe that the dispute affects what I say in this paragraph.
2. A reference to a needlessly savage one-act play by Christopher Durang, *Sister Mary Ignatius Explains It All for You.*

Homily 6

1. I have developed the ideas that follow somewhat more extensively in my homily "Let Go of Yesterday," *Tell the Next Generation: Homilies and Near Homilies* (New York: Paulist, 1980) 52–57.

Homily 7

1. Nestorius, *Liber Heraclidis* 2, 1; my translation is based on the French version by F. Nau *et al., Le Livre d'Héraclide de Damas* (Paris, 1910) 171.
2. Gerard Manley Hopkins, "As kingfishers catch fire . . . ," Poem 57 in W. H. Gardner and N. H. MacKenzie, eds., *The Poems of Gerard Manley Hopkins* (4th ed.; London: Oxford University, 1970) 90.
3. *Time* 121, no. 11 (March 14, 1983) 36.

Homily 8

1. St. Thomas Aquinas, *Adoro te supplex, latens deitas,* translated by Gerard Manley Hopkins, *The Poems of Gerard Manley Hopkins,* ed. W. H. Gardner and N. H. MacKenzie (4th ed.; London: Oxford University, 1970) 211.
2. In this final section, I am borrowing freely from David M. Stanley, S.J., *A Modern Scriptural Approach to the Spiritual Exercises* (Chicago: Institute of Jesuit Sources/Loyola University, 1967) 213–18, while shifting the emphasis from the ordained priest to the general priesthood of all the faithful.

Homily 9

1. In essence, this first point reproduces my sermon "The Last Supper: A Challenge to Love," published in my *All Lost in Wonder: Sermons on The-*

ology and Life (Westminster, Md.: Newman, 1960) 87–91. For the basic insight and outline of that sermon, and in some of its details, I was indebted to a splendid meditation in G. Longhaye, S.J., *Retraite annuelle de huit jours d'après les Exercises de saint Ignace* (4th ed.; Paris-Tournai, Casterman, 1932) 397–404.

2. St. Thomas Aquinas, *Adoro te,* in the translation of Gerard Manley Hopkins, "S. Thomae Aquinatis Rhythmus ad SS. Sacramentum 'Adoro te supplex, latens deitas,' " in W. H. Gardner and N. H. MacKenzie, eds., *The Poems of Gerard Manley Hopkins* (4th ed.; London: Oxford University, 1970) 211.

Homily 10

1. For the problem of identifying "the disciples" (Jn 20:19–20), see Raymond E. Brown, S.S., *The Gospel according to John (xiii-xxi)* (Anchor Bible 29A; Garden City, N.Y.: Doubleday, 1970) 1033 ff. "The question is of more than incidental interest, for it colors the discussion of those to whom the power to forgive sins (vs. 23) has been granted. There can be little doubt that what came to the evangelist from his pre-Gospel source was the story of an appearance to *the Eleven* (the Twelve minus Judas). . . . Thus, our real problem here concerns the intention of the evangelist. While the pre-Gospel narrative referred to the Eleven, does the evangelist now intend these disciples to represent a wider audience who would also be recipients of the mission in vs. 21, of the Spirit in 22, and of the power to forgive sins in 23?" (1033–34).

2. I was forcefully struck on reading this in David M. Stanley, S.J., *The Call to Discipleship: The Spiritual Exercises with the Gospel of St Mark* (Osterley, Middlesex, Eng.: The Way, c1982) 177.

3. On this see Brown (n. 1 above) 1046.

4. It is not clear whether this sentence is to be taken as a question or an affirmation. Many minuscule manuscripts and many modern scholars take it as a question; Brown "hesitatingly" accepts it as an affirmation ("You have believed because you have seen me") "since this is the more difficult reading" (1027).

5. Quoted in *Time,* Dec. 29, 1975, 48.

6. Ibid. 56.

7. *Time,* Dec. 15, 1980, 74.

Homily 11

1. I have been unable to recapture the author of this piece of verse, which I discovered almost four decades ago. Gratitude and apologies to my unknown creditor.

2. See C. H. Dodd, *The Johannine Epistles* (New York: Harper, c1946) 31.
3. So John L. McKenzie, S.J., in the article "Know, knowledge" in his *Dictionary of the Bible* (New York: Macmillan, c1965) 485–88, at 485. This is not to restrict the heart to emotions, for the Bible uses heart where in English we would use mind or will. The point is, what we are dealing with in this paragraph is something other than clear, cold intellect.
4. Here I am indebted to Roger Leys, *L'Image de Dieu chez Grégoire de Nysse* (Paris: Desclée de Brouwer, 1951) 82.
5. Vatican II, Constitution on the Sacred Liturgy, no. 7.
6. To avoid pitfalls on Scripture as "the word of God," the preacher might read Raymond E. Brown, S.S., " 'And the Lord Said'? Biblical Reflections on Scripture as the Word of God," *Theological Studies* 40 (1981) 3–9.
7. St. Thomas Aquinas, *Adoro te supplex, latens deitas,* translated by Gerard Manley Hopkins, *The Poems of Gerard Manley Hopkins,* ed. W. H. Gardner and N. H. MacKenzie (4th ed.; London: Oxford University, 1970) 211.
8. Thomas M. King, "The Teilhard Centennial," *America* 146, no. 16 (April 24, 1982) 318–19, at 319.

Homily 12

1. There are, of course, significant differences in Jesus' glorified body; see my Homily 10, "My Lord and My God?", in this volume.
2. For a detailed treatment of the four ruptures created by Sin, see my booklet *Towards Reconciliation* (Washington, D.C.: United States Catholic Conference, c1974).
3. Augustine, *Sermon 215,* no. 4 (PL 38, 1074).
4. I have taken the text, authored by Sydney Carter, from *Worship II: A Hymnal for Roman Catholic Parishes* (Chicago: G.I.A., c1975) hymn 128.

Homily 14

1. For much of the information in this first point, I am indebted to the commentary of Raymond E. Brown, S.S., *The Gospel according to John (i-xii)* (Anchor Bible 29; Garden City, N.Y.: Doubleday, 1966) 73–80, 510–12.
2. For this interpretation see the discussion in Raymond E. Brown, S.S., *The Gospel according to John (xiii-xxi)* (Anchor Bible 29A; Garden City, N.Y.: Doubleday, 1970) 1106–8, 1117–22.
3. Dietrich Bonhoeffer, *Gesammelte Schriften* 1 (ed. Eberhard Bethge; Munich: Kaiser, 1958) 320.

4. Dietrich Bonhoeffer, *Ethics* (ed. Eberhard Bethge; New York: Macmillan, 1962) 49.
5. Dietrich Bonhoeffer, *Letters and Papers from Prison* (enlarged ed. by Eberhard Bethge; London: SCM, 1971) 370.
6. Ibid. 35.
7. Ibid. 370.
8. See Dietrich Bonhoeffer, *The Cost of Discipleship* (2nd ed.; New York: Macmillan, 1963).
9. Ibid. 35–37.
10. Ibid. 271.
11. A reference to a popular TV-show title.
12. Two more references to TV programs.
13. See Thomas Merton, *Conjectures of a Guilty Bystander* (Garden City, N.Y.: Doubleday Image Books, 1956) 261.

Homily 15

1. Augustine, *First Catechetical Instruction* 1, 4, 8 (tr. J. P. Christopher, ACW 2, 23).

Homily 16

1. I suggest that it will be of advantage, not only to the preacher but to the faithful at large, to study the meaning of Lk 7:47: "Her sins, which are many, are forgiven, for she loved much." More probably, the sinful woman's love is not the condition but the consequence of her forgiveness. Already forgiven by God before she arrives, she now pours out signs of love and gratitude. Cf. Joseph A. Fitzmyer, S.J., *The Gospel according to Luke (I-IX)* (Anchor Bible 28; Garden City, N.Y.: Doubleday, 1981) 686–87, 692. See ibid. 683–94 for helpful information and observations on the whole incident.
2. See "Forgive Us As We Forgive," in my *Sir, We Would Like To See Jesus: Homilies from a Hilltop* (New York: Paulist, c1982) 46–51.
3. From "Amazing Grace!" by John Newton (1725–1807), in *Worship II: A Hymnal for Roman Catholic Parishes* (Chicago: G.I.A., c1975) 22.
4. I have used the text in Flannery O'Connor, *The Complete Stories* (New York: Farrar, Straus and Giroux, 1971) 488–509. I should acknowledge my debt to David Eggenschwiler's *The Christian Humanism of Flannery O'Connor* (Detroit: Wayne State University, 1972) 41–46, for a revealing analysis of the story.
5. "Revelation" 491.
6. Ibid. 499.
7. Ibid. 500.

8. Ibid. 506–7.
9. This paragraph borrows slavishly, at times verbatim, from Eggen-schwiler, n. 4 above.
10. "Revelation" 508.
11. Ibid. 509.

Homily 17

1. NC news release, in *Catholic Standard* (Washington, D.C.) 22, no. 33 (Aug. 19, 1982) 2.
2. I have reproduced this paragraph from a homily on the same subject in my *Sir, We Would Like To See Jesus: Homilies from a Hilltop* (New York: Paulist, c1982) 116. In that homily, however, I took a different tack, moving to the Suffering Servant theme and stressing obedience, humiliation, and death.
3. Cf. Thomas Merton, *No Man Is an Island* (New York: Harcourt Brace Jovanovich, 1978) 87.
4. Karl Rahner, *Mary Mother of the Lord: Theological Meditations* (New York: Herder and Herder, 1963) 98.
5. A reference to the delightful motion picture *Arthur*.

Homily 18

1. For helpful commentary on this story, see T. W. Manson, *The Sayings of Jesus As Recorded in the Gospels according to St. Matthew and St. Luke* (London: SCM, 1949) 298–301.
2. Quoted by Manson, ibid. 299, from *Besa* 32[b].
3. I have treated this puzzle, the radical Jesus and the moderate Jesus, at greater length in Homily 19 below, "Easier for a Camel."

Homily 19

1. I have profited from several New Testament commentators: Vincent Taylor, *The Gospel according to St. Mark* (London: Macmillan, 1957) 424–35; Rudolf Schnackenburg, *The Moral Teaching of the New Testament* (New York: Herder and Herder, 1965) 50, 121–32; Josef Schmid, *The Gospel according to Mark* (Regensburg New Testament; Staten Island, N.Y.: Alba [1968]) 189–97; Joseph A. Fitzmyer, S.J., *The Gospel according to Luke (I–IX)* (Anchor Bible 28; Garden City, N.Y.: Doubleday, 1981) 247–51. See also the article on rich and riches by Friedrich Hauch and Wilhelm Kasch in Gerhard Friedrich, ed., *Theological*

Dictionary of the New Testament 6 (Grand Rapids: Eerdmans, c1968) 318–32.

2. Besides the tradition where wealth is seen as a sign of divine favor, we meet (1) an attitude critical of wealth, especially in the prophets, and (2) an attitude that identified poverty with piety, riches with godlessness. See Schmid, *Gospel according to Mark* 193.

3. I have developed the problem of the "woes" more fully in my homily "Blessed Are You?" in my book *Sir, We Would Like To See Jesus: Homilies from a Hilltop* (New York: Paulist, c1982) 93–98.

4. Schmid, *Gospel according to Mark* 194.

Homily 20

1. Preachers should be aware of fresh approaches to, and more positive appreciations of, the Pharisees. See, e.g., Ellis Rivkin, *A Hidden Revolution* (Nashville: Abingdon, 1978); John T. Pawlikowski, *Christ in the Light of the Christian-Jewish Dialogue* (New York: Paulist, 1982); Leonard Swidler, "The Pharisees in Recent Catholic Writing," *Horizons* 10, no. 2 (Fall 1983) 267–87. On the parable itself, I have profited much from the manuscript of Joseph A. Fitzmyer's *The Gospel according to Luke (X-XXIV)*, scheduled for 1985 publication by Doubleday in the Anchor Bible series.

Homily 22

1. See Homily 19 in this collection.

2. See Mark Searle, *Liturgy Made Simple* (Collegeville: Liturgical, 1981) 11.

3. Cf. Reginald H. Fuller, *Preaching the New Lectionary: The Word of God for the Church Today* (Collegeville, Minn.: Liturgical, 1976) 449–50: ". . . a very different impression is created [by the Little Apocalypse of Mk 13] from Jesus' own proclamation which spoke of the inbreaking of the kingdom and the certainty of the speedy vindication of his message. We may believe that this apocalyptic elaboration spoke meaningfully to Mark's church, beset as it was by temptations of a divine man Christology and by persecution."

4. Fuller, *Preaching the New Lectionary* 453.

Homily 23

1. I employ a similar development for the same Sunday in the B cycle; cf. Homily 22 in this volume. There, however, I spend more time in my

second point on the "science-fiction" and the images in Mark 13:24–32; I see relatively little in Luke 21 to require such comment.

2. Joseph A. Fitzmyer, *The Gospel according to Luke (X-XXIV)*, scheduled for 1985 publication by Doubleday in the Anchor Bible series; I have used Fr. Fitzmyer's manuscript.

3. Here I am following Fitzmyer (ibid.) in interpreting Lk 21:7–24 of the destruction of Jerusalem, and vv. 25–36 of the end time.

4. See Josephus, *Jewish Wars* 5, 2, 1–5; 6, 2, 1; 6, 2, 7; 6, 5, 1; 6, 9, 3; 7, 5, 3; 7, 5, 5; 7, 5, 6.

5. To avoid needless confusion, note that what one reads as Mal 4:1–6 in some translations is 3:19–24 in the Hebrew. I am using the Hebrew numeration in this homily.

Homily 24

1. For historical information and for insights into the Paulist way of life, I am dependent in large measure on James M. Gillis, C.S.P., *The Paulists* (New York: Macmillan, 1932); Joseph McSorley, C.S.P., *Father Hecker and His Friends: Studies and Reminiscences* (St. Louis: Herder, 1952); and Vincent F. Holden, C.S.P., *The Yankee Paul: Isaac Thomas Hecker* (Milwaukee: Bruce, c1958).

2. See McSorley, *Father Hecker* 104.

3. See Walter Elliott, C.S.P., *The Life of Father Hecker* (New York, 1891) xiv, quoted by McSorley, *Father Hecker* 161.

Homily 25

1. Samuel H. Dresner, "Remembering Abraham Heschel," *America* 146, no. 21 (May 29, 1982) 414.

2. St. Thomas Aquinas, *Adoro te supplex, latens deitas,* translated by Gerard Manley Hopkins, *The Poems of Gerard Manley Hopkins,* ed. W. H. Gardner and N. H. MacKenzie (4th ed.; London: Oxford University, 1970) 211.

3. Ibid.

4. Lewis Carroll, *Alice's Adventures in Wonderland,* in *The Complete Works of Lewis Carroll* (New York: Random House, [1936]) 79.

5. Francis Thompson, "The Hound of Heaven," in *Francis Thompson: Poems and Essays,* ed. Wilfred Meynell (Westminster, Md.: Newman, 1949) 112.

6. In *Between God and Man: An Interpretation of Judaism from the Writings of Abraham J. Heschel* (New York: Harper, c1959) 40.

7. Ibid. 41.

8. Ibid.
9. Gerard Manley Hopkins, "God's Grandeur," in *Poems* (n. 2 above) 66.
10. Dresner, "Remembering Abraham Heschel" 415.
11. Gerard Manley Hopkins, "As kingfishers catch fire . . . ," in *Poems* (n. 2 above) 90.

Homily 26

1. *The Life of Henry V*, Act 4, Scene 1.
2. Lewis Carroll, *Through the Looking-Glass* (New York: Random House, 1946) 59.
3. An allusion to William Golding's 1954 novel *Lord of the Flies*.

Homily 27

1. William Blake, "Jerusalem," in Helen Gardner, ed., *The New Oxford Book of English Verse 1250–1950* (New York: Oxford University, 1972) 486.
2. Sister Mary Ignatius, "Discovery," *Messenger of the Sacred Heart* 77, no. 2 (February 1942) 58.
3. Cf. Carin Rubinstein, "Money & Self-Esteem, Relationships, Secrecy, Envy, Satisfaction," *Psychology Today* 15, no. 5 (May 1981) 29–44; see esp. 40–44.

Homily 28

1. See the reviews by Pauline Kael, "The Current Cinema: Anybody Home?" *New Yorker*, Aug. 8, 1983, 84, 87, and Richard A. Blake, "Thalia," *America* 149 (1983) 73.
2. This paragraph borrows liberally from my "Look, Love, Laugh," *Tell the Next Generation: Homilies and Near Homilies* (New York: Paulist, c1980) 109–15, at 110–11.
3. At Georgetown, ICC is the Intercultural Center, Yates is the main athletic facility, GUTS is the Georgetown University Transportation Society—bus transportation to various points in the District of Columbia.
4. Eugene O'Neill, *Lazarus Laughed*, Act 1, Scene 1; in *The Plays of Eugene O'Neill* (New York: Random House, 1955) 280.
5. Robert N. Bellah, "Religion & Power in America Today," *Commonweal* 109, no. 21 (Dec. 3, 1982) 652.
6. *Time*, March 3, 1980, 66, and Aug. 4, 1980, 61.

Homily 29

1. For this baccalaureate liturgy at Georgetown University, the Old Testament reading assigned for Trinity Sunday, Proverbs 8:22–31, was replaced by the Wisdom of Solomon 6:12–20, 7:7–12, to provide a fuller sense of wisdom's significance.
2. Vincent Canby in the *New York Times,* June 20, 1967, 34:1.
3. What follows in the next three paragraphs reproduces, with some changes in rhetoric, three paragraphs in my homily "The Man Who Lives with Wisdom," in *Tell the Next Generation: Homilies and Near Homilies* (New York: Paulist, c1980) 100–101.
4. The word "scoper," originating in a Greek word meaning "look at," is borrowed from campus rhetoric, where it refers to a pastime in which one gazes on and appraises members of the opposite sex.
5. Philip Rieff, *Freud: The Mind of the Moralist* (Garden City, N.Y.: Doubleday Anchor Books, 1961) 391, 390, 65, 361–62.
6. Title of an extraordinarily popular film fantasy.

Homily 30

1. For the interpretation of this Genesis passage, I have been helped by two authors in particular: Bruce Vawter, *On Genesis: A New Reading* (Garden City, N.Y.: Doubleday, 1977) 72–76, and Claus Westermann, *Creation* (London: SPCK, 1974) 82–88.

Homily 31

1. I am not implying that this is the precise meaning of the inspired text. Gen 1:26–27 has baffled the most competent of interpreters ancient and modern. Homilists might profit from Bruce Vawter's *On Genesis: A New Reading* (Garden City, N.Y.: Doubleday, 1977) 53–60.
2. This way of expressing the divorce rate in the U.S. might be misleading. If it is true that about half our marriages end before death, it is not necessarily true that *both* parties in each case disavow their vow.
3. The reference is to the best-known oddsmaker at the present writing.
4. Frederick Buechner, *The Hungering Dark* (New York: Seabury, c1969) 14.

Homily 32

1. In Wilfrid Ward, *The Life of John Henry Cardinal Newman* 2 (New York: Longmans, Green, 1912) 147.

2. Second Vatican Council, Constitution on the Church in the Modern World, no. 43.
3. The occasion of this homily was the 25th anniversary of Loyola Retreat House, Faulkner, Md.
4. Second Vatican Council, Decree on the Apostolate of the Laity, no. 5.
5. Here I have been aided by the summary but rich treatment in E. E. Larkin, "Spirituality, Christian," *New Catholic Encyclopedia* 13 (1967) 598–603.
6. See the wealth of historical and theological development on lay spirituality in Yves M. J. Congar, O.P., *Lay People in the Church: A Study for a Theology of Laity* (rev. ed.; London: Chapman, 1965) esp. 400–451 on being in the world and not of it—actually a chapter on lay spirituality.
7. For the deeper, theological meaning of this incident, see my Homily 14 in this volume, "What Are You Looking For?"
8. Translation from Michael Novak, *The Open Church: Vatican II, Act II* (New York: Macmillan, 1964) 84–87.
9. Ibid. 87.

Homily 33

1. Constitution on the Church, no. 4.
2. For documentation see Raymond E. Brown, S.S., "Role of Women in the Fourth Gospel," *Theological Studies* 36 (1975) 688–99, at 692–95. See also his treatment of the Samaritan woman in Jn 4 as having "a real missionary function" (691).
3. Decree on the Apostolate of the Laity, no. 3. My translation is from *The Documents of Vatican II*, ed. Walter M. Abbott, S.J. (New York: America, c1966) 492, save that at the end I turn *hominibus* as "men *and women.*"
4. Léon-Joseph Suenens, *Coresponsibility in the Church* (New York: Herder and Herder, 1968) 31.
5. Constitution on the Church, no. 48.
6. I have developed this theme at somewhat greater length in my homily "Joy: New Testament and New Christian," *Catholic Mind* 70, no. 1260 (February 1972) 28–33.
7. Eugene O'Neill, *Lazarus Laughed,* Act 1, Scene 1; in *The Plays of Eugene O'Neill* (New York: Random House, 1955) 279–80.

Homily 34

1. "Love Boat" is the title of a long-running TV serial, where "love" in myriad manifestations is a ceaseless part of the agenda on a cruise ship.
2. P. S. McGarry, "Thirty Years' War," *New Catholic Encyclopedia* 14 (1967) 98–100, at 100.

3. Decree on Ecumenism, no. 12 (tr. *The Documents of Vatican II,* ed. Walter M. Abbott, S.J. [New York: America, c1966] 354).

4. *WA* 7, 36, 3 f. (1520); cf. Gerhard Ebeling, *Luther: An Introduction to His Thought* (Philadelphia: Fortress, c1970) 212.